The Complete Idiot's Command Reference

Quick Reference to Quicken and Windows Shortcut Keys

Key Combination	Quicken Standard	Windows Standard
Ctrl+Z	QuickZoom selected amount in report	Undo
Ctrl+X	Go to Matching Transfer	Cut
Ctrl+C	Open Category and Transfer List	Copy
Ctrl+V	Void this transaction	Paste

Quick Reference to Data Entry Shortcuts

Function	Key Combination
Decrease date or check number	- (minus key)
Increase date or check number	+ (plus key)
Change date to today	**t**
Change date to beginning of month	**m**
Change date to end of month	**h**
Change date to beginning of year	**y**
Change date to end of year	**r**
Open Calendar tool	**Ctrl+G**

Quick Reference to Register Navigation

Function	Key Combination
Next field or column	**Tab**
Previous field or column	**Shift+Tab**
Next transaction	**Down Arrow**
Previous transaction	**Up Arrow**
Start of field	**Home**
First field in transaction	**Home** (twice)
First transaction in window	**Home** (three times)
First transaction in register	**Home** (four times) or **Ctrl+Home**
End of field	**End**
Last field in transaction	**End** (tw...
Last transaction in window	**End** (th...
Last transaction in register	**End** (fo...
Jump to next month	**Ctrl+Pg**...
Jump to last month	**Ctrl+Pg**...

Quick Reference to Quick Keys

Function	Key Combination
Open File	Ctrl+O
Back Up	Ctrl+B
Print Current Screen	Ctrl+P
Cut	Shift+Del
Copy	Ctrl+Ins
Paste	Shift+Ins
Find	Ctrl+F
Find Next	Shift+Ctrl+F
Account List	Ctrl+A
Category and Transfer List	Ctrl+C
Class List	Ctrl+L
Memorized Transaction List	Ctrl+T
Scheduled Transaction List	Ctrl+J
Security List	Ctrl+Y
Use Register	Ctrl+R
Manage Loans	Ctrl+H
Write Checks	Ctrl+W
Open Investment Portfolio	Ctrl+U
Get Help with Current Window	F1
Create New Transaction	Ctrl+N
Delete Selected Transaction	Ctrl+D
Insert Transaction	Ctrl+I
Void Transaction	Ctrl+V
Memorize Transaction	Ctrl+M
Go to Transfer	Ctrl+X

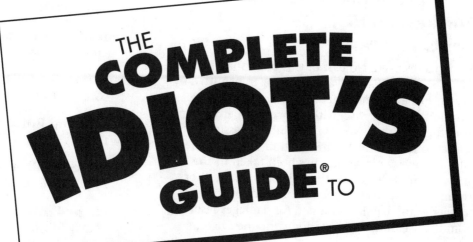

THE COMPLETE IDIOT'S GUIDE® TO

Quicken 2000

Stephen O'Brien

que®

A Division of Macmillan USA
201 West 103rd Street, Indianapolis, Indiana 46290

The Complete Idiot's Guide to Quicken 2000

Copyright © 2000 by *Que*

International Standard Book Number: 0-7897-2218-6

Library of Congress Catalog Card Number: 99-64717

Printed in the United States of America

First Printing: October 1999

01   00   99   4   3   2   1

Trademarks

Warning and Disclaimer

Publisher
Greg Wiegand

Acquisitions Editor
Angelina Ward

Development Editor
Gregory Harris

Managing Editor
Thomas F. Hayes

Project Editor
Leah Kirkpatrick

Copy Editor
Molly Schaller

Indexers
Aamir Burki
Kevin Kent

Proofreader
Tricia Sterling

Technical Editor
Robert Patrick

Team Coordinator
Sharry Gregory

Interior Designer
Nathan Clements

Cover Designer
Michael Freeland

Illustrator
Judd Winick

Copy Writer
Eric Borgert

Production
Liz Johnston
Lisa England
Steve Geiselman
Louis Porter Jr.

Contents at a Glance

Contents

About the Author

Stephen O'Brien is the author of 13 books about software, technology, and small business computing.

He has spent several previous existences counting widgets, designing irrigation systems, running a computer school, setting up an ISP, and working as a columnist, freelancer, and programmer. He co-founded a paralegal firm with Olwyn Kerr in 1992, and has been involved in personal and small business accounting since.

He lives on the Gold Coast, Australia, where he flies planes for fun, writes for profit, and likes to daydream about it being the other way around.

Dedication

To Olwyn Kerr.

Tell Us What You Think!

As the reader of this book, *you* are our most important critic and commentator. We value your opinion and want to know what we're doing right, what we could do better, what areas you'd like to see us publish in, and any other words of wisdom you're willing to pass our way.

As a Publisher for *Que*, I welcome your comments. You can fax, email, or write me directly to let me know what you did or didn't like about this book—as well as what we can do to make our books stronger.

Please note that I cannot help you with technical problems related to the topic of this book, and that due to the high volume of mail I receive, I might not be able to reply to every message.

When you write, please be sure to include this book's title and author as well as your name and phone or fax number. I will carefully review your comments and share them with the author and editors who worked on the book.

Fax: 317.581.4666

Email: office_que@mcp.com

Mail: Greg Wiegand
          Que
          201 West 103rd Street
          Indianapolis, IN 46290 USA

Introduction

Quicken 2000 is an amazing package. Yet while few would deny that it's a beautifully executed concept, it still isn't perfect.

That's why we've published this book.

Why an idiot's guide? If you plan to use this package to manage your finances, you're certainly not an idiot. In fact, managing your finances using Quicken 2000 is one of the best decisions you've made. But even the most user-friendly software has a way of making the brightest of us feel a bit dim.

This book was written to turn on the light. Not with long and complex series of steps that leave you wondering how you'll ever achieve the same on your own, nor with patronizing over-simplification. This book serves it up as it is, helping you to get results in specific areas without burying you in details, or swamping you with syntax.

Sit back, relax, and enjoy your journey. Only an idiot would want to miss out.

Why Do You Need This Book?

Quicken 2000 is the latest version of a very large package—large because it must cope with the ever-increasing complexity of the average person's finances.

If you are like most Quicken users, you have already established the need to use Quicken, and you want to get results, but you don't want to wade through thousands of minor functions and features.

After using this book, you'll be able to do far more than track your checking account's transactions. You'll also be able to coddle investments, play "what if" scenarios with your financial future, set up savings and "life" goals, check out your true net worth, optimize loan repayments, set up funds to send your kids to college, and, one day, hit your retirement running, with nary a financial speed bump in sight.

The above takes some doing, but this book makes it easy.

This book is a bit different than other Quicken titles. First, it doesn't assume you know too much, or even that you want to learn everything there is to know.

Second, it doesn't leave you floundering in a swathe of impossibly difficult steps.

Third, it gives you a great head start; one that's sufficient enough to ensure you won't have any trouble using Quicken's remaining features to their full potentials.

How Do You Use This Book?

Sure you're already using this book, but this is not that silly a question. If this is the first Complete Idiot's Guide you've ever read, there are just a few things you should know.

First, the best way to learn is to follow along with the explanation for any procedure. If you need to select a particular menu, you'll see the name of that menu appear in color, as in:

> Open the **File** menu and select **Print**.

The buttons and tabs in dialog boxes are also highlighted in color, such as:

> Click **OK** to save your changes when you're finished in the **General Options** tab.

Second, Microsoft Windows in general, and Quicken in particular, also include special accelerator keys designed to put us all on the fast road to wealth and happiness—or at the very least save a few mouse movements.

Accelerator key combinations appear in this book with a plus sign between them. For example:

> Click **New** or just press **Ctrl+N** to create a new category.

This means you should hold down the **Ctrl** key and tap the letter **N**, releasing the keys in any order.

These keys provide wonderful shortcuts to common commands, menus, and functions. They're a great way to work while your fingers remain on the keyboard: and they also help save your mouse from that embarrassing 10,000 mile grease and oil change.

You'll find Quicken's best accelerator keys on the tear-out card insider the front cover, and scattered throughout this book.

Finally, this book includes special notes that help you take that extra step beyond the basics. They also explain the lingo, and, if you have used previous editions of Quicken, explain the differences between the two versions. You'll see boxes such as the following:

Techno Talk

I can't help you walk the walk, but talking the talk is easy. In these boxes you'll find handy explanations, often with more detail than the Glossary.

Check This Out

These boxes are designed to tantalize. You'll read about helpful hints and short-cuts—perfect for jumping ahead of the crowd. You'll also learn some of the more obscure features and, if you have used previous versions of Quicken, get a quick heads-up on any changes.

Part 1
Boot Camp

There's not a lot you can't achieve with Quicken, at least in financial terms. In this section you'll learn how to set up your books, record transactions, work with categories and classes, and create great reports. But that's not all! You'll also learn how to get out of debt faster, set up accounts to handle almost any financial situation, and set up memorized and scheduled transactions that ensure you never miss an important payment again.

Chapter 1

Getting the Introductions Over With

In This Chapter

➤ Starting Quicken

➤ Setting up your first account

➤ Recording easy transactions

➤ Quitting Quicken

Quicken is an amazing product. It can revolutionize your finances, minimize your paperwork, prepare and file your taxes, and help you manage your investments. It isn't an exaggeration to say that Quicken has the potential to turn your financial life around, but it does ask something in return. You can't sit down and tap out a few transactions the way you might dash out a letter to mom using your favorite word processor. First you need to pave the way.

In this section of the book, you learn how to get Quicken started on the right foot. You also learn how to record all those checks you write, bank accounts you deplete, and credit cards you punish, as well as how to take complete control of your finances.

Are you ready? Great! Without more ado, let's get started.

Start Your Engines!

You can't walk a thousand miles without taking that first step, right? Well, the first step in using any software is to make sure it is installed on your computer. (If you just stare at the packaging, it runs kinda slow.)

So, before you start using Quicken, make sure you've followed those initial installation instructions included with the package. (If you know that your computer is running Windows 95, Windows 98, or Windows 2000—you should see a picturesque screen announcing the fact shortly after you turn on your computer—just slide the Quicken CD-ROM into your computer's CD-ROM drive. The installation software should start without your intervention. After you follow the onscreen prompts, you're ready to run. However, be sure to also consult Quicken's documentation.)

There are three sure-fire ways to start Quicken. If you see **Quicken's** icon on your desktop, just give it a quick double-click. If you've upgraded from a previous version of Quicken, you can also start Quicken from the Billminder window. (Billminder appears after you've been using Quicken for awhile and have outstanding transactions.)

What's a Double-Click?

Don't book tap lessons just yet. A double-click is when you click the left-mouse button twice in quick succession. You might have some trouble doing this when you first start using a computer, but it won't be long before you can click at a pace that would put Fred Astaire to shame.

Chances are you'll most often start Quicken using the Windows Start menu. To do so, click the Windows **Start** button, select **Programs**, click the **Quicken** menu command, and choose **Quicken 2000**. (Depending on the precise version of Quicken you purchased, you might also see Quicken's main program referred to as Quicken Basic 2000, Quicken Deluxe 2000, or Quicken Home & Business 2000.) You can see how to do this in the following figure.

After you've used Quicken for awhile, you might also find it more convenient to start Quicken by double-clicking the **QuickEntry 2000** desktop shortcut. Although you can use this to record a few transactions without launching the rest of the software, it isn't that much of a timesaver. To learn more about QuickEntry, see Chapter 3 "Hey, Big Spender!"

Another way is to double-click the
Quicken desktop shortcut.

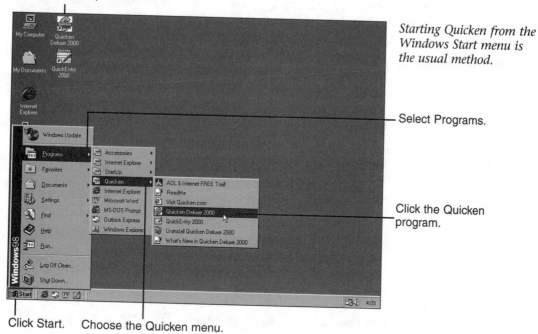

*Starting Quicken from the
Windows Start menu is
the usual method.*

Select Programs.

Click the Quicken
program.

Click Start.   Choose the Quicken menu.

Upgrading Old Data

You don't lose your old data when you move to a new version of Quicken. In
fact, Quicken 2000 can convert the data used in any previous version for
Windows, DOS, or Macintosh.

If you have used a previous version of Quicken, you might be offered the opportunity to upgrade your old data when you start Quicken 2000. If so, just click
OK when prompted. As soon as the conversion is completed, you find yourself at
the main Quicken screen. Your pre-conversion files are stored in a special folder
within your Quicken folder. The Quicken folder is called *quickenw* on your hard
drive. If you follow the default suggestions for installing Quicken, the full path to
Quicken 99 files is *c:\quickenw\qw99files*. Quicken 98 files are stored in
c:\quickenw\qw98files.

Quicken doesn't waste time when it starts. The first time you use it, you see a pleasant little dialog box called New User Setup. (The only time you don't see this box is when you are upgrading from a previous version and Quicken has detected your previous data. If that's the case, go ahead and approve the upgrade when it is requested.)

The New User Setup system takes a while to fill out, but after you've completed it you're all set for the rest of this book.

Six Easy Steps to Set Up Your First Account

Each time you launch Quicken, it attempts to determine whether or not you are a new user. If it doesn't find any old data files, it automatically launches the New User Setup. This is a friendly, question-driven system that has you up and running with a checking account in a matter of minutes.

Getting the Complete Multimedia Experience

If you use the CD-ROM version of Quicken, now is a good time to insert your program disc into the CD-ROM drive. The CD enables you to listen to the Quicken Audio multimedia help system. If you installed Quicken from floppy disks, you see a transcription of the audio instead of hearing it.

Creating your first account is as easy as pie. (Don't worry if you're not much good at baking pies. That just means you'll find it even easier!)

The figure below shows the first screen in the New User Setup system. Click the **Next** button on the right side of the dialog box to begin.

If you are a first-time Quicken user, you begin your Quickening here.

Quicken makes no bones about prying into your private life, and it doesn't keep its queries to financial matters alone. The questions you see on the next screen help it to create a set of categories most appropriate to your circumstances. For example, if you answer Yes to the question Do you have children?, Quicken adds a tax-related expense category called Childcare.

Don't be overly concerned with these questions. In Chapter 4, "It's a Category and Class Thing," you'll see how easy it is to import the categories associated with each of these queries.

Click **Next** when you've finished selecting the appropriate options, and move on.

That's Categories, Not Scattergories!

Categories are used by Quicken to group related transactions. For example, each time you go to the supermarket and put another crease in your credit card, you might assign a category to that expense transaction called "Groceries." A night's entertainment at the local *La Dolce Vita* would probably use a category called "Dining" or "Entertainment."

Quicken includes numerous categories suitable for almost any kind of income or expenditure. And if the ones that are included don't fit your needs, you can create your own!

In the next screen use the **Account Name** text box to record the name of your primary bank account, be it checking or savings. There's no need to precisely match the name shown on your banking records—indeed, the shorter you make this name, the better—but you should aim for something that's fairly indicative; for example, *Jamie's Savings*. You can't create additional accounts yet, but you can as soon as you've completed this series of dialog boxes.

If you want to use Quicken's online banking services (and why not, they're a great timesaver), select your Financial Institution from the list provided. Click **Next** when you're ready to continue.

Quicken takes over your finances from a specific date. From that point on you should use the program to record every transaction you make. The easiest way to coordinate the switch from manual to computerized accounting is to use the information shown on your most recent bank statement.

If you have your last bank statement handy, select **Yes** and click **Next**. The next screen asks you to enter the statement ending date, as well as an ending balance.

Record these exactly as they are shown on your bank statement. When you have finished, click **Next**.

If you don't have your bank statement nearby, select **No** and click **Next**. Quicken confirms that it will set up a $0.00 account as of today's date. You can update your account details later by reconciling this account. Click **Next** when you have finished.

Use the final screen to confirm your settings. When you've finished, click **Done** to jump to your checking account's register.

And that's all there is to it. Congratulations! You've just set up your first Quicken account. Now you're ready to start using Quicken's registers.

Read on to learn how to record your first transactions in the account you just created. If you'd rather continue with a leisurely overview of Quicken's main features, menus, and very helpful help system, turn to Chapter 2, "Exploring Quicken and Getting Help." If you want to leave Quicken for now, see "Closing the Door When You Leave" later in this chapter.

Starting Another Quicken File

You can create more than one file to use with Quicken. To do so, open the **File** menu, select **New**, make sure **New Quicken File** is selected and click **OK**. Give the file a name such as "My Accounts" and optionally click **Categories** to choose the category sets you want included. Click **OK** to create and open the file.

To move between files click the **File** menu and select **Open**. Use the File dialog box to select and open any other file.

Recording Your First Transactions

Transactions are the heart and soul of Quicken. To see how important they are, consider that Quicken doesn't store a particular account's balance, even though you can view your account balances in numerous screens and innumerable reports. Instead, it calculates the balance "on the fly" using the starting balance of that account and every transaction entered to-date.

If you created your account using the balance shown on your bank statement, one of your first tasks is to enter any transactions that have already occurred but have not yet appeared on your bank statement. This is the only way to make Quicken's version of your bank balance match reality.

You should try to add transactions as soon as they are made in real-life. It's a bit of a chore, I know, but after you are up and running, it should only take a few minutes each day. It also makes regular jobs such as an account reconciliation *that much* easier.

(How much is "that much?" It depends on how brisk the activity is in your account. Just remember that "that much" with Quicken is much less than "that much" with paper and pen.)

Reconciliation?

Reconciliation ensures the transactions noted on your bank statement match those you've recorded in Quicken. This process helps to keep the balance of your Quicken accounts in step with your real accounts. Reconciliation is widely regarded as a pain in the you-know-what, but Quicken really does make it particularly easy. Besides, as far as chores go, think of Cinderella and remember that things could be worse. That is, unless your checkbook turns into a pumpkin at midnight.

As soon as you have completed the New User Setup you see a screen filled with menus, buttons, gizmos, doodads, and an account register. (That last part is the big bit in the middle.) You can see an example of a register in the following figure.

Whoa! What's with the Renovations?

Brush off the sawdust. You're going to see some major changes in this version of Quicken. The icons have disappeared with Financial Activity Centers taking over most of the product. The menus are totally reworked. The QuickTabs that used to run down the right-hand side of the screen have the same names but now represent a hierarchical list that shows any windows already open under any of the Financial Activity Centers.

There are some big changes, but I think you'll decide they're for the better. Just don't trip over the scaffolding.

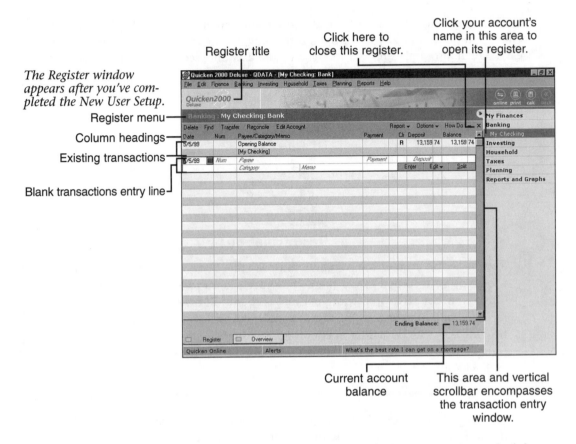

Click here to close this register.

Click your account's name in this area to open its register.

Register title

The Register window appears after you've completed the New User Setup.

Register menu

Column headings

Existing transactions

Blank transactions entry line

Current account balance

This area and vertical scrollbar encompasses the transaction entry window.

(If you leave Quicken and return, you see a screen called My Finances instead of the Register display. To get back to the register, open the **Banking** menu, select the entry called **Banking Activities**, and choose **Enter a transaction into my Register**.)

It's easy to record transactions. The previous figure shows a transaction created by Quicken from the account opening balance indicated in the New User Setup, but you'll find it just as easy to record them on your own. Just one hint before we get started: Even though you can use the mouse to move from one field in the register to the next, you'll probably find it easier to press the **Tab** key.

Every transaction needs a date. Type this into the first column of the first transaction in your register. This defaults to today's date, but you can change it in a flash, either by typing in a new date or by clicking the small **Calendar** icon to the right of that field. If you are recording a check, you might prefer to refer to your checkbook stub and provide the date you actually wrote the check.

Accounts and Registers?

Quicken's accounts are just like the checking, savings, investment, and other accounts you already use. Every time something happens to an account in real-life, you need to note that event in Quicken by recording a transaction in that account's register. Each register acts as a place to store all the transactions associated with a single account.

Use the next column (Num) to record a reference number. If you are recording a check, use the last three digits of that check's number. In the future you can select **Next Check Num** from that field's pull-down menu to number your checking transactions, or just press the plus (+) key. If you are recording a deposit, select **DEP** from the list instead—or just type DEP directly into that column. Although these selections are important, they are also for your own reference only. Quicken tells whether a transaction is an expense, deposit, or transfer using the transaction's category field.

Next, type in a payee. Quicken stores all payees in a list of memorized transactions, helping you to quickly recall that payee for future transactions. For now, though, you should enter the full name or, if you prefer, a convenient abbreviation.

Enter the payment amount or click the **Calculator** icon to use Quicken's built-in calculator. If this transaction represents a deposit, record the transaction's total amount in the deposit column instead.

Select a category. Click the **down arrow** to look through the list of existing categories and choose the most appropriate one. (You can always change it later.) If you have written a check, you most likely want to store it under an expense category. However, if you are recording funds flowing into your account, you need to use an income category, instead. If you don't want to choose a category, leave the field blank and answer **No** to Quicken's suggestion that you select a category from the list. However, keep in mind that if you don't assign categories, Quicken can't do so much of what it's really good at doing. (See Chapter 4 to learn more about categories.)

Type in a memo. The memo is a note to yourself that can contain extra information about this transaction, such as the transaction's purpose. This is your opportunity to improve on the microscopic space provided on most check stubs.

After you have completed the entry, click **Enter** to record the transaction and move onto the next.

Wasn't that just too easy? Give yourself a treat, because you've just created your first Quicken account and recorded your first transaction. Quicken was created to make it easy for you to do precisely this, and in that sense, in just a handful of pages, you've mastered 90% of the software.

Closing the Door When You Leave

Feel like a break before moving onto Chapter 2? Quitting Quicken is easy. Most Windows applications ask you if you would like to save the changes you've made to the open document or file when you exit that application. Things don't work the same way here.

Quicken is perfect for people who like to jump in and out of applications without bothering with the mechanics of keeping their data intact. Quite simply, there's no need for you to save your data when you leave.

To finish your current Quicken session, click the **Close** button in the upper-right corner of the Quicken window, or open the **File** menu and select **Exit**. There is just one potential hiccup. Every third time you exit Quicken, you trip over a dialog box that politely inquires if you would like to create a backup of your data.

If you decide to take note of this suggestion, click **Backup** and turn to Chapter 19, "Backing Up, Restoring, and Securing Your Data." If you would rather leave Quicken right away, select **Exit**.

The Least You Need to Know

➤ You don't need to be an expert at Quicken before you start to use it to manage your finances.

➤ If you haven't used Quicken before, use the New User Setup dialog box to start your file. Just follow the prompts to complete your first checking account.

➤ Quicken saves data every time you make a small change, such as adding transactions or adjusting a budget, ensuring the saved data always represents the most recent information you've recorded.

➤ The only way to revert to a previous saved version of your data is to restore a backup.

Chapter 2

Exploring Quicken and Getting Help

> **In This Chapter**
>
> ➤ Learning Quicken's menus, buttons, and screen layout
>
> ➤ Getting help when you need it

Quicken's a complex piece of work, no doubt about it, but don't let that daunt you. After all, it's just a collection of bits, bytes, and the inventive byproducts of someone else's graymatter. You've got a billion times more neurons than it has lines of program code, and you're really going to find this a cinch.

I'm at the Main Screen. Now What?

Despite its immediate appearance of complexity, there are quite a few sections of Quicken's screen that are repeated from one task to the next. These and the other main features are identified in the following figure.

*Each time you start
Quicken, it opens with the
My Finances Center
onscreen.*

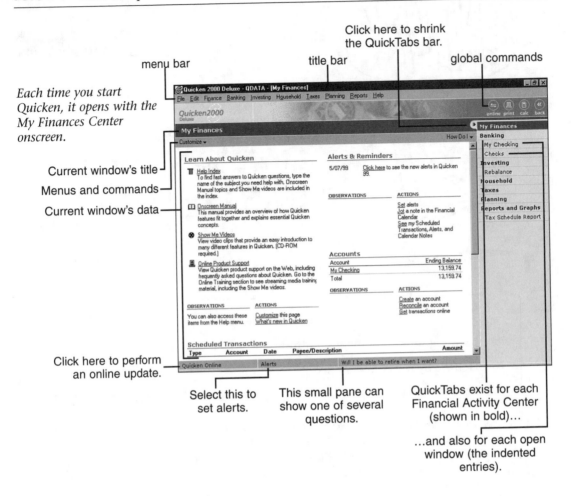

Click here to shrink
the QuickTabs bar.

menu bar   title bar   global commands

Current window's title
Menus and commands
Current window's data

Click here to perform
an online update.

Select this to
set alerts.

This small pane can
show one of several
questions.

QuickTabs exist for each
Financial Activity Center
(shown in bold)...

...and also for each open
window (the indented
entries).

Each section of the screen performs a certain task. Although some overlap occurs between each part's broader functionality, you'll find quite a few surprises in store for you.

Browsing the Menu Bar

Chances are you've already seen a Windows menu bar in action.

Quicken's menu bar, like other Windows programs, runs near the top of the screen and includes entries for File, Edit, Finance, Cocktails (sorry, that's my bar menu) and, well, you'll see soon enough.

The menu bar helps you to navigate to the different parts of Quicken and also to call up certain commands or perform particular operations.

For example, in the previous chapter you learned a little about the File menu. You can use it to access major program and file operations such as opening different files, changing printer settings, setting passwords, and backing up or restoring your data.

The Edit menu, the next one along, offers Windows' standard Cut, Copy, and Paste operations. However, it's also a little unpredictable, changing like a chameleon to offer commands that are in context with the current activity. You can use this menu to search and replace certain data, access the Quicken calculator, adjust Quicken's options, and numerous other tasks.

The Finance menu looks after the minutiae of your finances. You can use it to view and edit your Category List, access the Financial Calendar, and set Reminders and Alerts.

Under Banking you find just about everything that relates to working with transactions and accounts. If you click it now you see commands to reconcile accounts, set up online banking, and more.

The next menu is an important one. Every major feature and function relating to investments and capital gains is found under the Investing menu. Investment tracking is a huge part of the Quicken package. It is covered in Part 4, "Investing: Making Dollars with Sense."

Is your financial house in a mess? Check out the Household menu for a range of functions that help you to set up mortgages and loans, as well as research your credit and track your emergency records.

The Taxes menu is devoted to that second certain thing in our lives. You can use it to prepare your tax return and, even before then, work through strategies that might reduce your taxes. When you're done, the Tax Planner helps you to estimate your payments through the coming year.

Believe it or not, Quicken ships with an astonishingly complete financial planning system (actually, there are several). You can treat the Planning menu as a financial confessor, admitting your sins and taking the appropriate penance. "I will put 10% of my income into my IRA." Say it 100 times and believe it!

If you installed Quicken Home & Business, use the Business menu to set up receivables and payables accounts, generate invoices, record customer payments, and print statements. You can learn more about Quicken's business features in Part 5, "Minding Your Business."

Want to put your financial data on paper? Visit the Reports menu for a truly spectacular range of reports and graphs.

But wait, there's more! Before you move on, don't forget to try the Help menu. This menu includes a complete electronic manual along with access to Quicken's videos and more. You'll learn about Quicken's Help system shortly.

Accessing Quick Keys

You are probably familiar with how most Quick Keys work. (Windows calls them keyboard shortcuts.) For example, if you open the **File** menu, and look at the **Backup** entry, you see a little reminder telling you that this command is also available by pressing the key combination **Ctrl+B**, as shown in the following figure.

Quick Keys help you jump from one section of Quicken to another without resorting to the mouse.

The keyboard shortcut for Backup is Ctrl+B.

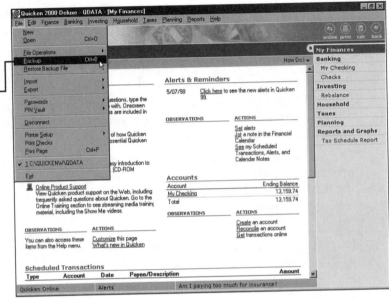

Quick Keys work throughout Quicken. You can, for example, complete writing a check and jump immediately to an account register simply by pressing **Ctrl+R**. (The only time this doesn't work is when there is a dialog box displayed onscreen at the same time.)

Some of Quicken's Quick Keys change according to the current activity. For example, pressing **Ctrl+N** with a Register window open creates a new transaction. However, with the Accounts List window open, **Ctrl+N** creates a new account.

The shortcuts used by Quicken are great for zipping from one part of the program to another. As you become more familiar with the program, you should also find that these shortcuts help you become more productive.

Table 2.1 shows keys with other special functions. (You'll see these and more on the tear-out card inside the front cover.) Not all key combinations are available in all situations. Note that the transaction shortcuts operate within a register but can have slightly different effects at other times.

Cut, Copy, and Paste

In previous versions of Quicken, the **Ctrl+Z**, **Ctrl+X**, **Ctrl+C**, and **Ctrl+V** keys performed tasks such as zooming into certain data, jumping to the matching transfer, opening the **Category List**, and voiding the current transaction. The X, C, and V combinations have been changed to the standard Windows shortcuts of Cut, Copy, and Paste, respectively. **Ctrl+Z** also stands for Paste. You can change these back by opening the **Edit** menu, selecting **Options**, clicking **Quicken Program**, choosing the **Settings** tab, and placing a check mark beside **Quicken Standard**.

Table 2.1   Special Key Combinations

Function	Key Combination
Open File	**Ctrl+O**
Back Up	**Ctrl+B**
Print Current Screen	**Ctrl+P**
Create New Transaction	**Ctrl+N**
Delete Selected Transaction	**Ctrl+D**
Insert Transaction	**Ctrl+I**
Memorize Transaction	**Ctrl+M**
Find	**Ctrl+F**
Find Next	**Shift+Ctrl+F**
Account List	**Ctrl+A**
Class List	**Ctrl+L**
Financial Calendar	**Ctrl+K**
Write Checks	**Ctrl+W**
Memorized Transaction List	**Ctrl+T**
Scheduled Transaction List	**Ctrl+J**
Use Register	**Ctrl+R**
Open Investment Portfolio	**Ctrl+U**
Security List	**Ctrl+Y**
Manage Loans	**Ctrl+H**
Get Help with Current Window	**F1**

Running Up a QuickTab

Quicken provides further shortcuts within the layout of the screen itself. The most useful of these is the QuickTabs bar.

This bar runs down the right side of the screen and at all times displays entries that take you to the My Finance, Banking, Investing, Household, Taxes, Planning, Business, and Reports and Graphs Activity Centers. Each time you open a new window under any of these centers, Quicken inserts another QuickTab. By clicking the tab with your mouse (there's no way to do so using the keyboard), you can quickly navigate between windows you've already opened.

All of the activity centers are shown in bold, while any windows you open are shown in a plain typeface and are slightly indented.

One of the most considerate aspects of Quicken is that it records the QuickTabs or windows that were open when you exit the program, restoring them for you when you return. You should try to get in the habit of closing those windows you no longer need before you quit the software. That way you avoid them gradually building up until they end up quite out of control. (This is especially important if your computer has limited memory, as each open QuickTab uses up a little more of that precious silicon RAM.)

To completely close a QuickTab and its associated window, just click the **Close** button (it's shown as a large **X**) that appears in that window's upper-right corner. (It's just to the right of the How Do I menu.) Alternatively, press your **Escape** (Esc) key to close the foremost open window, or click the appropriate tab with the right-mouse button and choose **Close: *Window Name*** from the menu that appears.

Techno Talk

Right-Mouse Button?

Believe it or not, this is one of the most under-utilized features of the Windows operating system. (Well, that and the Channel bar.) By clicking your mouse's right-mouse button, you can open a context-sensitive menu filled with commands that are perfect for the task you are currently performing. Try it throughout Quicken. You'll be surprised how easy it makes it to get certain things done. By the way, I'll just ask you to "right-click" your mouse whenever you need to access the right-mouse button menu.

As previously mentioned, Quicken recreates the same list of windows each time you start. You can also start with a specific set of windows rather than the last set open. To do so, set up the windows the way you want them. For example, you might open a register window, a check-writing window, and a particular Financial Highlights Center. Then arrange the order of their QuickTabs by dragging each up or down the list with your mouse. Open the **Edit** menu, select **Options**, and then **Desktop**. Choose **Save Current Desktop** and click **OK**. Then open the **Edit** menu once more, select **Options**, and click **Quicken Program**. Choose the **Startup** tab and select the option labeled **None**. Click **OK** and you're done.

Change the width of the QuickTabs bar by positioning the mouse over the border that the QuickTabs bar shares with the central window. (You can do this anywhere along the length of the border except where the QuickTab for the current window is located.) When the mouse changes to a double I-beam, click with the mouse and drag the border to the left or right.

You also can shrink your QuickTabs bar to make more room for the central window. Just click the small right-facing triangle that appears to the left of the **My Finances** QuickTab. (Click it once more to reopen the bar.) If you prefer to do this via Quicken's menu, open the **Edit** menu and select **Options**, then **Quicken Program**. With the QuickTabs tab selected, click to remove the check mark beside **Show QuickTabs**. Then click **OK** to save this change.

To turn your QuickTabs back on, just follow those steps once more, reinserting the check mark.

Note that even though you can shrink your QuickTabs, you can't make them disappear altogether. Apparently, more Americans prefer the look of QuickTabs over their nearest competitor.

Using the Window Navigator

The Window Navigator sits at the far right side of Quicken's screen, just below the menu bar. You can use this group of icons to go online, print the current window, open the calculator, and return to the previous window.

Hollering for Help

Although 90% of the work you do in Quicken is on familiar territory, there are times when you might need a little extra help. For instance, after you know how to use one register, you know how to use them all. Well, perhaps not the investment register, but I'm saving that for later. However, what about the more complex features? What about loan forecasting, budgeting, or creating scheduled transactions? Maybe you are a bit intimidated by a bank reconciliation. Although this book answers those questions, you can also turn to the online Help.

Quicken provides several ways for you to obtain the help you need:

➤ How Do I is context-sensitive help that accesses a database of common questions. The questions are filtered to reflect the current task. You can find the How Do I menu just beside the current window's close button.

➤ Press **F1** to get help with the current window. This, again, is context-sensitive.

➤ Open the **Help** menu to access a plethora of options, including a troubleshooter, the complete electronic help videos and text, and details for accessing Quicken's technical support hotline. Use the **Index** entry to search for help on particular features or topics and **Register** to tell Intuit a little about yourself. (Actually, you need to register online before you can use Quicken's online features.)

How Do I

Quicken's How Do I feature is the first place you should look for help. How Do I searches for help relating precisely to the issue at hand. For example, click **How Do I** with a standard account register to view topics about recording transactions, using categories, entering credit card payments, and more. Click **More** to open an even more detailed list, or **Troubleshooting** to try to work out where you're going wrong. The figure below shows one example.

Click How Do I to open the list of actions.

The How Do I feature helps you with your current task.

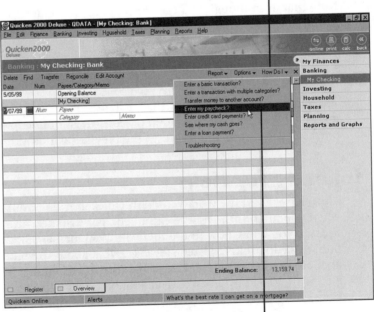

Select the action you need or click
More or Troubleshooting.

Formula F1

The F1 key provides help of a referential nature via a standard Windows help window. Use this window to read topics relating to the current cursor position or task, or click **Index** to access the complete Quicken help system.

Navigating the Help Menu

Quicken's help is scattered throughout the program. However, the major items are gathered under the Help menu, summarized in Table 2.2.

Table 2.2   Online Help Items

Menu Heading	Purpose
Index	Opens the main Help index. This is the same as selecting the Index button in the icon bar.
Current Window (F1)	Calls Quicken's context-sensitive help. This is identical to the Help button in the icon bar or pressing **F1** at any time.
Troubleshooting This Window	You don't always see this entry, but when available it opens the same window as selecting **Troubleshooting** from the How Do I menu.
Show Me Videos	It's not money, but this menu does open a window that enables you to browse all of the videos included with Quicken.
Onscreen Manual	Views Quicken's built-in electronic manual.
Product Support	Opens the Product Support dialog box.
Intuit Business Solutions	Learn about other Intuit business products such as QuickBooks and QuickBooks Pro.
About Quicken	Displays a small information window about your copy of Quicken.
Download Latest Version	Connects to the Internet and checks for updates to your Quicken software. If available, you can tell the update to download and automatically install. Quicken also checks for updates whenever you carry out a One Step Update. (See Chapter 13.)
Register Quicken	Registers your copy of Quicken online.

Thanks for the Memory

You can see how much of your computer's memory Quicken uses very easily. Just open the **Help** menu while holding down the **Shift** key, and select **About Quicken**. To summarize the number of transactions, accounts, and other data in your Quicken file, select the same menu option while pressing the **Ctrl** key.

Product Support

If all the other help resources fail, there are several more options under the **Help** menu's **Product Support** entry. Select this to open a dialog box that offers the following additional choices:

Are There FAQs on Quicken If I Get Really Stuck?

There certainly is. Try going to Quicken's site on the Web. Click the **Help** menu, select **Product Support**, and choose **Go to Web**.

➤ **Troubleshoot**   Choose this when available to help you solve problems rather than find answers to questions or learn about certain procedures. It's the first place to go when you discover that something doesn't work as you'd expected.

➤ **Go to Web**   This option takes you to Intuit's site on the Web. Obviously, you need to have a working Internet connection before you can do this, but when you're there you'll find a handy list of commonly asked questions and, even more conveniently, their answers.

➤ **Learn More by Fax**   This option gives you access to an automated fax-back system that might be able to solve your problem.

➤ **Call for Support**   Use this option when all else fails. This option can help you get in touch with the sensitive, caring, human side of Quicken's technical support.

➤ **System Info**   This option is only for tech-heads. Have a look, but don't run amok unless you really know what you're doing.

The Least You Need to Know

➤ Quicken's numerous onscreen features make it confusing when you're just starting out, but a quick exploration is all you need to take command.

➤ The icons and activity bar are, unfortunately, gone for good. However, the new menu structure makes it easier than ever to get to the sections of the program you need.

➤ Quicken works fine at a screen resolution of 800×600, but you should consider the next level up, 1,024×768, as the ideal working environment. Just remember that at that size you also need a large monitor—preferably one 17 inches or greater.

Chapter 3

Hey, Big Spender!

In This Chapter

➤ Transaction overview

➤ Writing checks to pay bills

➤ Correcting and deleting transactions

➤ Recording transactions with QuickEntry 2000

You've already seen how easy it is to record transactions in Quicken. Now it's time to take them to the next level.

Advanced Transaction Training

Transactions track the movement of funds through your accounts. Indeed, they record every financial move you make. (Something with which the IRS is fully cognizant.) In other words, you should never miss an opportunity to add them to Quicken.

You can record almost any kind of transaction in Quicken without knowing anything about debits and credits or other arcane double-entry accounting issues. By filling out simple transaction registers and dialog boxes, you can easily record transactions whenever you:

➤ Write checks

➤ Deposit or withdraw funds from an ATM

➤ Transfer funds to an IRA

➤ Record employer contributions to your 401(k)

➤ Make credit card or debit card purchases and payments

➤ Buy and sell shares

➤ Start and make payment to a mortgage or personal loan

➤ Create an invoice

Although Quicken's transactions are demonstrably simple, there are several powerful features that go beyond the basic transaction entry fields in your registers.

Paying Bills

It hurts to pay bills, but most are unavoidable. Although Quicken can't make your bills go away, it significantly lessens the pain.

You can pay your bills through Quicken in several ways:

➤ By recording that payment in your checking account register

➤ By using Quicken to both write and print the payment check

➤ If you paid by credit card, by downloading that payment from your online banking service

➤ By using electronic payments to pay the bill online

The online payment facility is a superb innovation, but it isn't for everyone.

If you prefer the feel of a physical check, consider recording your payments manually or, for a very professional approach, printing them on Quicken-compatible blank checks.

There are two advantages to printing your own checks: it's not as fraudulent as printing your own money; and you can add your address and logo to the checks, along with a fully itemized list of the items being paid, the payee's address, and more.

Of course, before you can start you need to order your checks from the IntuitMarket. Just call (800) 433-8810, or order them online. To do the latter, open the **Banking** menu, select **Banking Activities**, and choose **Order checks to print with Quicken**. Click the **Checks** icon to view the screen shown in the following figure. (The Order Checks button in the Write Checks window is discussed later in this chapter. In typical Quicken fashion, there are several ways to accomplish any single task.)

If you have trouble connecting Quicken to the Internet, check your connection settings by referring to Chapter 12, "Useful Connections," or use your Web browser to connect outside of Quicken. The IntuitMarket is available at www.intuitmarketplace.com.

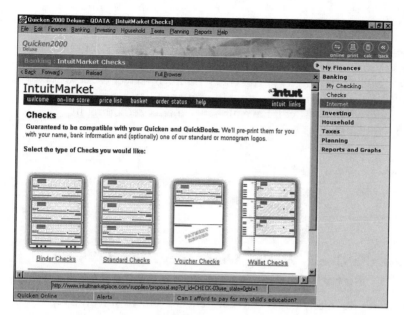

You can order four styles of checks online through the IntuitMarket.

Quicken is compatible with three primary check styles.

The Standard Checks look like ordinary business checks without a stub. Even though there are three checks per sheet, you're able to print them one at a time.

Wallet Checks provide a perforated stub that you can tear off after printing. They're useful for paying most personal bills because the voucher gives you a permanent, printed record. Like Standard Checks, Wallet Checks have three checks per sheet. Unlike the Standard and Voucher Checks, you can't print your own logo on Wallet Checks—although you can always pay Intuit a fee for doing so.

Voucher Checks are the Cadillacs of checks. With one check and two tear-off stubs, the single sheet of paper gives you and the payee generous amounts of space to use as a permanent record. These checks are the most convenient for accounts payable and payroll, but they are also the most expensive.

A fourth style of check is also available when you order online. Binder Checks are identical to Standard Checks and should be selected as such when you print them. The only difference between Binder Checks and Standard Checks is that you can slot the former into a binder supplied by Intuit with each delivery of 250 Binder Checks. When you're away from the office, write the checks by hand, tearing them off as required. When you're back at the office, remove entire sheets from the binder and run them through your printer.

Writing Checks

If you write your checks by hand, feel free to record them directly into your checking register. (It's a bit quicker than going through the Write Checks procedure.) Just use the Num field to note the last three digits of the check number—select **Next Check Num** from the drop-down list to jump to the next in sequence—and complete the payee, category, and memo sections as you have already experienced doing in Chapter 1, "Getting the Introductions Over With."

Is It Easier to Use the Check Writing Window or Record Checks Directly in the Register?

After you're used to it, it's definitely easier to record checks directly into the register. However, the first time you write a check you want to print to a new payee, make sure you use the Write Checks window and click the **address** button to add the address to the check. (Note: there's no need to do this if you address your envelopes by hand, rather than using the windowed envelopes with printed checks.)

If you decide to print your own checks, use Quicken's check writing facility instead.

Start by opening the **Banking** menu and selecting **Write Checks** (or just press **Ctrl+W**). The window shown in the following figure appears.

Use the tabs running along the bottom of the check writing window to move between those accounts with check writing privileges. The list might include checking accounts, savings accounts, money market accounts, investment accounts, and more. Click the one that corresponds to the account from which you are drawing with this check.

The check writing window is made up of two sections. Use the upper half to fill out the check. The lower section lists the checks waiting to be printed and includes checks created directly in the checking register when the Num field was set to Print Check. Sandwiched between the two are the category and split fields, and the Record Check button.

The date is set to today's, but you can also forward or back date checks by clicking the **Calendar** icon to select a date using Quicken's Calendar tool.

Click here to order
stationery through
the Intuit Web site.

Type in or
select a payee.

Enter the amount.

Choose a date.

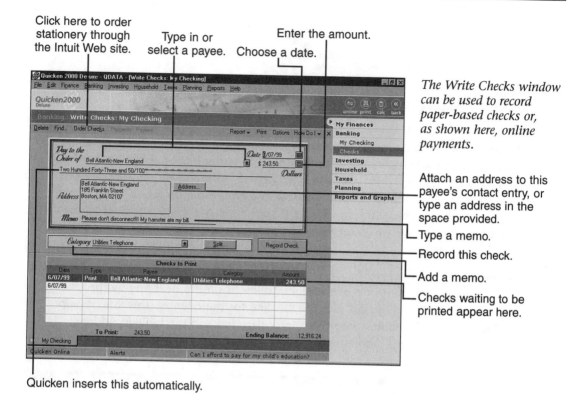

*The Write Checks window
can be used to record
paper-based checks or,
as shown here, online
payments.*

Attach an address to this
payee's contact entry, or
type an address in the
space provided.

Type a memo.

Record this check.

Add a memo.

Checks waiting to be
printed appear here.

Quicken inserts this automatically.

The Pay to the Order of field works the same way as the payee field you've used in other transactions.

The Address field is optional, but it's useful if you want to print the address on the check. The address prints perfectly positioned to appear in the clear section of Intuit's windowed envelopes.

The contents of the Memo field also prints on the check. The contents of this field can be seen through windowed envelopes, so don't use it for sensitive information. It is, however, a great place to include the payee's invoice number. This also means you can search for this check later by the payee's name, your own check number, or the payee's invoice number.

If you see a Message field, feel free to use it for items that are too sensitive to sit in the Memo field. Any information recorded in this field is hidden from view through the envelope's window, avoiding situations that could arise by including that message in the memo. To turn on the Message field, select the **Edit** menu, click **Options**, and open **Write Checks**. Click in the box **Allow Entry of Extra Message on Check**, then click **OK**, and type away.

Use the Category field as you have other category entries. You can specify categories, classes, splits (click **Split...**), transfers, or even leave it blank, although the latter is not recommended.

Storing Addresses

Quicken stores the addresses of all your past payees in its Address Book database. (You can open it by opening the **Finance** menu and selecting **Address Book**). This means that if you print your own checks and use windowed envelopes, you can actually skip the Write Checks window and type those payments directly into your account's register. Just select **Print Check** from the menu attached to the Num field to indicate you want to print this check. Quicken looks up the address and inserts it for you.

When you record addresses in the Write Checks window, use the standard format of the street on the first one or two lines, followed on the next line by the city, a comma, the state and the zip. Use the last line for the country. This format helps Quicken to slot the address into the appropriate fields in the built-in Address Book. For more on the Address Book, see Chapter 24, "Making Contact with the Address Book."

Can I Create Categories As I Go?

That's the easiest way, but take a good look through your category list to start with, just to make sure you're not duplicating an existing category. See Chapter 4, "It's a Category and Class Thing," for more information.

Click **Online Payment** to pay this check through the Online Center. If you haven't set up online banking for this account, you won't see this option. Also, if you haven't made an online payment to this payee before, you are asked to provide an address and specify the account and telephone number. You can read more about this in Part 3, "Online in No Time."

That's all there is to it. When you're finished, click **Record Check** to store this transaction and open a new, blank check window. To print the check, read on.

Do You Write the Same Checks Often?

If you regularly send checks for the same amount to the same payee, why not set up a scheduled payment? This process saves you time and ensures that the payment is made before the hairy-knuckled debt collector comes knocking on your door. You can learn more about this in Chapter 7, "Taking Control of Your Debt."

Setting Up to Print Checks

It is possible to save a lot of time by printing your own checks, especially if you print them in batches. (Batch printing means storing them up until you're ready to print several at once. Batch printing saves you from fiddling with partially printed sheets of checks.)

The first time you print your checks, you need to set up Quicken to use your printer and your particular style of blank printer checks.

Just open the **File** menu, select **Setup**, and choose **For Printing Checks**. This opens a small but very busy dialog box where you can set every printing option imaginable...and then some!

Use the **Printer** drop-down list to select your printer. Then choose between **Page-oriented** or **Continuous** paper. Page-oriented is used for laser and inkjet printers, whereas the continuous or fan-fold paper is only suitable for impact printers or inkjet printers with an appropriate ratchet feed. (You'd know if your printer supports these.)

Next, match the Check Style to the Standard, Wallet, or Voucher Checks you ordered.

Then set the **Partial Page Printing Style**. This setting depends on your printer. If your printer prints envelopes (and therefore partial checks) hard against the far-left edge of the paper feed, select **Edge**. (Most Hewlett-Packard laser printers are built like this.) If your printer prints envelopes with the envelope centered within the paper feed, select **Centered**. (Most Postscript printers behave like this.) If your printer prints envelopes with the long edge against the printer paper feed, select **Portrait**.

Okay, you're nearly there. If you chose to print page-oriented, select the appropriate printer trays provided beside Partial Page Source and Full Page Source. If you plan to load blank checks into your printer's tray, set the full page option to the paper tray you plan to use for your checks. If you plan to manually feed checks every time, set Full Page to manual feed.

If you chose Continuous paper, you can set two options for that type of paper. Bypass the driver tells Quicken to attempt to run your printer automatically, bypassing the Windows printer driver. This can fix some printing problems. Use low starting position is useful if your printer is printing too far up the page and requires a large adjustment. Use Align to further adjust the position.

Changing the Printer Font

The default check-printing font is set to 9-point Arial. To change this default, just click **Font** and choose another. This said, Arial is an economical and easy-to-read typeface, so you should probably leave it as is unless you have a very specific reason for changing it. What do they say about a little power?

There are three additional buttons in the Check Printer Setup dialog box. The first one's tricky; the other two are easy.

If your printer refuses to print in the correct position on your blank checks, click **Align** to open the Align Checks dialog box. You can adjust the position of both continuous and page-oriented checks, although the procedure differs somewhat. For continuous checks, follow the onscreen directions. Quicken does an excellent job of referencing a sample form to help you align your checks. For page-oriented checks, use the Align Checks dialog box to correct the printing of full and partial pages. Click each button shown to change the position of the printed information, using the Fine Alignment dialog boxes to adjust the fine alignment of each set of checks, and also to print a sample page. You might need to adjust each type of page several times to obtain an optimum result. However, save some trees and expense by printing the samples on paper cut to the same size as the Intuit-supplied checks. Hold them over a blank check and up to the light to check the alignment.

To change your printer's default settings, click the **Settings** button.

To add an optional logo to your Standard or Voucher Checks, click the **Logo** button. You can create a logo using any drawing package—including the version of Windows Paint that ships with Windows—and save it in the bitmap (.bmp) format. Remember, though, that it has to squeeze down to a size approximately 0.5 inches square. Click **File** in the Check Logo dialog box and choose your logo's bitmap. Click **OK** until you exit out of that series of dialog boxes. Quicken starts printing that graphic on all your checks.

Really Printing Your Checks

Now you're really ready. After you have your checks set up, printing them is easy. Here's how.

Open the register or account that corresponds to the checks you want to print. Then open the **File** menu and select **Print Checks**. The dialog box shown in the following figure appears.

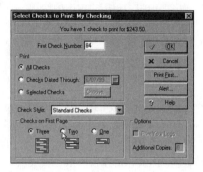

Use this dialog box to specify the number of checks on the page (in this case, there are two), and the first check number (in this case, that number is 84).

This dialog box looks complex, but it isn't really. Enter the number of the first check you want to print. This is the first check number shown on the page inserted into your printer. (It is important that you match this correctly—don't rely on Quicken's guess.)

In the Print group, select the checks you want to print. You can print:

➤ All Checks   Print every check not previously printed.

➤ Checks Dated Through   Print all checks recorded before or on a certain date.

➤ Selected Checks   Click the Choose button to print only those checks you mark in the list.

Select the **Check Style**. This must match the style of the blank checks inserted into your printer.

If you are printing page-oriented checks, indicate the number of checks there are on the first page in your printer. This isn't valid for continuous-feed checks or Voucher Checks, but is for those of the Standard or Wallet styles.

Use the Options group to toggle the printing of a logo on your checks (assuming you create one). Also, if you are using Voucher Checks, you can indicate how many additional copies of each you require.

How Can I Reprint a Check That Was Damaged or Lost?

Just find the old check in your checking account's transaction register and change the Num field that shows the old check number to **Print Check**. This adds the check to the list waiting to be printed. You'll see it when you print the next batch.

Click **Alert** to open the Alert window. From here you can set a warning for when this account approaches a minimum balance. This stops further checks from printing and helps you to avoid overdrawing your account.

Now you're ready to print. To print only the first check in the list, click **Print First**. This is an excellent way to ensure everything is running smoothly.

To print specific checks, click **Selected Checks**, then **Choose**. This opens the Select Checks to Print dialog box. All checks are selected by default. Just click in the Print column to toggle those checks you want to include in the batch. Click the **Close (X)** button and then **OK** to print the checks you selected.

To print the entire batch, click **OK** with the **All Checks** option selected.

As soon as Quicken is finished printing, it opens a final dialog box to make sure everything printed as promised. Don't automatically click **OK**. Carefully look over the checks you have printed. If you spot any mistakes, enter the number of the first check to show a mistake. Quicken will keep it and all remaining checks on the to-be-printed list, letting you have another shot at automated check printing after you've solved the problem.

Doing the Transaction Splits

It's easy to write about simple transactions where the transaction uses a single category. The only problem is that you'll almost certainly find situations where your basic mono-categorical transaction simply doesn't cut it.

If you work from home, for example, you probably pay your utility bill using a single check, even though you can divide the payment between your home and your work—the latter for its tax deduction.

You could record this as two separate transactions that show the appropriate percentages of the total targeting each category, but that's rather inefficient.

Instead, let's limber up for some splits.

A split transaction uses more than one category—in fact, it can use up to 30 at a time!

You probably haven't seen any just yet (although you certainly will after you record your first paycheck—see Chapter 9), but they're easy enough to recognize. Just look for the Split in the category field. To see what made that split, click the small green tick to the category's right. Alternatively, press **Ctrl+S** or click **Split** in the Transaction toolbar.

To create a split, fill out the transaction as you normally do, making sure you enter a total amount into the appropriate register field. However, after you reach the category field, click the down arrow and select **Split**. The following figure shows an example of a rental expense split across the business and home components. Even though each split has its own memo, the transaction as a whole also has its own. It's useful to explain the reasoning behind each split using that split's memo, and the reason for the entire transaction (such as the dates of this rental payment) in the transaction's memo.

Set a category,
sub-category, or class
for each part of the split.　Type a memo.

Enter the amount
or use the
Calculator tool.

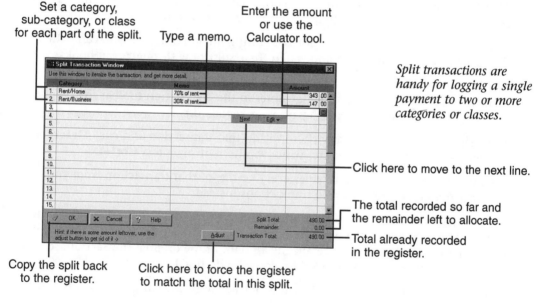

Split transactions are handy for logging a single payment to two or more categories or classes.

Click here to move to the next line.

The total recorded so far and the remainder left to allocate.

Total already recorded in the register.

Copy the split back
to the register.

Click here to force the register
to match the total in this split.

Select the category as you would in a nonsplit transaction, either by typing in the first few letters or selecting it from the drop-down list. You can also mix transfers and categories in the one split. If you are recording a transfer, simply type in the account name surrounded by square brackets. For example: [**My Savings**]. You can use this technique to record payments on loans, splitting the transaction between an Interest Expense component and the Principal. However, Quicken can also do this automatically for you when you set up a mortgage and home account.

Press **Tab** and type a memo. The memo prints on the check stub; the category doesn't.

Press **Tab** again and enter the amount. This is the component of the transaction applicable to this line of the split. You can also use the calculator to work out a percentage amount rather than a straight dollar figure. Just leave the total "as is" and click the **Calculator** icon. Type the percentage and press %. Quicken inserts the total into the split's amount.

Click **Next** or press **Enter** to move to the next line and repeat the process for any other splits. Check the Remainder to make sure you have allocated the original total in full. Otherwise, click **Adjust** to balance the split.

When you finish, click **OK** to record the split and return to the register.

Type a memo and press **Enter** to record the split transaction.

Editing, Deleting, and Voiding Transactions

Many accounting systems treat recorded transactions as if they were carved in stone. After they have been entered, that's it. Forgeddaboudit! There is literally no way for an operator to delete a transaction once it has been typed into the system.

Quicken isn't quite such a stickler for accounting integrity. In fact, you can edit, delete, or void any transaction and watch the results flow through your books.

To edit any transaction, find the transaction and click the field you need to edit. Make the change as required and click Enter in the Transaction toolbar to save the change. (Or just press the **Enter** key on your keyboard.)

To delete a transaction, click anywhere within that transaction and click **Delete** in the upper-left corner of the register window. Alternatively, press **Ctrl+D**.

Even though deleting is easy, it wipes every vestige of that transaction from your account. You might prefer to void transactions instead.

Voiding deletes the effect a transaction had on your books but leaves a copy in the register. This is handy if you want to retain a permanent record of that register entry. Unfortunately, voiding doesn't retain the amount of the original transaction, so make sure you copy that to the Memo field before you do the deed.

You can spot voided transactions because Quicken adds the word Void before the Payee's name and deletes the transaction amount.

Using QuickEntry 2000

QuickEntry 2000 provides a convenient way to record transactions in your books without launching the full complexity of Quicken.

You can start QuickEntry in two ways:

➤ Click the Windows Start button, select **Programs**, click the **Quicken** menu command, and click **QuickEntry 2000**.

➤ From the Windows desktop, double-click the **QuickEntry 2000** icon.

QuickEntry is a standalone register pane, as shown in the following figure. You can access any account—with the exception of investment or 401(k)s—and you can record income, expense, and transfer transactions.

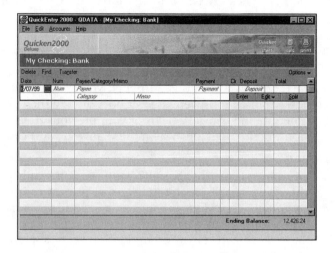

Use QuickEntry to quickly record a few transactions, or to set someone else's recording transactions without laying your financial records open before them.

However, don't panic when you don't see any transactions in the QuickEntry window. QuickEntry can only record transactions, preventing you in its default setup from viewing those that are already there.

Displaying Past Transactions in QuickEntry

If you wish, you can easily set Quicken so that it displays past transactions in QuickEntry. Just open the **Edit** menu from within Quicken (not QuickEntry), select **Options**, choose **Register**, click the **Miscellaneous** tab and click to place a check mark beside **Show Transaction History in QuickEntry**.

To open Quicken, click the **Start Quicken** button in the top-right corner of the window.

If you have set password protection for your data file (see Chapter 19, "Backing Up, Restoring, and Securing Your Data"), you or anyone else can access that file and enter transactions through QuickEntry—although they aren't recorded until you enter Quicken. However, it isn't possible to open the file through the **Start Quicken** function without supplying the password.

Can I Delete the QuickEntry Shortcut?

Sure. Given that it's really just Quicken running in different clothing, feel free to delete the shortcut from your desktop. Just click once to select it and press your **Delete** key.

If you start Quicken after recording transactions in QuickEntry, you see an Accept Transactions dialog box. Use this to edit, delete, or accept certain or all transactions, or click **Finished** to continue with Quicken and keep these transactions in the QuickEntry pending file.

QuickEntry is a great concept, but it does lead to a word of warning: the Payee field in QuickEntry acts like any other payee field, displaying a list of all your memorized transactions. Although you can't see when these transactions were used, it does display the payee, amount, and category fields of your previous transactions, perhaps giving away more than you want casual eyes to know.

So what can you do about it? Well, about the only thing you can do is set a password to protect your file. By default, QuickEntry refuses entry to a file that has been protected by a password unless that password is applied. The only time it won't do that is if the password option has been deselected under the Miscellaneous tab of Quicken's Register Options.

The Least You Need to Know

➤ Every transaction you record in Quicken eventually ends up in a register. You can adjust almost any aspect of a transaction through the register, including those recorded using one of Quicken's transaction tools; for example, the Write Checks window.

➤ It's easiest to record checks you want to print using the Write Checks window. However, if you don't plan to use windowed envelopes, you can also record these checks in the register. Just set the Num field to Print.

➤ Deleting a transaction removes if from your register for good. Consider voiding it instead, copying the transaction's total amount to the memo field.

➤ QuickEntry 2000 is a great way to record transactions without starting the complete Quicken program. However, be careful of the security issues that relate to the Payee field. Set password protection if you are worried about your data's security.

It's a Category and Class Thing

Categories and classes help you to make sense of your transactions. You already know the basics, but this chapter will teach you how to use categories and classes to turn Quicken into a powerful data-extraction tool. And you want to know the best news? There isn't a dentist in sight!

Using Categories and Classes

Remember when library catalogs were built of row upon row of tiny wooden drawers? Those were the days when library cards knew their place, and didn't get all uppity just because they'd been sent to the Library of Congress. It's enough to make old librarians go all Dewey about the eyes.

Quicken uses a method similar to the old box-based cataloguing system to track, sort, and group transactions.

Just as each book's cataloguing card was assigned a particular drawer, each transaction in Quicken is assigned a particular category.

You can use the categories later to group and browse related transactions. You also can set up all the cross-referencing you need by assigning a certain class to transactions stored in different categories.

Without categories and classes, Quicken would be little more than a system for recording a long list of transactions—something you can achieve with notepaper, a few vertical lines, and a pen.

With them, the story is quite different. You can use categories to:

➤ **Tag your income and expense transactions** This helps you see where your income originated and how it was spent. Quicken provides numerous graphs and reports to dissect that information in a number of very useful ways.

➤ **Automate taxes** Categories help you assign your income and expenses to specific deductible and nondeductible line items on the Form 1040 and its accompanying schedules. This is quite a job, but Quicken also includes a great feature called the Paycheck Wizard that makes it easy. You can learn more about this in Chapter 9, "Paychecks and Tax Categories."

➤ **Stick to a budget** By comparing your income and expenses against budgeted amounts, you can see precisely how well you are doing.

➤ **Plan for the future** Categories help you project your spending.

➤ **Track income and expenses across multiple categories** This is great for generating profit and losses on specific projects or jobs.

Subcategories, Classes, and Subclasses

Subcategories further differentiate related transactions; classes and subclasses act as filtering tools, helping you to view related transactions that fall into multiple categories and subcategories.

Categories are easy to master. However, they are also extremely powerful. In fact, after you start adding subcategories, classes, and subclasses, Quicken is able to track just about any group of transactions you can imagine, at any level of detail you desire.

Using Categories in Your Transactions

Quicken has three basic rules when it comes to using categories in transactions:

➤ You can record a category in any category field simply by typing in the first few letters of its name or selecting it from the drop-down list that appears in the category field of any transaction. Quicken uses its QuickFill feature to complete the category with the closest match from its list.

➤ If Quicken gets the QuickFill wrong, continue typing. As long as that category actually exists, you will eventually type enough letters to arrive at a match.

➤ If you try to use a category that doesn't exist, just create it "on-the-fly." Type in the full category name and press **Tab**, as if to move to the next field. Quicken stops you with a New Category dialog box. Click **Yes** to move to the Set Up Category dialog box explained in "Creating New Categories," found later in this chapter.

Although Quicken's default categories make a good place to start, you'll probably find plenty of excuses to add your own. For instance, want to track how much you spend on Oreos? (Hey! It's a hobby!) Just add an Oreos subcategory to the Groceries category.

You can add, edit, and delete categories via the Category & Transfer List.

To open it, select the **Finance** menu and choose **Category & Transfer List**. The window shown in the following figure appears.

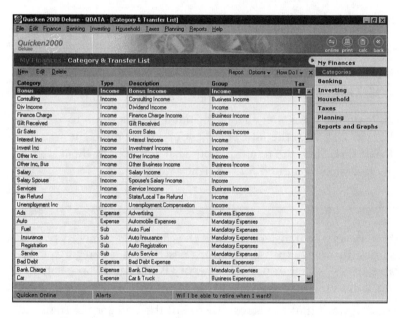

The Category & Transfer List is a great place to discover the categories Quicken has already set up for your accounts.

This list shows every category included in your Quicken file, but you can use the **Options** menu to switch between displaying all categories, income categories, expense categories, account transfers, or tax-related categories.

The list also shows available account transfers. Although account transfers aren't really categories, they are used in place of them, hence their inclusion in the list.

Can I Make Quicken's Categories Match the Codes Used in My Old Accounting System?

It takes a bit of work, but the answer is yes. Start with a new set of books and delete all of Quicken's categories. Then create your own using the old code as the name for each category and the description as the plain-English category description used by your other accounting system.

Learning the Category List

One of the best ways to learn the categories already included in Quicken is to print the Category & Transfer List. With the list open on your screen, open the **File** menu and select **Print List**. Stick the results to your wall and consult them whenever you feel yourself scratching around for the right category to use in a transaction.

The five columns in the Category & Transfer List show the category's name, its type (there are three possibilities: Income, Expense, or Sub), a description, a category group name, if applicable, and whether or not this category is marked as tax-related. (If you see a T in the Tax column, it's tax-related.)

The New, Edit, and Delete buttons that run across the top of the Category & Transfer List window are self-explanatory. The others need some work.

Click the **Report** button to generate a category report that shows all transactions flagged to the selected category. (If that category hasn't been used, you will be told "No Matching Transactions Found".)

The Options menu performs several tasks. You can use it to filter the categories displayed, to select the columns displayed in this window (try selecting **Show Tax Item**), to set up Category Groups, to match tax-related categories to specific questions on your tax forms, and to add categories from Quicken's list of preset groups.

More on the last three in a moment.

Finally, How Do I answers common questions relating to categories.

Tax-Related

The transactions flagged to tax-related categories are included in tax-related reports as part of your income and expenses. If you plan to use Quicken to prepare your tax—something it's darn good at doing—you should ensure all your taxable income flows into a tax-related income category while all your deductible expenses flow through tax-related expense categories.

Creating New Categories

Feel free to create as many categories as you need; the standard categories don't always do the trick.

To start creating categories, open your **Category & Transfer List** and click **New**. This opens the Set Up Category dialog box shown in the following figure.

Creating Categories As You Go

You can also create categories when recording transactions. Just type in the category name and, if Quicken doesn't find it in the list, fill in the New Category dialog box that appears just as is described in the following paragraph.

Categories help you to view related income and expense transactions.

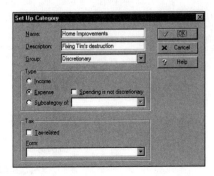

Enter a name for this category using up to 32 characters. Then type a description. The description appears in report headings. If you don't enter a description, Quicken uses the category name instead.

Optionally select a category **Group**. Groups are supersets of categories that help you to budget. (Instead of specifying precisely how much you want to spend on dining, cinemas, and so on, you can just set a budget for the group called *Discretionary*.) You will learn more about groups later in this chapter. To create a new group, click the **New** button that appears in the group selection drop-down list.

Nearly all your categories are **Income** or **Expense** categories, and you should select either of these options in the Type section of the New Category dialog box. Also, you can make creating a budget easier by selecting **Spending is not discretionary** if this is an unavoidable regular expense such as rent, mortgage or loan repayments, certain medical expenses, or college fees.

If you want to create a subcategory under an existing category, click **Subcategory of** and select the parent category from the list. (Subcategories are discussed in the next section.)

To include this category in a Tax Summary report click **Tax-related**. To also include it in your Tax Schedule report, select the appropriate tax form line item from the list. Tax Summary reports are useful when you have a taxation professional working by your side and on your side. The Tax Schedule relates directly to specific Form 1040 line items and is more useful if you want TurboTax or some other software to try to reduce the amount owed to Uncle Sam. You can learn more about tax-related categories in Part 2, "Taxing Times."

When you have finished, click **OK** to save the new category.

Adding Categories from the Preset List

The category presets are those loaded when you started using Quicken. Particular sets were chosen according to the responses you gave to the first set of questions in the New User Setup.

There are five special lists of categories built into Quicken in addition to the standard set that appears with every new file. The first four are called Married, Homeowner, Business, and Children. The fifth set, Investment, is automatically loaded when you create your first investment account.

If your circumstances have changed since you first started to use Quicken, you might want to add extra categories from one of these sets.

To do so, first open the **Category & Transfer List**. Then pull down the **Options** menu and select **Add Categories**. This opens the Add Categories dialog box.

Use the **Available Categories** menu to select the appropriate set.

The categories included in that set are shown in the left-hand list. Select the categories that you want to copy across by clicking to place a check mark in the far-left column of that list. (You can also select them all by clicking **Mark All**.) Click **Add>>** to copy the categories you marked to the list on the right.

You can select more categories and category sets if you like, adding them to the right-hand list. When you've finished, click **OK** to add all those categories you copied to your actual category list.

Editing a Category

To edit a category, select it in the **Category & Transfer List** and click **Edit**. The Edit Category dialog box takes the same form as the Set Up Category dialog box, and you can use the details given previously as a guide.

You might change any aspect of a category including its name or description and its tax status. Categories can also change from income to expense or vice versa, but take care—you could do very interesting things to your profit and loss reports.

Deleting and Merging Categories

To delete a category, select it from the list and click **Delete**.

Deleting a category doesn't delete any transactions in which it was used. Instead, those transactions stay right where they were, but with a blank category field.

Merging categories is almost as easy as deleting them.

Just edit the original category, changing its type so that it becomes a subcategory of the destination category. Then delete the original category. When you delete a subcategory, Quicken shifts all of the transactions contained in that category to the parent category. By deleting the original category, you transfer those transactions to the destination category.

If you want to merge some of the transactions assigned to one category but not all of them, use the Recategorize utility described next. This makes it easy to separate those that need to be merged from those that don't.

Recategorizing Transactions

You can recategorize your transactions in two ways. The hard way is to search for them by scrolling through the account registers, and editing them one at a time. The easy way is to use Quicken's Recategorization tool.

You can find it under the Edit menu. Click **Find & Replace** and select **Recategorize**.

Specify the old category in the **Search Category** field, or use the down arrow to select it from the category list. You can search on categories and transfers.

Click **Find All** to search for all transactions flagged to that category. Any transactions found are displayed in the list below the search box. Quicken searched through split transactions as well as normal transactions. To bypass the split transactions, click to remove the check mark from **Show Matches in Split**.

Only marked transactions are converted to the new category. You can mark them by clicking to place a check mark in the leftmost column beside each transaction.

To mark all the transactions in the list, click **Mark All**.

Select or type the new category into **Replace With** and click **Replace** to perform the conversion.

Creating and Using Subcategories

Subcategories are the ideal way to extract more detail from broad-based categories. For example, Quicken's default categories help you to track just one set of bank charges. But what if you have two bank accounts? How can you differentiate between the charges applied to each?

The obvious way is to create another bank charges category. You've already seen how easy this is. However, it's not that great an idea in the long run. For instance, while those two categories make it easy for you to see how much in the way of charges that bank has slugged you in each account, you can't combine both amounts for a true overview of your bank charges across all accounts.

The answer lies in retaining the original *Bank Charges* category but also in creating two new categories beneath it (hence, the "sub" in subcategory).

You can still assign transactions to the parent category, but you can also assign them individually to each of the subcategories. Even better, you get to determine which level of category you see in Quicken's reports and graphs. The subcategory level shows the charges broken down by bank, while the category level neatly totals the subcategory amounts.

To create a subcategory, follow the instructions for "Creating a New Category." However, instead of specifying an income or expense type, click **Subcategory of** and choose the parent category from the list. The subcategory inherits the parent category's income or expense type.

You can use subcategories as easily as you do standard categories. For example, to assign any transaction to a subcategory, enter the parent category followed by a colon (:) and then the subcategory. For example, *Bank Charges: Bank of America*.

When you delete a subcategory, all of its transactions are automatically assigned to the parent category.

Creating and Using Category Groups

Category groups enable you to group categories (and any subcategories within them) into larger groups yet again. Remember that ditty about larger fleas having smaller fleas and so on, ad infinitum? That's what it's like.

You can use category groups to summarize the data contained in various categories and subcategories, providing you with a simplified view of your finances.

They are also ideal for use in budgets and reports.

The standard set of Quicken categories includes three category groups: Discretionary, Income, and Mandatory Expense.

The first is made up of expense categories that are not absolutely essential. For instance, one common discretionary category ideal for this group would be entertainment.

The Income category group bundles together all your income categories. You can use this for all your income including salaries, wages, tips, bonuses, and so on, but you might prefer to create an Other Income category group to handle your tips and bonuses, dividends from investments, and so on. The first is easier to count on when constructing a budget than is the second, so separating those categories makes sense.

Category Groups

If you've used versions of Quicken prior to the 1999 release, you'd know Category Groups as Supercategories. The change is only in the name. They work the same way, do the same things, and, like roses, smell as sweet.

The last category group, Mandatory Expenses, used to be called non-discretionary. It groups expense categories that must be met, no matter what. As mentioned previously, these include rent, regular fees, and the like.

If you mentioned when you first set up your books that you were also running a business, you see two additional category groups. Business Expenses, as its name suggests, should be used for grouping all categories relating to your business expenses. And Business Income, well, I'm sure that doesn't need explaining.

If you do run a business, pay special attention to category groups because they can prove very useful indeed. For instance, most small business accounts try to divide the business's income and expenses into:

➤ **Income**   Income derived from your primary business.

➤ **Other Income**   Income derived from secondary sources, such as that earned on investments.

➤ **Cost of Goods Sold**   Expenses relating directly to the manufacture of your goods. These are usually unavoidable expenses such as the cost of raw materials.

➤ **Expenses**   Expenses that are necessary but not directly related to the manufacturer; for instance, marketing costs, office space, computers, word processing software, and telephone bills.

➤ **Other Expenses**   These expenses include travel and accommodation, entertainment, and anything else that tends to lie on the periphery of the business.

Category groups are ideal for shuffling categories into these rather broad areas. Just bear in mind that they behave a little differently compared to categories and subcategories. For example, there is no way to assign a transaction to a category group. Instead, that transaction is assigned to a category that just happens to be part of the destination group. It appears under that group in reports and budgets, but is never directly linked to it. Also, deleting a group has no effect on the transactions underneath it.

To view your category groups and the categories that are assigned to them, open your **Category & Transfer List**, open the **Options** menu and select **Assign Category Groups**. The dialog box shown in the following figure appears.

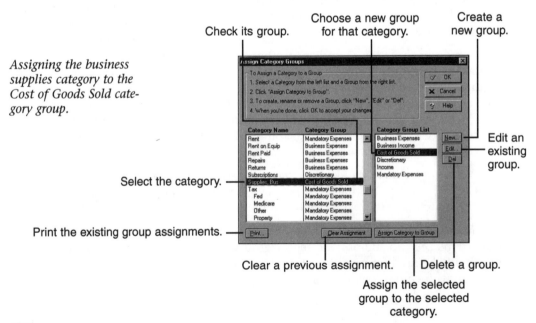

Assigning the business supplies category to the Cost of Goods Sold category group.

The list on the left shows every Quicken category and its assigned group, if any. The list on the right shows all available groups.

You can create, edit, or delete groups using the buttons to the right of the Category Group List.

To create a new category group, just click **New**, enter a **Group Name**, and click **OK**.

After you've created the group, you need to assign categories to it. You can also use these steps to assign categories to existing groups.

Using the **Category Name** list in the Assign Category Groups dialog box, select the categories you want to assign to the category group. You can select more than one category by holding down the **Ctrl** (Control) key while you click each one.

Click the **Category Group List** to select the group you're going to assign. Then click **Assign Category to Group** to assign those categories to the category group. You see the group name appear beside each category's Category Group listing. To remove a group designation, select the category and click **Clear Assignment**.

Click the **Print** button to generate a handy list of your group assignments.

Category groups help you to build budgets and create financial forecasts. They are also useful for collating the figures to be used in a report. Although reports are discussed in Chapter 8, "Powerful Reports and Great Graphs," remember that you can often select a category group using the Organization field when customizing any report. This gives you an easier way to print a report that, for business anyway, shows all Business Income category groups followed by Cost of Goods Sold groups and, finally, Business Expense category groups, just as it would appear in a profit and loss report.

Creating and Using Classes

Wow! Your head's probably spinning from the number of ways you can categorize transactions beyond categories alone.

Want one more? Even if you can't conceive of any reason why you'd want to arrange your transactions in yet another way, take the time to brush up on classes.

Classes are incredibly useful because you can use them to grab related transactions, no matter in which sub- or normal categories they occur.

Okay, enough of the waffle. This definitely calls for an example.

Let's assume you own two homes. You live in one and rent out the other. Expenses occurred in maintaining the rental property are tax deductible and you need to track them separately from those associated with your residence.

There are two ways you can do this: Create duplicate sets of categories or subcategories for each home—an unwieldy, inelegant solution—or use one set of categories with classes to differentiate the transactions that were incurred on behalf of each property.

The second method enables you to view subtotals for transactions relating to both properties or filter them by their classes so that you only see those relating to one property at a time.

Classes are easy enough to use—it's understanding how they work that takes some time. So before we get started, here are some general notes that should give you a heads-up:

➤ A class is just a means of tagging transactions no matter to which category those transactions were assigned. You shouldn't use classes in place of categories, rather you should use classes in conjunction with them.

➤ By filtering your data through particular classes, you can create individual profit-and-loss centers. Using the earlier housing problem, it would be possible to print a profit-and-loss report filtered through the class designated to the rental property. This would immediately reveal the income and expense transactions directly associated with that house, telling you how much profit or loss you made. You can use this information to fine-tune your tax return.

➤ Classes are ideal if you work more than one job or operate more than one business. Just define a class for each business or job and use those classes when recording job- or business-related income and expense transactions. Quicken can automatically segregate the transactions targeted at each business, making it easy for you to file individual returns.

➤ Classes save you from creating a host of subcategories. For example, many categories apply to each of the properties discussed above. These include rates, repairs, telephone, electricity, and so on. Rather than creating subcategories for one house or the other under each of these categories, simply create one class for each home and save yourself a bunch of time.

Are you convinced? Then read on.

Open the **Finance** menu and click **Class List**, or just press **Ctrl+L**.

The Class List displays all your existing classes. Chances are it's empty because, unlike with categories, Quicken doesn't set up any classes for you. Click **New** to open the Set Up Class dialog box.

Enter a name for this class using up to 32 characters, and type an optional description. The description is used for report headings. If you don't record one, Quicken uses the class name instead.

The copy number helps Quicken prepare multiple copies of certain tax-related forms. (Copy number information is also passed to TurboTax.) Why do you need it? If you run two or more businesses, you can use the copy number to generate multiple Schedule Cs. You can also use the copy number if you work two or more jobs and receive more than one Form W-2. Just create a class for each business or job and assign one copy number *1* and the other copy number *2*. Add the appropriate class to each transaction concerning one business or the other and Quicken will have all the information it needs to prepare separate returns.

Classifying with Classes

You can use a class with or without an associated category. However, as with categories, some basic rules apply to their use:

➤ The class must be preceded by a forward slash (/), for instance: /Bus 1.

➤ When used with categories, classes are recorded like this: Category/Class. Transfers between accounts can also stand in for categories. Therefore, a register entry could read: [Transfer Account]/Class.

➤ You can mix classes with subcategories if you record them in the following order: Category:Subcategory/Class.

➤ You can also treat any class as a subclass, even though subclasses aren't explicitly supported the way subcategories are. To use a class as a subclass, type in the first class followed by a colon, followed by the subclass as in: Class:Subclass. The full notation looks something like this: Category:Subcategory/Class:Subclass.

➤ Almost anywhere Quicken calls for a category, you can use a class instead. For example, many reports support classes. Just customize the report so that row headings in the Report Layout section of the customization dialog box are set for **Class** rather than **Category**.

Check This Out

Reclassifying Classes

Quicken doesn't provide a reclassification tool, but you can search for and reclassify classes using the standard Find & Replace function. Just type a forward slash in the **Find** field followed by the class name. Do the same for the destination class in the **Replace** field. Click **Find All**, then **Mark All**, and finally **Replace** to make the switch.

The Least You Need to Know

➤ Categories and classes are the key to not only collecting and organizing your transactions into like-minded groups, but also to extracting oodles of information about them from Quicken.

➤ Subcategories are a great way to break down a single category into sections that make more sense. Use them when you need to include a whole lot of different sections under Income, Auto, Home, Education, Entertainment, and so on.

➤ Category groups are mostly used for budgeting. They were called Super-categories in versions prior to Quicken 99, and while their name has changed, they remain "super" in many ways.

➤ Classes help you to join transactions scattered through numerous category groups. They are handy when you need to track the income and expenses associated with a particular item, project, or job.

Chapter 5

Accounting for Accounts

In This Chapter

➤ Creating more accounts

➤ Editing existing account details

➤ Reconciling your accounts and statements

➤ Transferring funds between accounts

Creating Additional Accounts

There's no accounting for taste, but Quicken certainly has a taste for accounts. At last tally, Quicken Deluxe 2000 offered some 14 flavors, and there are even more accounts in Quicken Home and Business!

The checking account you created with the New User Setup dialog box might prove to be the only account you need. After all, it can record all of the transactions associated with your primary bank account, and it can assign those transactions to any number of income and expense categories.

On the other hand, if your financial situation is just a little more complex, you need to create additional accounts. These can help you to manage your credit card, invest in property and shares, maintain an inventory, or do any of the other things for which Quicken's so useful.

Here's a quick guide to the major types:

➤ **Checking**   This is the best way to use Quicken's time-saving check-writing and printing facilities, but you should also use these accounts to manage any checking account, or to send your payments electronically across the Internet.

➤ **Savings**   These accounts differ from a checking account only in that you record withdrawals from this account using the transaction register rather than an onscreen checkbook.

➤ **Credit Card**   As its name suggests, you use these accounts to manage your credit card. This type of account also contains a few extra features including the capability to specify a credit card limit (Quicken keeps you constantly appraised of available funds), as well as the capability to generate a reminder when you exceed your own set limit. By the way, if you use a debit card, just track it using an ordinary checking account instead of a credit card account.

➤ **Money Market**   These accounts are another variation on the checking/ savings account theme.

➤ **Cash**   Simply an asset account with slightly different register column headings. That is, Spend and Receive rather than Increase and Decrease. You can use these accounts to track the funds in a savings jar, petty cash tins, or if you run a small business, your actual cash registers.

➤ **Brokerage**   These are asset accounts used to track units in a trust as well as individual stocks. They are very different from Quicken's other accounts. To learn more, read Part 4, "Investing: Making Dollars with Sense."

➤ **IRA or Keogh**   These are tax-deferred investment accounts that can track a single mutual fund or a complete portfolio. There are several variations within this type of account to cover the various tax-advantaged investment schemes developed by Congress. You can use the IRA or Keogh account type for the standard IRA or Keogh, but also for a Roth, SEP, or Education account.

➤ **401(k)**   Quicken automatically marks your retirement savings accounts as tax-deferred as soon as you create them. The software also treats this type of account as an investment account, following the fluctuating value of one or more funds. This account can be used for any tax-deferred retirement account used to track investment funds. It is only available in Quicken Deluxe 2000 and Quicken Home and Business 2000.

➤ **Dividend Reinvestment Plan**   It is said that plumbers always have dripping taps. Conversely, it seems that financial advisers always know how to tap DRIPs. Quicken's DRIP are yet another form of investment account, but one that works the same way as the standard investment account.

➤ **Other Investment**   This is another standard investment account. There is no particular reason to use it in place of an ordinary investment account, unless you have some securities investments that you don't want included in your standard portfolio. For example, shares that you hold but that you would never usually trade.

With So Many Account Types, Are They All Different?

Actually, there are only a few types of accounts, at least in so far as the way they operate internally. Most accounts fall into the asset or liability groupings, and nearly all accounts, with the exception of retirement savings and investment accounts, present an almost identical transaction register. Indeed, the only things that change are the background colors and the Debit and Credit column headings.

➤ **House**   In this latest version, Quicken has added specialized House and Vehicle asset accounts. You can use these to track the value of your major assets with or without an associated mortgage. Quicken also can download the latest median prices for houses in your area.

➤ **Vehicle**   Use this account to track the value of your automobile (one per account) with or without a mortgage. Quicken can also download the used value of your car from the Internet. If you don't see your car's make or model in the drop-down lists when creating this account, feel free to type in the actual make or model.

➤ **Asset**   Use this type of account to track assets large and small, including your home inventory, property equity, funds owed to you, vehicles, expensive toys such as boats and aircraft, and so on. If you lend money to someone, link this account to an amortized loan to track the repayments due.

➤ **Liability**   Useful for tracking your short- and long-term liabilities such as personal loans, mortgages, bills to be paid, and so on. You can attach these accounts to amortized loans to remind you when payments are due.

➤ **Invoices/Receivables**   Quicken Home and Business also supports this final type of account. You can learn more about this in Part 5, "Minding Your Business."

➤ **Bills/Payables**   This is another account unique to Quicken Home and Business. Use this account to track amounts you owe. Learn more in Part 5, "Minding Your Business.

Open Your Accounts List

Your list of accounts is the best place from which to create, edit, or delete accounts. To open it, select the **Finance** menu and choose **Account List** (or press **Ctrl+A**). You can also use this list to access each account's register and adjust that account's optional information.

Creating a new account is easy, but the steps differ according to the type of account you decide to create. Although Quicken's dialog boxes can guide you through the process, there's also a shortcut that works for every type of account except the 401(k).

To create a new account, first open your list of accounts (**Ctrl+A**). Then click **New** just above the list or open the **Edit** menu, select **Accounts**, and choose **New**; or just press **Ctrl+N**. However you get there, you eventually launch the Create New Account dialog box shown in the following figure.

This is the first step in creating a whole range of accounts.

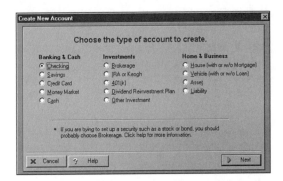

Select the type of account you want to create and click **Next**. Now, rather than working through Quicken's step-by-step instructions—the steps differ for each account type—click the **Summary** tab to follow a handy shortcut.

Fill in the fields in the Summary window using the following information as a guide. If you don't see one of the fields mentioned, don't panic; this simply means it isn't supported by that type of account. Skip that field and move on to the next.

The Account Name appears on the Account tab in the Register window. You can use any combination of letters, spaces, and numbers with the exception of the following characters: [ ] / : ¦ ^. Keep the account name short so it doesn't completely fill the register tab.

> ### Should I Create an Account for Every Real-World Account?
>
> It depends on how important those accounts are to you. For instance, there's probably no need for you to track the value of an old savings account with just a few dollars in it. Frankly, it's not worth the effort. However, you should try to create accounts for those items of great value that don't actually have their own real-world accounts. For example, you might like to create an account to hold the value of any antique furniture you own, and you should most certainly create accounts to track your retirement savings.

The Description is used in various Quicken reports. If nothing else, it makes up for a short account name.

If you are creating one of the investment accounts, you see two more options. Select **Account Contains a Single Mutual Fund** if you only want to track a single unit trust or mutual fund using this account. In the Cash Balance area select **Use a Linked Checking Account for my Cash Balance** if your investment account includes check-writing capabilities. You are then able to select an existing checking account or create a new one on the spot.

For other accounts, fill in the Balance… by referring to the most recent statement you have received for this account. Enter the ending balance shown on the statement along with the date the statement was issued. If you don't receive statements and you only want to track the value of a single asset or liability with this account, use the balance and date fields to record the cost (or value) and date you purchased or received that asset or incurred that liability. To track a mix of assets or liabilities, leave the opening balance and date at zero and record the value of those assets or liabilities by recording individual transactions in the account register.

If shown, select your **Financial Institution** from the list. This is the first step in setting up your account for online access. If you don't want to use online access, ignore this setting.

Click to select if your account is supported by a compatible financial institution. Online credit card accounts are particularly useful because you can automatically download every transaction relating to that card, saving on significant typing.

Financial Institutions

This placement of the list of financial institutions represents a change in the way Quicken handles online transactions. You'll see numerous instances in which online banking and bill paying have moved from the Online Financial Center to take a more central role in the rest of the software. The good news is that the system now works better than it ever has.

Do I Need to Set Up for Online Banking Right Away?

Although it is convenient to download statements for your accounts, and even to pay your bills electronically, you can avoid the urge for as long as you like. It's easy to make the shift to online banking at a later date.

Click to select **Online Payment** if you want to use this account with the Intuit Services Corporation (ISC) electronic payments system. ISC pays the payees electronically if they are registered on their system or mails them checks if they aren't. It's that easy.

If you are creating an investment account, the online options are in the Online Information area. Choose your Financial Institution using the **FI** menu, and click **Online Investment** or **Online Payment** to enable these options.

After you have selected an online option, clicking **Next** takes you to the online financial institution setup system. You can find out more about this in Part 3, "Online in No Time."

When creating a credit card account, you can also specify **Credit Limit, if Applicable**. Quicken uses this to trigger an Alert (see Chapter 6, "Memorized Transactions Are Made of This") when you approach a preset limit. This doesn't have to be the credit card's actual limit but an amount you determine.

Use the buttons under **Optional Information** to record extra information that you want to associate with this asset account. For example, click **Info** to record your financial institution's contact details and the account's interest rate. Quicken doesn't use this information for any of its reports or calculations, but it's good to have it on hand. Click **Tax Info** to set this account as tax-deferred. This is useful for IRAs and other tax-deferred investments. If you do and you also want Quicken to help you prepare your tax, make sure you also click **Transfers In** and select **W-2:Salary or wages, self**. This decreases your reported income (and thus income tax) by however much you transfer to that account.

Okay, you've finished. Click **Done** to save the account. If you have created a liability account, Quicken also offers to set up an amortized loan that is attached to that account. You don't need to accept the offer; you can learn more about this procedure in Chapter 7, "Taking Control of Your Debt." Otherwise, click **No** to create the loan later.

Editing Accounts

There are several ways you can edit accounts.

In previous versions of Quicken it was easiest to select the account in the Account List and click the **Edit** button at the top of the Account List pane. This opened a dialog box similar to that used to create the account.

In Quicken 2000 you can still use this method, but it simply opens the Overview pane, just as if you had clicked the **Overview** tab down by the bottom of the screen when you had that account's register pane open.

Once the Overview pane is open, click any aspects of the account that appear under the heading Account Attributes. Type in the new details, or select a new entry from a drop-down list.

Either way, any changes you make are automatically saved for you.

Reconcilable Differences

A reconciliation is a simple affair...I promise. By comparing each of the transactions you've recorded with those shown on your bank statements, you can ensure that Quicken's account data is kept accurate and up-to-date. You can also verify that you have included all bank charges and any other fees that have been automatically deducted. A reconciliation also helps you to keep track of those checks that have cleared and those that are still waiting to be presented, and to accurately determine the availability of funds.

Quicken offers you two methods of reconciliation. You should use one or the other depending on whether you are using paper-based statements or performing the reconciliation through an online account.

I'm going to take you through a paper-based reconciliation below. To learn how to reconcile an online account, see Part 3.

If the register belonging to the account you want to reconcile isn't open on your screen, open it now and click the **Reconcile** button at the top of the Register window, or open the **Banking** menu, select **Reconcile**, and select the **Reconciliation account** in the dialog box provided.

Are you ready to begin?

You should see the dialog box shown in the following figure. Take a look at your most recent bank statement and enter the ending balance. (The opening balance is calculated for you from your last statement's ending balance.)

Enter your bank statement summary information. Quicken uses this as the basis for the reconciliation.

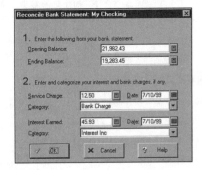

You can also use the additional fields provided to show service charges and interest earned, but Quicken only allows for one of each transaction, so you need to calculate the total if you've received more than one instance of either. (Personally, I prefer to enter these transactions directly into my register after I move past this first dialog box.)

Click **OK** to open the main Reconciliation window shown in the following figure.

Use the transaction lists to complete the reconciliation. Mark off every transaction that appears on your statement. Withdrawals are listed on the left, and deposits are listed on the right. Keep in mind that your statement might not show the transactions in the same order they occurred in your register because your checks probably didn't clear through your bank in the same order you wrote them.

Chances are you'll see several transactions on your statement that don't appear in the reconciliation window. Use the **New**, **Edit**, and **Delete** buttons in the upper-left corner of the Reconcile Bank Statement window to add, edit, or remove transactions from your register. When you're finished, select **Return to Reconcile** from the Transaction toolbar to jump back to the Reconcile window.

Use these buttons to add, edit, or delete transactions in this account's register.

Click here to adjust your statement details. For example, opening and closing balances.

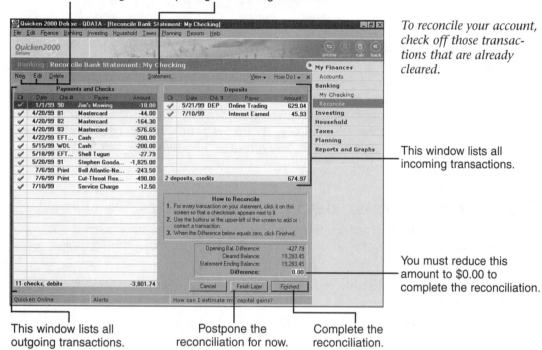

To reconcile your account, check off those transactions that are already cleared.

This window lists all incoming transactions.

You must reduce this amount to $0.00 to complete the reconciliation.

This window lists all outgoing transactions.

Postpone the reconciliation for now.

Complete the reconciliation.

Taking a Reconciliation Break

Reconciliations can prove long and tedious. If you decide you'd rather complete this reconciliation later, have no fear. Just click the **Finish Later** button. Quicken marks all the transactions you indicated as cleared by placing a c in those transactions' Clr column. (You can see this when you return to that account's register.) When you are ready to return, open the register and choose **Reconcile**. Click past the opening dialog box and complete the reconciliation.

After you have marked (or added and marked) every transaction that appears on your bank statement, check the difference in the lower-right corner of the Reconcile window. If it equals zero, you're done. Just click **Finished** to complete the job and optionally print a reconciliation report.

If you can't get your account to reconcile, look through your past transactions, making sure you've recorded each one as shown on your statement.

If you deposited several checks at once, you might find these assigned a single transaction in your statement and a total deposit amount. Make sure the total matches your check stubs and mark off all the individual deposit transactions. You should also try looking for duplicate entries, misplaced decimal points, and so on. The good news is that as long as you reconcile often, you limit the detective work involved in tracking down an error when an account doesn't balance.

Transferring Funds Between Accounts

Sometimes you need to transfer funds from one account to another. Even if you don't walk up to the counter of your bank and specifically request the transfer, there are occasions when you need to do just that in Quicken.

For example, you will need to record transfers if you have set up accounts for any of the following:

➤ **Credit card**   Any checks you write or online payments you make to your credit card provider should be recorded in Quicken as transfers to your credit card liability account. If you don't track your credit card in a separate account (this isn't recommended, because it doesn't allow you to track the credit card's balance), create a Credit Card expense category and log the payment to that.

➤ **Debit card**   Transfer funds on a regular basis to save it from running out of gas.

➤ **Mortgages or loans**   Each repayment is recorded as a transfer to the mortgage or loan liability account. Use Quicken's loan management facilities discussed in Chapter 7 to set up automatic repayments.

➤ **Investments**   Whenever you add money to or draw money from an investment account, you probably need to record it as a transfer to or from the originating or deposit account. The only time you needn't is if you write checks against the account using a linked cash management facility.

Transferring funds between accounts is easy. Just open the account register from which you want to transfer funds, and click the **Transfer** button at the top of its window.

Make sure the correct accounts are selecting in **Transfer Money From** and **To Account**, and provide a **Date**, **Description** and the **Amount**. Click **OK** to record the transfer.

Type-Thru Transfers

The fastest way to record a transfer transaction is to type it directly into the register. Just type a left square bracket in the category field followed by the account name to which you are transferring those funds. (At some point while you are typing, Quicken completes the name so that it is surrounded in square brackets.) For instance, to record a transfer to an account called **Investment**, you probably only need to type Inv. Quicken completes this for you, recording the category as **[Investment]**.

Quicken replicates transfers in both the destination and originating accounts. You can move between each side of the transaction by right-clicking it and selecting **Go To Transfer** from the drop-down list. This takes you to the matched transaction in the other register.

Incidentally, if you delete one half of a transfer transaction, Quicken automatically deletes the other.

The Least You Need to Know

➤ Accounts are as necessary to Quicken as transactions and categories. They provide the easiest way for you to track the value of your assets and liabilities, no matter their form.

➤ It's easy for the version of your account held in Quicken to fall out of lockstep with the actual account held by the bank. A reconciliation is the best way to force them to march in time. A reconciliation is also the ideal way to detect banking errors; something that happens far more often than the bank's confidence in their electronic systems would have you believe.

➤ Transfers are the only way to move funds between accounts. Even if you write a check that makes a payment from your savings account to your investment account, you should not record that transaction as an expense. It's a transfer because your asset level remains the same.

Chapter 6

Memorized Transactions Are Made of This

In This Chapter

➤ Storing a transaction for future use

➤ Locking transactions

➤ Using the Financial Calendar

➤ Scheduling transactions

➤ Setting alerts

Memorizing Transactions

Remember Jeeves, the butler from P. G. Wodehouse's novels? Quicken isn't so dissimilar.

There'll be numerous times when you are happily plugging information into one of Quicken's registers or templates when Quicken automatically takes over your typing, completing the category, the payee, or, in some circumstances, the complete transaction. No fuss, no bother. It almost seems to sense what you're intending to do.

How does it do it? Quicken isn't prescient, despite its simulation of a crystal ball with its financial forecasting feature—mind you, prescience would be useful when downloading stock prices. (I'd like the next two months of the Dow Jones, please.)

Is It Safe for Quicken to Memorize All Those Transactions? Isn't There a Security Issue?

There is, but only if you don't set password protection, see Chapter 19, "Backing Up, Restoring, and Securing Your Data," for more information. Remember also that your list of memorized transactions is also visible in QuickEntry 2000, even if previous entries remain hidden from view.

Quicken completes your data entry by first memorizing every transaction you record—up to 2,000 in all—storing them alphabetically by their payee. The next time you start recording a similar transaction to one of those memorized, it can complete that transaction for you.

You see a list of the memorized transactions every time you click the down arrow next to any payee selection field. You can also view the list in a separate window, and edit or delete those that are no longer required.

Deleting Memorized Transactions

There's an easy way to keep your list of memorized transactions tight and trim. Quicken includes a setting that automatically deletes transactions not used in the past so many months. To adjust this setting, open the **Edit** menu, select **Options**, then **Quicken Program**. Select the **General** tab and click **Remove Memorized Transactions Not Used in Last**...**Months**. Enter the number of months and click **OK**.

To view your list of memorized transactions, open the **Banking** menu and select **Memorized Transaction List** (**Ctrl+T**). You should see something similar to the window shown in the following figure.

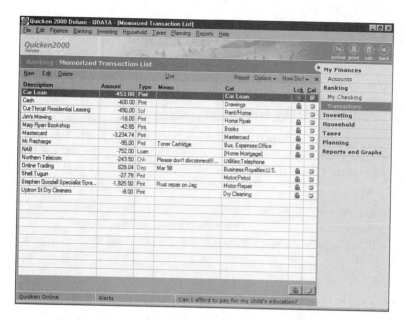

A trip down memory lane? Every transaction you record is added to this list.

Use the buttons at the top of the list to create New memorized transactions, Edit existing memorized transactions, or Delete memorized transactions.

Although most of the columns in the memorized transaction list take their information from the columns used in the register, the two at the end are a little unusual. They indicate Locked and Calendar transactions. You'll learn how to use these next.

Working with Locked Transactions

Imagine you make a regular home maintenance payment such as $20 per month for someone to mow your lawns. The first time you record this transaction Quicken adds it to your list of memorized transactions. It's easy to use it from then on simply by calling up the payee, say *Vern Gogh's Mowing, Plumbing, and Portraiture Service* (he's a talented guy), and selecting that transaction from the list.

But what if the rates go up to $25 per month?

If you use a memorized transaction and change it by adjusting the amount, category, or memo, Quicken automatically updates the stored transaction. The next time you call up that transaction you call up the most recent version used. (This doesn't change examples of that transaction you have already used.)

Although there are innumerable instances where automatic updating is very convenient, there are also times you want to prevent Quicken from changing that transaction. For example, if one month you also asked Vern to dash out a quick portrait of your pet poodle, you might need to pay $125, but you don't want the memorized transaction changed because you will need to go back to the regular amount the next month.

A locked memorized transaction is protected from change. No matter how often you use and adjust that transaction in the future, it does not change the memorized transaction.

To lock a transaction, just find it in the memorized transaction list and click in the **Lock** column of that transaction to place a padlock icon. This prevents the transaction from being inadvertently changed by future register entries.

You can edit a locked transaction by locating it in the list and clicking **Edit**. You can also use this function to convert a memorized transaction to an online payment. This is perfect if you have been using Quicken for awhile but have only just started to utilize the online services.

Alternatively, use the transaction once more and adjust it as required. However, before recording it in the register, select **Edit**, **Transaction**, and **Memorize** (**Ctrl+M**). You can choose to **Replace** the existing transaction or **Add** this copy as a new memorized transaction.

Setting Calendar Transactions

The final column in the Memorized Transaction List is used to flag transactions that should appear in the list attached to the Financial Calendar. You can learn more about the Financial Calendar later in this chapter.

Preparing for Upcoming Payments

Even with the money of Croeseus, bills are still a pain in the you-know-what.

Quicken makes bill payments easy, but if you're the type to forget when a payment falls due, only to find yourself drowning in a flood of increasingly terse reminders, you'll appreciate the software's bill management facilities.

Quicken can help you stay sane and meet your payments on time in the following ways:

➤ Notes placed in Quicken's Financial Calendar can nudge your memory on almost any matter from when payments are due to when you should take your cat to the vet for its annual checkup.

➤ Scheduled payments automatically create the payment transaction, adding it to your list of checks to be printed.

➤ Alerts warn you when an account balance falls below a certain level, when a stock hits a certain price, and when tax payments are due. There are many more alerts besides these. They help you avoid situations that could prove as costly as they are embarrassing.

➤ The Reminder view combines notes, scheduled payments, alerts, and more to show you what you can expect up to 30 days in advance.

➤ By printing your Financial Calendar, you can create a complete schedule for the upcoming month that you can tape to your wall.

➤ And even if you ignore that, you may see a Billminder pop up when you start Windows that lists all your extant reminders and alerts.

Using the Financial Calendar

The Financial Calendar is the best place to get a fast heads-up on what's happening in your financial world. You can use it to note previous transactions, schedule future transactions, and set reminders.

To open the calendar, open the **Finance** menu and select **Financial Calendar** (**Ctrl+K**). You'll see a window similar to the one shown in the following figure.

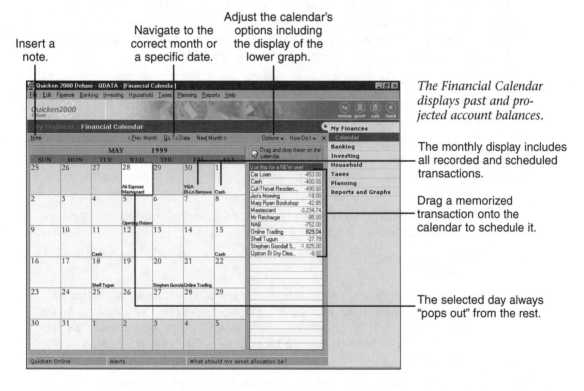

Insert a note.

Navigate to the correct month or a specific date.

Adjust the calendar's options including the display of the lower graph.

The Financial Calendar displays past and projected account balances.

The monthly display includes all recorded and scheduled transactions.

Drag a memorized transaction onto the calendar to schedule it.

The selected day always "pops out" from the rest.

The Options menu controls several important aspects of this window. The first two Options menu entries turn on or off the display of transactions in the calendar itself. You can choose to show recorded transactions (those you've already entered into an account register), as well as scheduled transactions (those that are set down to occur at a future date).

The third and fourth options enable you to control the display of an account balance graph, as well as the memorized transaction list shown to the right of the calendar display.

Customizing the Account Balance Graph

The account balance usually displays the aggregate of your bank accounts. These are the liquid assets you can readily use to pay bills, decreased by the balance of your credit card accounts. If you prefer to view your net worth or the balance of some other accounts or group of accounts, pull down the **Options** menu and select **Calendar Accounts**. Place a check mark next to those accounts you want to include. To display your Net Worth, just click **Mark All**.

Use the Financial Calendar to immediately record transactions in a register or to schedule transactions to occur at a future date.

Scheduled transactions are particularly useful. Not only can you set a transaction date any length of time ahead, Quicken also reminds you before it falls due and takes that transaction into account in any forward-looking reports (for instance, a projected account balance).

Even better, a scheduled transaction can occur once, a limited number of times, or continually at predetermined intervals.

Use scheduled transactions for regular events such as loan repayments, utilities and rental, and so on.

The calendar is a great place to record transactions or to schedule repeating transactions. You can simply drag a previous example of the transaction you want to create from the Financial Calendar's Memorized Transaction List, dropping it onto the target date. (Use the **< Prev Month**, **Go To Date**, and **Next Month >** buttons at the top of the calendar to navigate to the target date.)

Alternatively, click the calendar once to select the target date and then again to open the list of transactions recorded or scheduled for that date. After you see the small transaction window, click **New** to create a new, paid, or scheduled transaction, **Edit** to change the selected transaction, **Delete** to delete the transaction, **Register** to jump to a paid transaction's position in its register, or **Pay Now** to record a scheduled transaction in its register.

Whether you start a new transaction in the Financial Calendar or drag an existing one, you eventually see a New Transaction dialog box similar to that shown in the following figure. Using it is easy.

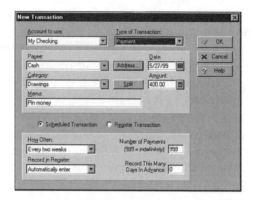

The Financial Calendar is an easy place from which to schedule transactions. Just make sure you set the repeating options so you don't get any unpleasant surprises.

First select an **Account to use**. You can select any of your accounts from the pull-down list. Then indicate the **Type of Transaction**. Just choose from a **Payment**, **Deposit**, **Print Check**, or **Online Pmt**.

Type in a **Payee** or select a memorized transaction from the pull-down list.

The **Address** button is optional and only works when the Type of Transaction is set to **Print Check**. If you are using preprinted checks and windowed envelopes, click **Address** and fill in the Address Book record. (For more information on the Address Book, see Chapter 24, "Making Contact with the Address Book".)

Set a **Date** for the first time this transaction falls due and choose a **Category**. You can specify one category, a transfer, or a **Split** that divides this transaction between two or more categories or transfers.

How Do I Print the Financial Calendar?

With the calendar visible on your screen, open the **File** menu and select **Print Calendar**. Before you do so, you might also want to turn off the display of past transactions. (To do this, click the **Options** menu and click to remove the check mark beside **Show Recorded Transactions in Calendar**.)

Enter the total **Amount** of this transaction and record an optional **Memo**.

To record a scheduled transaction, select **Scheduled Transaction** and fill in the lower part of the dialog box shown using these additional scheduling options:

- ➤ **How Often**   The default is **Only Once**. This means this transaction is enacted only on the selected date. However, you may specify a range of repeating frequencies from weekly to yearly, in which case it appears as often as you like.

- ➤ **Record in Register**   If you want this to be a hands-off transaction, select **Automatically enter**. Select **Prompt before enter** if you want Quicken to ask you to confirm this transaction before it goes ahead.

- ➤ **Number of Payments**   Use this field to specify how many times you want this payment to occur. For instance, if you have 36 payments to make on a personal loan, enter **36** here. Use **999** for an infinite number of payments. You cannot edit this field if you have specified a one-time only transaction.

- ➤ **Record This Many Days in Advance**   Use this field to specify the number of days in advance of the due date that you want this transaction recorded in the register. The transaction is recorded on that date as a postdated transaction. For example, a payment set to record 5 days in advance that is due on January 20 would be recorded in the register on January 15. If the payment is to be made by check, the check will be printed with the date payable set to January 20. This field helps you make your payment in advance, to take into account any delays in mail delivery.

Caution!

If you use Billminder, Quicken notifies you of a scheduled payment by adding Billminder's own advance notice to the notice you specified when recording the scheduled transaction. Therefore, if Billminder is set to give you 7 days notice on all your scheduled transactions, and you have selected an additional 5 days under the transaction's **Record This Many Days in Advance**, you receive a total of 12 days notice (7 days plus 5 days) before the transaction falls due.

To record a register transaction, select **Register Transaction** and use the **Number** pull-down list that appears to the right of Memo to select what you want to appear in the transaction's Num/Ref column when it reaches the register. For printed checks, select **Next Check Num**, or just press the **N** key when you reach that field.

After you have finished, click **OK** to save the transaction.

Setting Notes

Is the world a better place since the creation of the Post-It? Not since Bic's revolutionary ballpoint pen has a low-end technology made such a ubiquitous impact on the office.

Quicken doesn't include Post-Its as such, but it does provide the electronic equivalent in the form of colored notes that you can attach to any day of the calendar. And unlike Post-Its, these don't clutter your work area.

The easiest way to create a reminder is to add a note to the day that reminder falls due. Quicken is limited to one note per calendar day, and that note is limited to a maximum of 500 characters. However, feel free to squeeze in as many subjects as you can.

Even though the notes system is rather rudimentary—you wouldn't use it for scheduling appointments, for instance—if you just want to give yourself a mental prod to call the stockbroker, send your mother a birthday card, renew your club membership, or something similar, it should prove more than adequate.

Can I Share My Notes with Others?

Although you can't print your notes, you can view them attached to a printed copy of the Financial Calendar. Unfortunately, even though notes appear in the Reminders window, you can't print that list.

To set a note, select the target calendar day and click the **Note** button that resides in the upper-left corner of the calendar window. Alternatively, use the right mouse button to click the target day and select **Note** from the menu that appears.

Use the Note dialog box to record a message, as shown in the following figure. Select a color for the note (yellow, if you like Post-Its) and click **Save** to chisel it into your calendar.

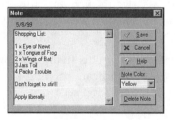

A Note is an easy way to attach a short reminder to a calendar day.

The text of the note isn't displayed in the calendar because it would probably fill more than the available space, but you do see a small icon. However, the text appears in printed versions of the calendar and also in the Reminders and Billminder windows.

Using the Scheduled Transaction List

Although the Financial Calendar is useful for recording scheduled transactions, you might find it easier to manage them via the Scheduled Transaction List.

To open the list, open the **Banking** menu and choose **Scheduled Transaction List** (**Ctrl+J**). (If you have set up an account for online payments, you see three tabs at the top of this window. Click the tabs to move between all scheduled transactions, normal scheduled transactions only, and scheduled online payments only.)

The list is a great place to create new scheduled transactions, edit or delete transactions, bundle transactions into groups, and force early payments of transactions.

Click **New** to start creating a new scheduled transaction.

If you have created an account for online payments, select **Single or Multiple Scheduled Payments** instead of **Repeating Online Payments**. (You don't see this dialog box if you haven't set up any accounts for online payments.)

The instructions for completing a scheduled transaction are almost identical to creating a scheduled transaction using the Financial Calendar.

First select the account to use and the type of transaction. Choose between **Payment**, **Deposit**, **Print Check**, or **Online Pmt**.

Type in a **Payee** or select a memorized transaction from the pull-down list.

The Address button is optional and only works when the Type of Transaction is set to Print Check. If you are using preprinted checks and windowed envelopes, click **Address** and fill in the Address Book record.

Set the **Next Date** to the first time this transaction falls due and choose a **Category**.

Enter the total **Amount** of this transaction and record an optional **Memo**.

Now fill in the lower part of the dialog box using these additional scheduling options.

Use **How Often** to determine the frequency of this payment and **Record in Register** to choose whether you want to be prompted to record this transaction or if you just want it to occur automatically.

Specify the **Number of Payments**, or **999** for an effectively infinite number, and use **Record This Many Days in Advance** to indicate the number of days in advance of the due date that you want this transaction recorded in the register.

After you have finished, click **OK** to save this transaction.

Scheduled transactions are easy to create and a great way to see how your cash flow will appear in a month, week, or even a full year's time. The more scheduled transactions you create, the more automated your bookkeeping becomes. They are also the perfect way to never miss another important loan repayment.

Marking Scheduled Transactions As Paid

Unless you have instructed Quicken to automatically record your scheduled transactions, you need to record them when they fall due.

Your scheduled transactions are listed in the following areas when they are ready to be paid:

➤ **Financial Calendar**   From within the calendar, click on the day the transaction falls due and then again to open the transaction list. Select the transactions and click **Pay Now**.

➤ **Reminders List**   Open the Reminders List from the Finance menu by selecting **Reminders**. You also see this list if you access Quicken from the Billminder. Select the transaction and click **Enter in Register** or click **Skip Payment** to defer it until next time. You can also use this window to view reminders from other Quicken files.

You can set reminders to show reminders for more than the current week. In fact, you can display them up to 30 days in advance. To do so, open the **Edit** menu on Quicken's Menu bar (not the one directly below the top of the Reminders window pane), select **Options**, and choose **Reminders**. Set your advance notice for all reminders using **Days in Advance**. You can also use **Show notes for** to specify the period over which notes are shown.

➤ **Scheduled Transaction List**   From within the list, select the transaction and click **Pay**.

➤ **Billminder**   This is the perfect place for scheduled transactions, but you need to click **Run Quicken** before you can pay.

Each of these methods takes you to the Record Scheduled Transaction dialog box. Use this dialog box to edit the transaction, type in a memo, and specify a check number, if that's applicable. When you finish, click **Record**.

Although it is easy to set up scheduled transactions so that they are recorded without any interference from you, keeping this step in place gives you the opportunity to verify the payment and also to make any last-minute edits. For example, if you are recording a regular rental payment, you can use the Record Scheduled Transaction dialog box to also record a memo giving the period over which that payment is valid.

Setting Alerts

Alerts are the closest Quicken comes to doing your worrying for you—and anything that can do that must be pretty good!

Stock Price Alerts

The stock price alerts do not take stock splits into account. If the stock splits and you don't know about it, you might find the true value of your stock is soaring or plummeting and didn't trigger an alert.

You can set alerts to warn you when your credit cards are getting close to their limits, when you have exceeded some aspect of your budget (the two are probably related), when stocks rise above or fall below a certain price, and more.

To set an alert, open the Alerts window by selecting the **Finance** menu and choosing **Alerts**. The dialog box shown in the following figure appears.

Use the tabs across the top of the screen to target your area of interest. As you can see, you can set alerts for Accounts, Investments, General, Taxes, and New. (New alerts are those downloaded from Quicken.com.)

Alerts are one of Quicken's handiest features. You can set them up to flag you after certain events have occurred.

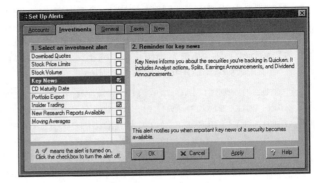

How Can I Download New Alerts?

You need to perform an update. Pull down the **Finance** menu and select **One Step Update**. Any new alerts are added under the **New** tab in the Alerts dialog box.

The list on the left shows all alerts available under that category. Use the area on the right to set the characteristics of that alert.

The characteristics change according to the type of alert, but in general you can set numerical limits, select items with check boxes, and specify dates.

When you have finished, click **OK** to save your changes.

If you can't see any alert options under a particular alert, it probably means you aren't using an account or other feature appropriate to that alert. For instance, if you haven't set up any stocks, you won't be able to specify Stock Price Limits under the **Investments** tab.

Quicken makes you aware of its alerts through pop-up dialog boxes in the Reminders window and in the Billminder utility. An alert doesn't prevent a transaction from taking place or some other event from occurring, and you can ignore it with the click of an **OK** button, but it sure beats knotting string around your fingers!

Need a Quick Budget?

Try the **Monthly Expenditure** alert under the **Accounts** tab. You can set a total expenditure value for any or all of your expense categories, and you can be sure the alert will let you know about it if you exceed that figure.

The Least You Need to Know

➤ The key to keeping yourself financially prepared is to know what's coming up. Quicken's huge range of transaction scheduling and financial alerts keep you appraised no matter what's around the corner.

➤ Memorized transactions are a great way to save your fingers. Don't be surprised when Quicken shows a surprising amount of insight into the transaction you are currently typing; it has memory longer than an elephant's.

➤ Lock your transactions to prevent Quicken from updating them each time you use them and make a small change.

➤ The Financial Calendar is a little like an electronic year planner. It's a great place to keep appraised of upcoming bills and scheduled transactions.

➤ Quicken provides a large number of alerts, but you also can download additional alerts through the One Step Update. Keep a close eye on these; you may find the perfect alert just an Internet connection away.

Chapter 7

Taking Control of Your Debt

In This Chapter

➤ How to reduce your debt

➤ Creating budgets that fit your needs

➤ Tracking money you borrow or lend

➤ Meeting goals through saving

A Plan with Elan

Quicken's budgeting, financial planning, and transaction recording features all help you keep a tight rein on your expenses. But what should you do if your debt has already spiraled out of control?

Don't give up. Just make a plan!

There are five easy steps to paying off your bills. If you follow them through, your future should appear rosy, even without tinted glasses:

1. First, pay off your high interest debt as fast and furiously as possible. The Debt Reduction Planner helps you prepare this frontal assault.

2. Set a budget. Budgets don't necessarily curtail your spending—just look at rising government expenditure—but they're great at helping you spend your funds in the most effective way.

3. Use Quicken's loan management functions to set up automatic repayments on your loans and keep track of the future effect those payments will have on your finances.

4. Prepare a financial forecast that shows how fast (or how slowly) you're getting ahead. Quicken's forecasts are great for long-term planning.

5. When everything else is settled, set some savings goals. As soon as they are met, you can start to seriously enjoy the fruits of your labor.

What Are the "Planning Assumptions" in the Planning Center?

The Financial Planner built into the Planning Center uses assumptions you have recorded in the Planning Center and elsewhere for its calculations. You can change your assumptions by opening the **Planning** menu and selecting **Assumptions**. Provide as much information as you can about yourself and your existing and future financial situation. You'll see the plan the next time you return to the Planning Center. The easiest way to adjust the plan is through Quicken's "What If" tool. It is under the **Planning** menu called **What If Event Scenarios**. As its name suggests, you can use it to build multiple scenarios, seeing what effect any and all might have on your future funds and, ultimately, retirement budget.

Planning for Success

This chapter looks at several of Quicken's financial planning tools, but there are many more you can discover on your own. Take a look at the **Planning** menu right now. Included on it are planners that can help you prepare for retirement, meet college fees, and more. You'll also see a submenu that includes a range of useful financial calculators.

Reducing Your Debt

The Deluxe and Home and Business editions of Quicken include a superb utility called the Debt Reduction Planner.

To open it, open the **Planning** menu and then select **Debt Reduction Planner**.

It takes a little bit of effort to work through this plan, but it's definitely worth your time.

The planner helps you to pay off your debt in order of the highest interest rate to the lowest. It also helps you track down lump sums that you can use to pay off your debt more quickly. This planner also can review your budget, searching for possible cutbacks in your spending. All in all it's a rather clever piece of work, but there is one thing you should do before you begin: the planner produces a more realistic plan if you ensure your liability accounts are up-to-date before you start it.

Like many other utilities built on Quicken's edifice, the planner operates through a series of linked dialog boxes with the final plan appearing in the main window. If you've used the planner before, you see your previous plan onscreen. If that's the case, start another plan by clicking **New Plan** and selecting **Yes**.

After you're on your way, click **Next** to skip past the introductory window.

Insert your Quicken Deluxe or Home and Business CD-ROM when prompted, and make sure the volume controls on your computer's speakers are turned up so you receive the full multimedia experience of the planner's movies. If you don't have your CD-ROM handy, just click **Next** to skip past those windows.

Your debt reduction starts with the How Much Do I Owe? dialog box shown in the following figure. You should see your existing debts and several buttons to the right. You can adjust almost any aspect of any debt, but at the very least you should select each, click **Edit**, and make sure the balance (not always adjustable), interest rate, and minimum repayments are correctly set. If you go back to your registers and change your liability data, click **Update Debts** to re-import those details. Add any other debts, such as personal loans, that aren't already listed. When you're finished, click **Next**.

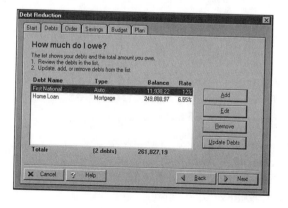

Use this dialog box to edit listed debts or to add other debts.

The next window summarizes your existing debt situation. It shows you how long it is going to take you to pay your existing debt as well as the total interest you will pay along the way.

Click **Next** to read the next screen, and click it again to move on.

The best way to save money is to pay off the high interest debts first, no matter their sizes. After they're satisfied, you can apply the money you save on the high interest to your other debts, setting up a reinforcing loop that's as advantageous to diminishing debt payments as compound interest is to your investments.

The next dialog box you see displays an optimized payment order for ridding yourself of your debt. You can adjust this by selecting **Change Payment Order?** and clicking **Next**. Use the subsequent screen to adjust the position of each repayment with the **Move Up** and **Move Down** command buttons. The Results window shows how the changes reduce the interest you save. To return to the Planner's recommended plan, click **Reset to Optimized Order**. If you'd rather stick to the optimized results, just click **Next** without selecting **Change Payment Order?**

Okay, you're almost there. Watch the video and click **Next** to proceed.

The next screen is a great one for getting a handle on the compound interest that adds so much to long-term debt. It summarizes your savings and investments, allowing you to test a one-time payment that reduces your debt by a lump sum. Just enter the amount and click **Recalculate**. Remember that the money in your savings account is probably earning less interest than the liability is costing you. Therefore, applying your savings to your liabilities always works in your favor. If you decide to apply a one-time payment, enter it here.

By the way, if you do decide to make this payment, you must record it in your books. The planner does a lot, but it won't take that extra step.

When you've finished experimenting, click **Next** to watch the subsequent video and then click **Next** once more.

Shouldn't I Pay Off a Larger Amount, Even If It Has a Lower Rate of Interest Than a Much Smaller Amount with a Higher Rate of Interest?

No. Even though this might seem counter-intuitive, if you pay off you biggest interest rate debts first, no matter how much interest that equates to in dollar terms, you're able to apply the money you save to the debt with the lower interest rate, paying them both off significantly quicker.

You're just about there. Use the final screen, Where Can I Cut My Expenses?, to free up funds that could go towards paying off your debt.

The planner searches your books, looking for the largest categories held in discretionary category groups. (It ignores non-discretionary items because they are not reducible.) It then works out your average monthly spending. By clicking the down arrow next to each category, you can select any category in your books, whether discretionary or not, although you need to press the **Tab** key before the planner replaces the old average monthly expense.

Record the amount you intend to trim from each category using the Amount to Cut Back fields. Provide an aggregate for any other categories in the Other/NA field. Then click **Recalculate** to see the effect this has on your interest payments.

To learn more about category groups and discretionary/non-discretionary items, see Chapter 4, "It's a Category and Class Thing."

Okay, you're finished! Click **Next** to view your debt reduction plan. (The following figure shows one example.)

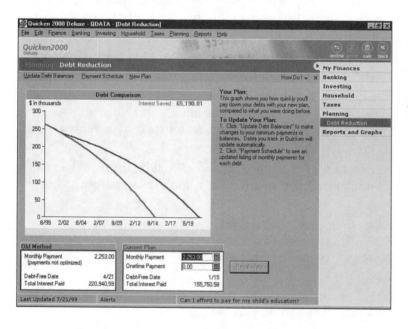

The curved lines in the Debt Reduction Planner's main screen show your original debt reduction against the improved plan. Compared to most budget cuts, this one's a very smooth shave.

You should now have an effective debt reduction plan that tells you how much you're going to save and how soon you'll be out of debt. Click **Print This Action Plan** for a hard copy. The Payment Coupons tell you how much you should pay through to the remainder of the year.

Click **Next** and then **Done** to return to the main Debt Reduction window. You can use this window to adjust your monthly or one-time payments, but don't forget to click **Recalculate** each time.

Every so often you should return to this screen and click **Update Debt Balances**. This copies the most recent data from your books and updates the plan. You can also print a **Payment Schedule** to show your debt payments over the next few years.

Big Budget Productions

Some people think of budgets as scrimping and saving, but that isn't necessarily the case. Like a healthy diet, a good budget is really about planning and balance. Indeed, the Debt Reduction Planner helps you drop those liability pounds, but the Budget puts you on a maintenance diet that keeps you at a level of debt you find both healthy and comfortable. The good news is that like any good diet, a balanced budget also allows you the occasional splurge. With my appetite for profiteroles, (what does it profit thee? not a lot, but they taste darn good) that was all the convincing I required.

The great thing about budgets is that they actually give you an excuse to spend. By helping you stick to a plan, you can set goals for yourself that are probably met far sooner than they would have been if you were relying on a vague notion that you'd like to one day do this or that. After you meet a goal, there's no reason you shouldn't also satisfy it!

Creating a budget in Quicken is easy. Your most important decision is working out which are your discretionary and non-discretionary items.

Typical non-discretionary items include groceries, mortgage repayments or rent, education, medical, utilities, taxes, basic clothing, and automotive. You can't avoid spending a certain amount on these, so you can't budget for them at a reduced amount.

However, the rest of the world are your oysters. Why you would want the world to become a small bivalve with a penchant for grit I really don't know, but each to their own.

Feel free to add as many discretionary items as you like. These might include your holidays, entertainment, Internet and cable connections, theater tickets, eating out in style once or twice a week, and so on. These are items you enjoy but can probably do without.

A budget establishes how much income you need to set aside for your bare essentials, and then helps you decide what you can do to cover the rest.

It's that easy.

Knocking Your Budget Into Shape

To open the budgeting tool, click the **Planning** menu and choose **Budgeting**.

Before you start creating your budget, you need to decide how particular you want to be. You can create a budget for the current month, quarter, or year, or you can create a budget for every month or quarter in the year. You can also stick to the category groups, which take less planning, or you can look at individual categories by clicking the **Categories** button and marking those you want to include.

Where Are My Categories?

If you've used previous versions of Quicken, you're probably used to seeing a bunch of categories in the budgeting window, rather than the optional category groups. This time around, Quicken assumes you'd prefer to generalize and work with category groups instead of specific categories. To display all your categories, click the **Categories** button, click **Mark All** in the dialog box displayed, and then click **OK**.

To change the frequency of the budget, open the **Options** menu at the top of the budgeting window and take your pick from the top five items.

You don't have to set a budget for every single item. Just leave those you'd prefer to ignore at zero.

You might also want to record transfers to other accounts, such as for loan repayments or contributions to a retirement account. However, it's best to define these first using scheduled transactions. After you've done that, Quicken automatically takes them into account when defining your budget.

Can I Change My Budget If I Find That I Have Extra Expenses Through the Year?

The budget is a flexible spending and savings plan that you can change as often as you like. Just change the dollar amounts in any column or update a single column, open the **Edit** menu at the top of the budgeting window, and select **Fill Columns**.

Recording Budgeted Amounts

As soon as you've decided on the general framework for your budget, it's time to start recording the budget amounts.

The hard way is to record figures in each column for each category group or individual category.

Quicken has a shortcut, but you can only use it if you already have been recording your transactions in Quicken, giving the software a base from which it can extrapolate your future income and expenses.

The shortcut is under the **Edit** menu at the top of the budgeting window (that's *not* the one in the menu bar).

To create a budget using your existing data, open the **Edit** menu and select **Autocreate**. You should see the dialog box shown in the following figure.

Autocreate helps you build a new budget based on your previous Quicken values. To create a budget for the 2000 financial year, you could use your 1999 values as shown here.

Use the **From** and **To** fields to bracket the transactions you want to include in the Autocreate calculation. For example, if you started a new job three months ago, you would probably want to use the first of the month in which that new job began as the base for calculating your most recent financial profile. However, if your finances haven't changed too much, you might prefer to base your Autocreate on the entire past year. If you want to take seasonal spending patterns into account, try basing the budget on the entire previous year's history.

To round the budgeted values to the nearest $1, $10, or $100, select one of those amounts from the Round Values to Nearest pull-down list.

If you select **Use Monthly Detail**, Quicken creates the budget by replicating the amounts month-by-month for the bracketed period. Select **Use Average for Period** instead to average the amounts for each category or category group over that period, and spread the average over each period in your budget.

Click **Categories** to select the categories and accounts you want to include in this Autocreation. (By default, Quicken uses every possible category and account.)

There's also one final fine-tuner. Quicken usually ignores categories with a single transaction of less than $100. These are spurious, irregular amounts that it assumes you don't want to include in your budget. If you do, also select the check box **Include all nonzero transaction amounts**.

That's all there is to it. Click **OK** to create the budget. To create additional budgets, open the **Options** menu and select **Other Budgets**.

Other Budget Shortcuts

Use the **2-Week** command under the **Edit** menu to include items in your budget that you receive every 14 days rather than every second calendar week. Click **Copy All** under the same menu to copy the budget data to the clipboard. This is great for pasting that data into another program such as a spreadsheet. Finally, use the **Fill Row Right** and **Fill Columns** commands to copy existing row and column data through the rest of the budget.

Tracking Your Budget

There's little point building a budget if you don't stick to it. Fortunately, Quicken provides a couple of easy tools you can use to see how well you're doing.

The first, the Budget Report, is a **Reports** menu, click **Spending** and choose **Budget Report**. Quicken compares your income and your expenses against the budgeted amounts. This report works on the year-to-date and provides simple, totaled figures.

The second, the Budget Variance Graph, is useful for showing how closely you managed to stick to your budget. The graph calculates the totals accrued by each budgeted category and shows you first how favorably or unfavorably those totals compare to your budget, as well as those categories that were the worst offenders.

To create the graph, select the **Reports** menu, click **Spending**, and choose **Budget Variance Graph**. A graph similar to the one shown in the following figure appears.

The upper half of the graph shows your budget variance in dollars, month by month. Quicken displays each month as a favorable or unfavorable amount. The more favorable the amount, the higher your net income.

Although the upper columns tend to bundle all of your categories together, you can view the breakdown for any month by double-clicking that column. To go back to the original graph, click the back arrow or close button in the graph's title bar.

Use your mouse pointer to extract precise figures from the graph or double-click to delve further into that column.

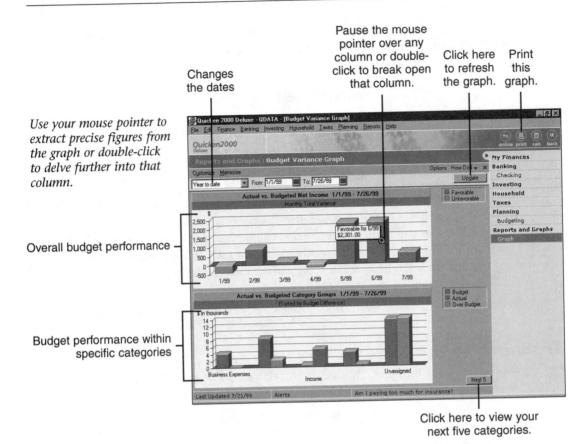

Changes the dates

Pause the mouse pointer over any column or double-click to break open that column.

Click here to refresh the graph.

Print this graph.

Overall budget performance

Budget performance within specific categories

Click here to view your next five categories.

The graph in the lower portion of the window shows the budget variance for your individual categories calculated across that entire period. The categories are arranged by their budget difference. This time, double-clicking any column shows the performance of that category across the entire period.

If you have more than five budgeted categories, click **Next 5** in the lower-right corner of the graph window to scroll to the next five categories. Keep clicking and you should eventually go full circle, returning to the first five.

Becoming a Loan Ranger

Quicken provides an extensive armory of tools designed to help you reduce your debt; plan, track, and complete budgets; and manage your loans.

Unlike debt reduction and budgeting, it is very important that you tell Quicken about all your personal loans, mortgages, leases, and so on. Without this information, there's little for Quicken to work with when creating a financial forecast or planning your tax.

Before you start setting up your loan, gather all the loan documents. You will need the original agreement as well as statements from the loan account.

Can You Afford That Loan?

The easiest way to tell is to check out the Loan calculator. Open the **Planning** menu, click **Financial Calculators**, and select **Loan**. This calculator takes less time than the financial planners arranged under Life Events in the Planning Center window, but you should use the latter to include more conditions and assumptions into your calculations.

To begin, open the **Household** menu and select **Loans** (**Ctrl+H**).

If you've run Quicken's Loan Setup previously, click **New** at the top of the window to start the Loan Setup system. If you haven't run it before, it starts automatically.

After you're in, click **Next** to move to the first question.

You can track loan situations where you have borrowed or loaned the funds. Indicate whether this loan is for you to **Borrow Money** or **Lend Money** and click **Next**.

Quicken tracks money you have borrowed in liability accounts and money you have lent in asset accounts. You need to set up a separate account for every loan that you track. Even though you can do this by first creating the account and then setting the loan, I prefer to do it the following way.

Simply type a name for the loan (for example, *Personal Loan*) into the New Account field. If you have already set up an account for this loan, select **Existing Account** and find it with the pull-down list. Click **Next** when you're done.

Select **Yes** or **No** in the next screen as appropriate and click **Next**.

Type in the initial loan information including the Opening Date and the Original Balance—not the current balance! Then click **Next**.

A balloon payment is a final payment that is larger than your regular payments. Often it can amount to 40% or more of the original loan. If your loan has a balloon, indicate it here and click **Next**.

Now you need to specify the original length of the loan in years, months, weeks, or a certain number of payments. The length is shown on your original loan documents. Click **Next** when you've finished.

Specify the payment period in fixed calendar terms (monthly, biweekly, and so on) or as a certain number of payments per year. Then click **Next**.

The compounding period is important for calculating the interest accrued through the course of the loan. For large sums across long periods, the compounding period can have enormous impact. You must specify the correct compounding period for Quicken's own calculations to be accurate. Click **Next**.

If you know the current balance of the loan, select **Yes**, click **Next**, and provide the date and amount. You can find this information on the last statement you received for the loan.

If you don't know the current balance, select **No**. Click **Next** to move on.

Provide the date the next payment is due, and click **Next**.

Do you know the amount of the first payment? If you do, click **Yes**, then **Next**, and record the Payment Amount. If not, click **No**. Quicken calculates the repayment for you before you leave this loan setup procedure. Click **Next** in both cases when you're done.

Finally, provide the current Interest Rate and click **Next**. If this is an adjustable or variable rate loan, use the most recent rate known because you can easily adjust the interest rate later. Click **Next** again.

What a haul! You now have a final opportunity to confirm your loan data. Just work your way through the three Summary screens, adjusting any entries as necessary. The calculated payment is shown in the field Payment Amount (P+I). Click **Done** to leave the Loan Set Up and define your regular repayments. If you didn't specify the regular payment amount earlier, Quicken calculates and inserts it for you before allowing you past the final screen.

Making Payments

You've set up the loan; now you need to keep the sharks at bay by attaching regular or scheduled payments to the loan. Quicken takes you there automatically, but you can open the Set Up Loan Payment dialog box at any time by clicking the **Edit Payment** button in the View Loans window.

The Edit Loan Payment dialog box is shown in the following figure. You can adjust both the payments and the interest rate. More importantly, you can edit the payment to include other amounts unrelated to the requisite principal and interest. These might include some form of state tax, a borrowing fee, or any amount you want to use to pay your loan a little faster.

To set up loan repayments, look to the Payment section of the Edit Loan Payment dialog box. Indicate the Current Interest Rate and, using Principal and Interest, the amount of the regular payment. This payment is the minimum you are expected to make under the terms of your loan agreement.

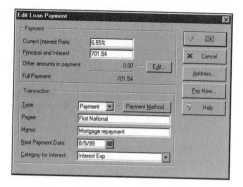

Regular loan payments ensure your loan never gets out of hand.

To add extra payments, click the **Edit** button and record those payments using the Splits window. In the window, assign each extra payment to an appropriate expense category for payments you make or an income category for amounts you receive. Extra payments used to pay off the loan sooner should be recorded as a transfer to the loan account. Click **OK** to close the Split. In the previous figure, I recorded an extra payment of $100 as a transfer to the account "[Personal Loan]".

Now select the type of payment in the Transaction area. Choose **Payment** for handwritten checks or direct debit payments. To record online payments or print your own checks, select **Print Check**. Use the Payment Method dialog box to choose between a **Scheduled Transaction** or a **Memorized Transaction**. Use the first if you want Quicken to generate the payment for whenever it falls due. Use the second to manually initiate the payments each period. If you have set up your Online Center you also see **Repeating Online Payments**, and you can select **Checkfree Fixed Payment** if you have set up a Checkfree account. (You can learn more about online payments in Chapter 12, "Useful Connections.")

How Do I Make Extra Payments on a Loan That I've Already Set Up Using the Loan Planner?

The best way is to avoid adjusting the amount of your regular payment. Instead, click **Make Payment**, choose **Extra**, and provide the amount you want to pay. Extra payments recorded in this way are one-off payments. You can use them to record lump sum payments and also whenever you have a few spare dollars you want to throw the loan's way.

If you set a Scheduled Transaction, don't forget to set the Scheduled Transaction options. In the Register Entry field select **Automatically Enter**; this is great for direct debits. Use the Account to Pay from and the Days in Advance fields to specify when you want that payment generated. If it takes an average of three days for your printed checks to arrive at their destination, set the Days in Advance field to 3. The check won't be cashed until it falls due, but it can be generated and posted in plenty of time.

Click **OK** to save your changes.

Okay, you should be back at the Edit Loan Payment dialog box. You're not out of the woods yet, but there's not far to go, and we're nowhere near grizzly country.

Enter the Payee and a Memo. The memo is recorded alongside each loan repayment when it's written into your register.

Check the date for the next payment due and make sure there's an appropriate category selected in the category for interest. It's typically called Interest Exp but if someone's paying you money, it will be called Interest Inc.

Finally, if you print your own checks and post them using windowed envelopes, make sure you also click **Address**. Use the message line in the address box to specify your loan account number. (If you mail your payments with slips from a payments book, ignore the memo.)

Click **OK** to save the payment and you're finished. Well done!

If you decide to create a memorized transaction instead of a scheduled transaction, you need to keep track of when the payment falls due. When each payment period expires, return to the View Loans window and click **Make Payment**. Select **Regular** and record the transaction. If you set up a scheduled transaction, Quicken does all the worrying for you, but you still need to record the transaction when prompted.

In both cases, don't forget to adjust the **Number** field when recording the payment to indicate a check number for a handwritten payment or **Print Check** for one you print yourself. Use **Transfer** for direct debits.

Managing Your Loan

So far you've defined a loan and set up a transaction to handle the payments. Several other features in the View Loans window make it easy to track your progress.

➤ If you have more than one loan, use **Choose Loan (x)** just below the View Loans title bar to move between them.

➤ Use the **Payment Schedule** and **Payment Graph** tabs to view more information about the principal and interest components of your loan.

➤ Want to know how much interest you will end up paying through the course of your loan? Click the **Payment Schedule** tab and select **Show Running Totals**. Scroll to the end of the schedule and read off the final figure in the

Interest column. Add this to the amount shown for Principal to calculate the total you'll repay over the life of the loan.

➤ Because Quicken maintains your loan in a regular Quicken account, it can easily follow the balance and curtail your payment schedule if you finalize the loan early. Open the **File** menu and select **Print Loan** to produce a hard copy of the schedule.

When you have completed the loan, Quicken automatically tidies it up. However, if you want to cancel the loan, just select it using **Choose Loan (x)** and click **Delete**. All previous payments are retained but future payments are deleted.

That's it! Loan management in a nutshell. When combined with Quicken's budgeting, forecasting, savings goals, and tax planning features, it represents a superb final part to Quicken's comprehensive financial management tools.

Forecasting Your Finances

Quicken doesn't include a crystal ball, not even your stock standard *foretell the future* incantation, but it can do a reasonable job of showing you how your finances will look several months or even years into the future.

Back to the Future

The clarity of Quicken's forecast depends on the quality of the information you have previously provided. However, if you have built up a pattern of transactions showing your income and expenses and taken the time to tell Quicken all about your loans and any dividends you receive from investments, it is able to give you a reasonably accurate picture.

You can generate a forecast based on the current budget or by summarizing the flow of funds using a combination of past history and future scheduled transactions. The forecasting center also enables you to record one-off or repeating transactions. However, you can't convert these to actual transactions. Rather, they let you test possible income or expenditure situations to see how they will affect your future finances. You can even develop different scenarios and compare them side-by-side.

After you have worked out what's possible and what's not, it's an easy matter to update your budget with the figures derived from your experimentation.

The forecaster works over a period of one month to two years, starting at any time.

To create a forecast, open the **Planning** menu and select **Cash Flow Forecast**. The first time you open the Forecasting window, you see a dialog box called Automatically Create Forecast.

Quicken bases its forecast on the date range you specify. This means that if you think the last quarter is representative of the next year, specify only those dates in the **From** and **To** fields. If you think the last year is a better bet, set the dates accordingly.

Click the **Advanced** button in this box to gain more control over how Quicken creates the forecast. However, some of the options do require careful consideration. If you're not interested at this point, click **OK** and move on to the forecasting graph. If you do click **Advanced**, you have the following additional choices:

➤ **Known Items (from Scheduled Txns)**   Select this to only include data taken from scheduled items. This is useful if you don't want Quicken to make too many assumptions based on your past spending.

➤ **Estimated Items**   Select this to ignore scheduled items but include amounts Quicken believes you will spend based on your pattern of previous spending or the budgets you've set.

➤ **Create Both**   Obviously this uses both options above.

You can also choose the origin of the estimated item data:

➤ **From Register Data**   Select this to create estimated items based on your previous spending.

➤ **From Budget Data**   Choose this to create estimated items based on your budgets.

Finally, you might also want to limit these advanced conditions to specific **Accounts** and **Categories**.

Click **Done** when you've finished and click **OK** to create the forecast.

The figure below shows a forecast created from both estimated and known items. The diagram below the graph marks the occurrence of past or future events. Click any triangle to create a new event or examine those that are affecting the graph at that point. (You can read about this in "Creating New Forecast Events," which follows this section.)

You can do many other things to tailor the forecast to your needs:

➤ Select the length of your forecast using the pull-down list in the lower-left corner. Shift your frame of reference forward or backward by clicking the **<< Prev** and **Next >>** buttons directly below it.

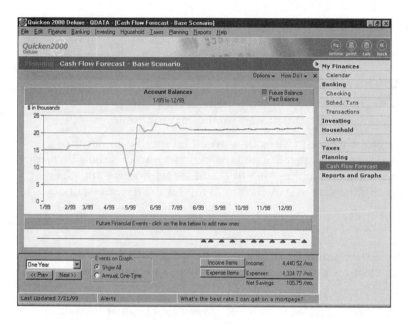

Do a forecast and admire those rising balances!

➤ Use **Events on Graph** to determine whether you want to **Show All** your scheduled events or just those that occur on an **Annual, One-Time** basis. Use the first if you are dealing with a tight time frame and the latter if you prefer to look one to two years into the future.

➤ Adjust the total for each category of known and estimated items. You can change **Income Items** or **Expense Items** and use the subsequent dialog box to change the amount assigned to each.

The **Options** menu at the top of the screen helps you create, copy, and combine your forecasts. The menu commands are:

➤ **Manage Scenarios**   Open a dialog box to create a new scenario based on the current scenario or start from scratch. You can also use this dialog box to compare two scenarios at the same time. Just click **Compare Current Scenario with** and choose the second scenario from the drop-down list.

➤ **Select Accounts**   Choose the accounts you want to include in your forecast. Usually, Quicken selects your banking and credit card accounts, but you can also select other accounts you have created on a case-by-case basis.

➤ **Update Forecast**   Create a new forecast with the same Automatically Create Forecast dialog box described previously.

➤ **Update Budget**   Copy the values used in your forecast categories into the current budget.

If you like what you see after you've completed the forecast, consider printing it out. You'll find a **Print Forecast** command under the **File** menu.

Creating New Forecast Events

By defining your own forecast events, you can experiment with different financial scenarios. For instance, can you afford that new car, holiday, or home?

Like a budget, you can create forecast transactions based on specific amounts or average amounts. Average amounts are spread across the period selected as their frequency (that is, divided so only a little is paid on each day) and are known as estimated items, whereas specific amounts are executed once in full on the day they fall due.

To create a new forecast item click **Income Items** in the Forecasting window and select **New**.

In the Create New Income Item dialog box specify a **Description**, **Amount**, and **Frequency**. If you are creating an expense item, you should also select **Expense**.

To create a known item, select **Next Scheduled Date** and specify the first day this item is to occur. To create an estimated item, select **Average Amount** instead.

If you intend copying your forecast workings into a budget, click **More** and set a **Category (for tracking)**.

If you have specified a frequency greater than **Only one**, you also need to set the **Number of Payments**. Click **OK** when you're done.

Click **OK** on both screens to save the transaction and return to the Forecasting window. You should see your new item appear as a red or green triangle under the line on the second graph.

Techno Talk

The Red and Green Triangle Show

Every time a repeating or one-time transaction is scheduled to appear, it shows on the second forecasting graph as a red or green triangle. Green triangles are used for repeating transactions; red ones are used for those that occur one time only.

The Forecasting tool is a powerful one. There's no doubt about that. It's also very flexible, but in that flexibility there lies a lot of complexity. Probably the best way to really get a handle on interpreting the graph through estimated and known income and expense items is to set up several scenarios and start experimenting.

Who knows? The future might look so bright you've gotta wear shades.

Setting and Creating Savings Goals

If your debt is down to a manageable level, you can start setting savings goals. Savings goals are easy to create, easy to update, and best of all, they "hide" your money from you so you aren't tempted to spend it.

Quicken creates a new asset account for each savings goal you create. Any amounts you contribute are deducted from the account doing the contributing, you'll see this reflected in their balances. However, Quicken also keeps track of the real balance, so it's not really cooking your books. (More like a quick microwave.) Indeed, each time you reconcile your accounts, Quicken negates any transfers made to savings goals for the duration.

Creating a savings goal is easy. First, open the **Planning** menu and select **Savings Goals**.

Click **New** at the top of the window and provide a Goal Name, the Goal Amount, and the Finish Date—that is, the date you want to arrive at that amount. The name must not be in use by an existing Quicken asset account or category. Click **OK** to save the goal.

When you have the funds to spare, you might decide to contribute some to your goal. To do so, just click **Contribute**. It's just below the Savings Goals title bar. Specify the account from which you are contributing the amount (Quicken calculates an amount for you based on the number of months left to run), and the date it was contributed. This transaction is recorded as an account transfer, removing the funds from the original account (thus changing the available balance), and depositing them into the savings goal account.

To withdraw funds, click **Withdraw**, specify the account to which you are transferring those funds, as well as the transfer date. Unless you transfer to a completely different account, withdrawing funds restores your original account's balance by the amount of that withdrawal.

If you need to adjust any aspect of the savings goal, either click the **Edit** button at the top of the window, or change those values in the Goal, Start, and Finish fields directly onscreen.

To record regular payments to the goal, schedule a transfer as you would any other regular transaction.

After you contribute funds to your savings goal, you can still see how much money you have in your real-world account. Go to that register, pull down the **Options** menu, and toggle **Hide Savings Goals** on and off. (You won't see this entry until you have contributed from that account.) When this feature is selected, Quicken temporarily hides all of the transfer transactions. This converts the balance of the account to its real-world status.

When you attain your savings goal, remove it by selecting it from the Savings Goals list and clicking **Delete**. Quicken asks you what you want to do with the savings goal account. Click **Yes** to keep the transactions and the savings account as a permanent record, or click **No** to delete the account and transfer the funds back to your real account, ready for spending.

The Least You Need to Know

➤ Quicken's debt reduction, budgeting, loan management, savings plan, and financial forecasting features exist for just one purpose: helping you meet your financial goals. They are some of the software's most innovative features, going far beyond the tasks of balancing a checkbook and tracking basic assets and liabilities.

➤ Budgets are the best way to rein in your spending. However, more than this, they are a great way to meet your financial goals.

➤ Always use Quicken's mortgage and loan management system to track funds you borrow or loan to someone else.

➤ While it isn't perfect, Quicken's Financial Forecasting is useful for plotting your future income and expenditure. You can, at the very least, gain a broad understanding of whether your income will exceed your expense in the near future.

➤ Once you have your budget worked out, look towards Savings Goals as a way to set aside funds destined for a special purpose.

Powerful Reports and Great Graphs

Data Mining

The titans of industry have an excellent system for getting the data they need. It's called "send a minion" and, for them anyway, it's an Executive Information System that works just great.

Quicken provides its own take on the EIS, and it doesn't involve berating the computer department, tangling with the intricacies of an arcane data query system, or puffing threateningly on a cigar from behind a three-acre desk.

In fact, you're often able to find the data you need before you even start looking. Financial information, upcoming payments, important financial news, reminders, alerts, and a whole lot more are scattered throughout the main Activity Centers, hidden just beneath the surface of the EasyAnswer system, and only a mouse-click away in Quicken's numerous reports and graphs.

In short, Quicken can turn a mass of information into a series of highly informative reports and graphs that help you concentrate on a general overview of your finances rather than every retreat or rally. You can see what's happening and why.

Finding Your Way Around the Financial Centers

Before we get into the reports and graphs, let's take a look at Quicken's most dynamic reporting function.

Financial Activity Centers

If you have used earlier versions of Quicken, you're at least partly familiar with the concept of the Financial Centers. Previously, they were called the Financial Activity Center, and before that, Financial Snapshots (these were windows you could customize to display between two and six small-sized panes of graphs, reports, or calendar notes). Those instant photo-sized panes have grown into complex multi-screen displays that provide far more information and flexibility then Financial Snapshots or the Financial Activity Center did in earlier versions of Quicken.

There are seven financial centers, and each is filled with customizable options, links to other parts of the software, and more. They are so adaptable that the best way to learn about them is to plunge right in; just start scrolling and clicking until you're familiar with all they have to offer.

You can open each financial center by opening its menu and selecting the first option therein. Alternatively, click the center's name in the QuickTabs area to the right of the main window.

Here's a quick overview of what you'll find:

➤ **My Finances**   This center (see the following figure) summarizes the most important information from your other centers and acts as a launch point to your accounts, vital data, and the other centers.

➤ **Banking Center**   Useful for summarizing data from all your banking accounts.

➤ **Investing Center**   Displays your watch list, portfolio balances, and current asset allocation.

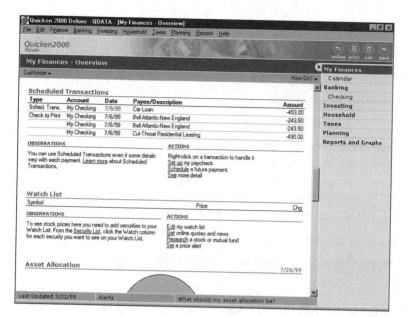

Feel free to customize the My Finances window to provide the information you need. In this case, it provides a list of upcoming scheduled transactions.

➤ **Household Center** This is the place to look for a summary of your home and automobile equity.

➤ **Taxes Center** With a tax calendar, your projected tax, income to date, and more, this center is a great place to go as you get closer to April 15.

➤ **Planning Center** Who's really prepared for the rest of their lives? The planning center, at the least, gives you a good start. Visit it to see how well you are keeping up with plans you have already established, and also to use Quicken's numerous built-in financial planners.

➤ **Business Center** You'll only see this if you use Quicken Home and Business. It's a great place to track your business accounts, payables, and receivables.

➤ **Reports & Graphs** The other centers have more than their fair share of instant reports and quick graphs, so this center exists only to provide an easy way to access Quicken's entire selection. Click the report that interests you and then the **View Sample** button to get an idea of what's included in that report.

If you aren't interested in viewing My Finances each time you start Quicken, open the **Edit** menu, select **Options**, and choose **Quicken Program**. Then click the **Startup** tab and select **None**.

Customize My Finances

The My Finances center is the only one you can customize. With it open, click the **Customize** menu at the top of the window and select **Customize this View**. Use the Customize View dialog box to choose new components for your page from the list on the left. (Clicking **Add>>** adds them to the page.) You can also create additional pages using the **Customize** menu's **Create a new view** function.

You cannot, unfortunately, change the size of any of the elements displayed.

Getting Answers with Reports and Graphs

Quicken's reports and graphs can present your data in a clear, concise format that makes it easy to not only gain an overview of your finances, but also to focus on the detailed data that makes up the broader picture.

There are two ways to get the answers you need. You can either open the **Reports and Graphs Center**, or you can open the **Reports** menu. (Selecting the first item in the Reports menu, **EasyAnswer Reports and Graphs**, takes you to the Center anyway.)

EasyAnswers

The EasyAnswers system no longer exists as a series of separate dialog boxes. However, you can find the old EasyAnswers report under the first entry in the Reports and Graphs Center.

The EasyAnswers section of the Reports and Graphs Center attempts to provide answers to questions already phrased in plain English. However, use the customization fields in the lower part of the screen to give it a hand.

The other sections listed down the left side of this window correspond to the additional menus provided under the Reports menu. Again, use the customization field to give Quicken a better idea of the categories, dates, or other data in which you're interested.

(Yes, you can get the same result by customizing a report or graph, but EasyAnswers' structure makes it a lot easier.)

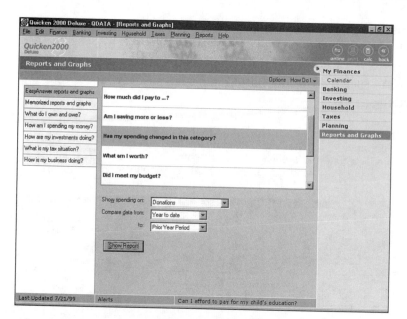

EasyAnswers finds the right report or graph for you.

If the EasyAnswers system doesn't answer your question, you need to delve more deeply into Quicken's reports and graphs. Read on.

All the reports and graphs are available from the **Reports** menu.

To generate a report or graph, simply select it from the menu.

Just one quick note: Until you are familiar with Quicken's reports, use the Reports and Graphs Center rather than the Reports menu to find the ones you need.

Working with Reports and Graphs

Quicken's reports and graphs are anything but static displays. The following figure shows a Cash Flow Report. The contents of the report aren't important right now. Instead, look at the date fields and pull-down menus that run across the top of the window.

You can use these to change how that report or graph appears, as well as the information it conveys. From left to right, these fields enable you to:

➤ Specify a defined period such as the current year or quarter, last year, the previous quarter, month to date, all dates, and so on.

➤ Set a custom date using the fields **from** and **to**.

➤ Add columns to the report. This enables you to break down the information displayed by using a repeating period such as biweekly or monthly, or by category, class, payee, or account.

These fields and menus are common to every report. Indeed, you will even see the date sections duplicated when creating reports such as the Profit and Loss Comparison.

However, you do need to click the **Update** button to see any of the changes you make reflected onscreen.

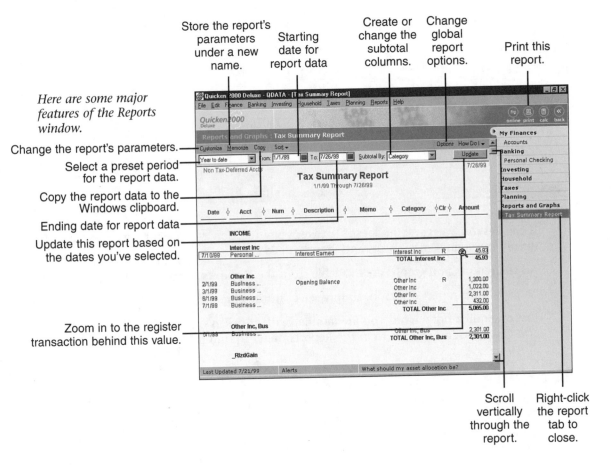

Here are some major features of the Reports window.

Just above the date fields and menus is an additional row of buttons. This is common to all reports and graphs.

Click **Customize** to change the structure and look of your report or graph. You learn how to use this feature next.

Select **Memorize** to store a customized report or graph's parameters so you can quickly recall them in the future.

Reports and Graphs with Zoooom!

There's a neat trick you can perform with your reports and graphs. Pause the mouse pointer over any detail line in any report and double-click to zoom through to the transaction or transactions that contributed to it. The same applies to graphs. For instance, double-click one of the bars in a graph showing your investment performance of your entire portfolio based on the year to date and Quicken gives you the performance of that double-clicked security instead.

Use the **Copy** button to copy a report's data to the clipboard so you can use it in other software. The report contents are copied as plain text with columns replaced by tab marks. You can format the report using any word processor or desktop publishing package. (This button isn't available in graphs.)

Finally, click **Options** to change the default date ranges and the overall "look" of all your reports and graphs. Additional coverage on report and graph options is available in Chapter 20, "Program Options: Doing It Your Way."

How Can I Import My Reports Into a Report I'm Preparing?

If you're using software such as Microsoft Office or Corel Perfect Office, open **File**, select **Print Report**, and select the **123 (.PRN) Disk File** format. Open the file in your word processor (or DTP package) and set it as a table. Word's **Convert Text to Table** and **Table AutoFormat** commands can turn the report into something of which any spin doctor would be proud.

Customizing Reports and Graphs

Between the built-in reports, graphs, and the EasyAnswers system, it is very easy to extract the information you need, when you need it. However, there will also certainly be occasions when the report or graph doesn't give you precisely what you need.

The good news is that with very little effort you can create reports and graphs that are superbly tailored to your needs, turning Quicken and your books into the ultimate financial analysis tool.

In fact, there are many reasons you might decide to slip on the work belt and start customizing your reports and graphs. For instance:

➤ There's no problem sharing the one Quicken file between you and your business. When you want an overview, Quicken's standard reports and graphs will provide you with precisely that. However, when you want to separate that information, a customized report that only considers data belonging to your business's Class (see Chapter 4, "It's a Category and Class Thing") will tell you just want you want to know.

➤ Do you share your file with your partner? If you file separate returns, customizing the report by class will again help you to separate your data.

➤ Work to a different financial year? A customized profit and loss report saves you from changing those dates every time.

➤ Need to generate a report with certain information but nothing you consider confidential? Just choose those categories you want included in the report and let Quicken do the rest.

To start customizing a report or graph, click the small **Customize** button in the top-left corner of any displayed report or graph.

The customization dialog boxes differ depending on whether you are working with a report or graph. When customizing a report, you see one similar to that shown in the following figure.

Use the Display tab to adjust your report's overall presentation.

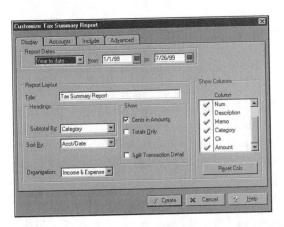

The tabs at the top of the dialog box group broad areas of functionality. Select each to do the following:

➤ **Display**   Adjust the included dates, the grouping of lines, ordering of columns, and other aspects of the overall layout, such as the title and detail displayed in each line.

➤ **Accounts**   Choose which account types should be included in this report. Even if you select every account, not all will be included. For an account to make a showing, that account must contain transactions of the type required by the report.

➤ **Include**   Select the categories, classes, or transactions that will be searched for the data to complete your report. If the report targets an investment account or your investment portfolio, use this tab to select specific securities.

➤ **Advanced**   Select tax-related categories, the types of transactions to be included (deposits, payments, unprinted checks, or all), the status of checks (blank, newly cleared, or reconciled), and the inclusion of transfers and subcategories.

You can use numerous customizable options in these tabs, and one of the best ways to see how they work is to put them into action.

Select accounts and categories by clicking to place a check mark in the spare column to the left. Dates work the same way as the date fields and menus you see at the top of any report. Use the Include tab's **Matching** section to filter all your transactions so you only view those by payee, category, class, or memo.

When you've finished setting options, click **Create** to generate the new report. To fine-tune your settings, click **Customize** at the top of the report window to return to the customization dialog box.

The dialog box used for customizing graphs is a little different than that used for customizing reports. Depending on the type of graph you customize, you will see tabs named **Accounts**, **Categories**, and **Classes**, or **Accounts** and **Securities**. Despite their differing titles, each of the tabs works the same way. All you need to do is place a check mark beside those items under each tab that you want to include in your graph.

How Do I Import Graphs Into Another Program?

There is no way to export a graph from Quicken. However, if you press the **PrintScrn** key when the graph is displayed on your screen, you should be able to go to the program you want to import that graph and paste in its picture. To tidy things up, consider using an image editing program to crop the image to remove Quicken's menus and other screen artifacts. (These tools might also be built into the software you're already using.)

Memorizing Customized Reports and Graphs

Memorized reports and graphs can save you a lot of time, especially if you have performed an extensive customization on a particular report or graph. (Memorizing not only saves you time when you next view that report or graph, it also saves you from trying to remember exactly what it was you did to customize it. Now that's the memory for me!)

To memorize a graph, click **Memorize** after your customized graph is displayed onscreen, and provide a **Graph Name** in the **Memorize Graph** dialog box. Click **OK** to save the graph.

Memorizing reports is a little bit trickier, but not much. When you have the report onscreen, click the **Memorize** button. Then, in the dialog box that you see, assign a **Title** and optional **Description**. When you recall this report in the future, Quicken can either calculate new dates according to the **Named Range** you select in the report window, use data between two **Custom** dates you specify, or simply use the default for this type of report (**None**). Make your choice. The **Named Range** is suitable if you have created a report which is always used for the year to date, the last quarter, the last month, and so on.

When you complete this dialog box, you see the title and description appear in the **Memorized** sections of the Reports menu and the Reports and Graphs Center.

The 10 Most Useful Reports and Graphs

Sometimes the harvest can prove too bountiful. Take Quicken as a case in point.

Quicken Deluxe provides some 36 reports and graphs, not counting those you might care to customize and memorize, and the Home and Business edition provides even more.

So, which ones are the most important?

Well, from a financial management point of view, there are some reports and graphs you simply shouldn't be without. Let's run through the best:

➤ **Net Worth Report**   A handy summary of your true value—that is, assuming you've entered all your assets and liabilities. This report is especially useful when applying for a loan.

➤ **Net Worth Graph**   How similar are they? You'll be surprised how different they are. Use the Net Worth Graph to drill down through your major assets and liabilities to the actual transactions that are provided in the Net Worth Report. This is a great way to see how your financial situation has changed over time, and I sincerely hope it fits an exponential curve.

➤ **Cash Flow Report** It's depressing when your income doesn't exceed your expenses. This report breaks them down by category, so you can see where you're falling behind. Print a **Cash Flow Comparison Report** to compare one period to another; for instance this year to last year.

➤ **Transaction Report** This report creates a statement showing all transactions logged to an account over the selected period. It's a handy one to print and store with the electronic backup of your data. (You do have one, don't you?)

➤ **Itemized Categories Report** This one is handy when trying to find a mis-recorded transaction or to make sense of a strange category total. It breaks down all your transactions by the category to which they were assigned. It's also a handy report to pass on to a tax professional as it shows all your transactions neatly filed away without making any assumptions about those that might be tax deductible.

➤ **Budget Report** Okay, it's probably not something you want to rush home to, but the budget report (and the related Budget Variance Graph) is a great way to see how well you're doing with the belt tightening—or loosening, as the case might be.

➤ **Capital Gains Report** If you are an active investor, you need to keep abreast of and plan for capital gains. This report considers only the taxable realized gains. Any unrealized gains are, and please pardon this, not included.

➤ **Investment Performance Report** I have a confession to make: I love this report. It shows what is known as an annualized or internal rate of return for your investments. All that really means is that this report shows the annual interest a bank would need to pay to match the annual rate of growth shown by your securities.

➤ **Tax Summary Report** Even if you don't use Quicken's more advanced tax preparation features, this report shows the breakdown of profit and loss (or income and expense) in all categories marked as tax-related. It's an important report because it shows your starting point for estimated tax payments, adequate withholding, and so on.

➤ **Job/Project Report** This is a profit and loss (or cash flow) report broken down by class. If you use more than one class to, say, track different businesses, profit and loss centers, or just the combined transactions of two people, you'll like this report. Each class gets its own column, but this report also totals everything at the end, giving you several ways to look at your financial data.

The Least You Need to Know

➤ Quicken's reports and graphs serve unique purposes not found in other financial software. Usually a report is something that prints on your printer. If it prints to the screen, it's simply a replica of the printed output. Graphs usually print to the screen, but are non-interactive. Quicken's reports and graphs are dynamic data displays that automatically update whenever you change the underlying data. Double-click to zoom in, click the **Close** button to zoom out. It's that simple...and fun!

➤ Customize your reports and graphs so they display only the information you are interested in.

➤ Memorize highly customized reports and graphs so that you can recreate them with new data simply by selecting the memorized report or graph from the reports and graphs menu.

Part 2
Taxing Times

Taxes aren't all bad. Sure they can jangle the hip nerve, cause night sweats, and make people's lives just darn miserable, but those people probably don't use Quicken. (If Congress had their way, they'd probably ban it.)

In this section you'll learn how to plan and prepare your taxes. It's remarkably easy, and the perfect analgesic for that pain in the pocket.

Chapter 9

Paychecks and Tax Categories

In This Chapter

➤ Using Quicken to prepare your taxes

➤ Recording your paycheck

➤ Using tax-related categories to track your income and expenses

➤ Linking categories to the tax forms

Understanding Your Income Tax

Let's not kid anyone. Not even Quicken can take the pain out of paying taxes. Certainly it saves you time, and it might even save you some money by tracking down extra tax deductions. However, whichever way you look at it, taxes are a regular drain in the pocket.

So where does Quicken shine? Even honest mistakes in an erroneous return can attract significant penalties. Quicken significantly decreases this opportunity for error, no matter if you base your filing on the data contained within Quicken, use that data as the basis of a TurboTax return, or print out a report of all your transactions and send that to your taxation professional for finalization. In short, the advantage to Quicken is that every transaction you have recorded throughout the financial year remains fully annotated and categorized.

How Can You Use It?

Quicken helps you to complete your taxes in the following ways:

➤ Electronically track all of your income and expenses. The Paycheck Setup system (see "Setting Up Your Paycheck," later in this chapter) helps you sort your income and track amounts already deducted or paid on your behalf by your employer.

➤ Categorize items so they are automatically targeted for certain parts of the Form 1040 and its related Schedules.

➤ Calculate in advance your withholding and estimated tax.

➤ Generate reports that will help you fill in your tax forms or provide a tax professional with everything he or she needs.

➤ Ensure your calculations are always accurate and up-to-date.

➤ Enable electronic filing, reducing your waiting time for a refund from 40 to 21 days.

➤ Track down valid deductions.

➤ Interface with various editions of TurboTax, giving you one of the most powerful software combinations for personal, business, corporate, and Federal and State tax preparation.

Helping Quicken Help You

At the end of each financial year, you need to follow a few simple procedures to produce your tax return or, at the very least, report on your finances in a way that a taxation professional can easily turn to your advantage.

First ensure Quicken is up-to-date at least through the end of December. Tally its data with the information shown on the returns you have received throughout and at the end of the year. These returns should include all Form W-2s, Form 1099s, and so on. Be very accurate; copies of these forms also go to the IRS where they are stored and checked by computer against the amounts you report in your own return.

If you plan to use a tax professional, print out the Tax Summary, Investment Income, and Capital Gains Reports. Although some of the information contained in those reports is redundant, it provides a useful breakdown of your financial information from several points of view.

If you are preparing your own tax return, print a Tax Summary or Tax Schedule report, or just export the data to TurboTax and follow that product's instructions from there.

Tax Summary and Tax Schedule?

These are Quicken's most tax-competent reports. Print the Tax Summary when all you are interested in are the transactions from each category marked as tax-related. Print the Tax Schedule when you want Quicken to assign totals to specific tax-form line items. You can set up or verify the assignments with the Tax Link Assistant discussed in Chapter 10, "Deductions and Capital Gains."

Create a copy of your data by opening the **File** menu, selecting **File Operations**, and then **Year-End Copy**. You can **Archive** your transactions, creating a copy of your existing file but retaining your previous transactions through the new year, or you can select **Start New Year**, saving a copy of your current file but starting the new year with a completely fresh set of books. The first method is useful to spin off a copy of last year's books for your accountant. The second option is useful if you record thousands of transactions during the course of a single year. With your books wiped clean, save for their new opening balances, it also helps Quicken run faster and smoother. Even though Quicken creates a copy of your file, you should also make a backup before choosing to start a new year.

Can I Retrieve Data from the Previous Financial Year After Starting a New Year?

Unfortunately not. Always make a backup of your data before you start a new year. This gives you the best of both worlds: a comparatively clean and fast Quicken file to use through the new year, and a backup of all the transactions to date.

Finally, print a Transaction report, customizing it to include all your accounts. Print this on paper and store it with the electronic copy of last year's books, as created through the archiving procedure described previously.

Although tracking your income and expenditure is an essential part of managing your finances, you should also use the Paycheck Setup system described next to track your gross rather than net income, as well as any deductions already made. Let's take a look at that right now.

Setting Up Your Paycheck

Quicken is as good at tracking money you don't actually receive as it is any other funds. There's no better example of this than your paycheck.

The Paycheck Setup system built into Quicken simplifies the tracking of your paycheck by helping you specify, in advance, how your gross pay becomes net pay.

It is important that you use the Paycheck Setup for this purpose rather than simply recording the net income component. This is especially true if you want to use your Quicken data to create tax reports or use other tax-preparation software.

It takes between 5 and 15 minutes for you to complete all the steps in the dialog boxes the first time. However, you only need to do this once. Thereafter you can log your paycheck and its associated transactions in a matter of seconds.

Is It Absolutely Necessary to Use the Paycheck Setup System? Can't I Just Type in the Net Amount I Receive and Record That As Income?

You can, but you'd only be using Quicken on its simplest level. It's a bit like chopping the fourth leg off a table because it can mostly stand on three. By recording all the components of your paycheck through the Paycheck Setup System, you give Quicken an enormous amount of information about yourself. You also help it to accurately calculate your net worth, predict whether you are saving sufficiently for your retirement income, and also prepare a more advantageous tax return.

Just one tip before we begin: You'll find it much easier to complete this section if you have your most recent paycheck handy. If it doesn't list the breakdown of your income and deductions, turn to your most recent Form W-2.

Okay, here we go.

Start the Paycheck Setup system by opening the **Taxes** menu, selecting **Tax Activities**, and choosing **Set up my Paycheck**. You should see the dialog box shown in the following figure. If you see a Manage Paychecks dialog box instead, you've already created a paycheck. To set up another paycheck, click **New**.

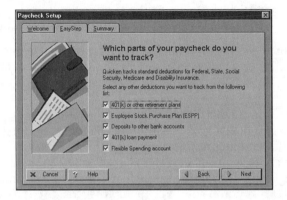

If you don't mind taking the longer route, just check every box and ignore those you don't need until later. This saves possible back-tracking.

Read the introductory screen and click **Next** to continue.

Quicken can track a wide variety of deductions. For example:

➤ Federal Income Tax

➤ State Income Tax

➤ Social Security (FICA)

➤ Federal Medicare

➤ State Disability Insurance

If you make any other deductions, you need to indicate their nature here. Other deductions include amounts paid into a retirement fund, automated mortgage reduction payments, long-term savings accounts, employee stock purchases, and more. These might not necessarily reduce your taxation liability, as deductions can be made to other than tax-deferred accounts. Each box that you check relates directly to a later dialog box. For instance, select **Deposits to other bank accounts** to move to a step later on where you can indicate amounts you transfer to other Quicken accounts. To play it safe, you can also check every box shown, skipping them later if they don't apply.

Click **Next** to proceed.

Use the next screen to provide a name for the paycheck (this is the name used when the transaction is recorded as a deposit in your register) and also to indicate how often you are paid. You can set up any number of paychecks—handy if you work two or more jobs, although you need to set up further paychecks under the Manage Paychecks dialog box. Click **Next** when you're finished.

Record the date shown on your most recent paycheck and the Quicken account into which it was deposited. As soon as you complete this setup system, Quicken records a paycheck transaction at the date you enter here. Therefore, you should only enter the date shown on your last paycheck if you haven't already recorded that paycheck manually. If you have already recorded that paycheck, set the date as the date that you receive your next paycheck. Quicken still records the transaction, but forward-dates it so it doesn't take effect until you receive your next check.

If the paycheck is paid into more than one account, record the principal deposit account. You're able specify the other transfers later.

Click **Next** to move on.

Now you need to start recording the financial data attached to your paycheck. Enter the **Gross** and **Net** amounts in this dialog box and indicate the income **Category**. The default category is Salary, but you might need to change this. For example, if you are recording your spouse's paycheck, you can edit this to read Salary Spouse. Fortunately, you can create categories or subcategories whenever you want. Simply enter the new name, press the **tab** key, and click **Yes** to approve creating the new category. You should define your salary-related categories as tax-related. If you want to use the Tax Planner or TurboTax to prepare your return, assign these to the "Form W-2, salary" tax form line item.

Click **Next** when you're finished.

If you receive other income as part of your salary (commissions, bonuses, a car allowance, or the like), indicate so here. Just click **Yes**, choose an **Income Category**, indicate the **Amount**, and click **Next**.

The next dialog box helps you to record the standard deductions taken from your paycheck. This information should be shown on your paycheck stub and is certainly shown on the W-2. The categories are already set up, so simply run down the list, recording the amounts for each. If you need to change them—to, say, record your spouse's deductions—feel free to do so. Click **Next** when you're finished.

If there are any other taxes, click **Yes** and record them now. Quicken uses the category Tax:Other, but you might need to be more specific. If you don't have any other taxes, leave it as it is.

After you click **Next** to exit this dialog box, you move into a series of dialog boxes relating to each option selected in step 2. These are optional steps because you might or might not need to perform them.

➤ Enter your 401(k) or other Retirement Plan deductions; select the account and the amount. If you contribute to more than one plan, you should manually edit the scheduled transaction after you complete this interview. If you haven't already set up this account, select **Create New Account** from the pull-down menu and set up the account. You can do this in any of the dialog boxes that request you to specify a Quicken account. Click **Next** to continue.

➤ Enter your Employee Stock Purchase Plan (ESPP) deduction. Again, select the account and the amount. Click **Next** to continue.

➤ Enter the name and amount of other accounts into which you have deposited funds. You are limited to checking, savings, and money market accounts, so you can't record a contribution to, say, your mortgage liability account. However, you can set up a direct debit facility with your bank to do that and record it as a scheduled transaction separate from your paycheck. Click **Next** when you're done.

➤ Record the repayment of a 401(k) loan. You must have the loan set up as a liability account. Click **Next** to move on.

➤ Record your Flexible Spending deduction and click **Next**.

Are there any other deductions listed on your paycheck? If so, click **Yes**, and specify the category and the deduction amount. Don't worry if you don't have the appropriate deductions category set up yet—simply enter the new name and click **Yes** to create and save the category. Then click **Next**.

The final step in the Paycheck Setup interview asks you if you would like Quicken to automatically ask you if it should enter your paycheck on the next pay period. Click **Yes** to create a permanently scheduled transaction. Click **No** if you prefer to create a memorized transaction—you can easily call this up and record it each payday.

The displayed summary screen shows the paycheck transaction as it is recorded in your register. The top line shows the gross amount with various deductions along the way. The Net Amount obviously displays the net amount. If it all adds up, click **Done**. If not, I'm afraid you have to go back and check over the numbers.

If you set up Quicken to automatically remind you when your paychecks are due, a subsequent dialog box tells you about your scheduled transaction. Click **OK** to move past this and look over the details of the scheduled transaction. All of the data is taken from the questions you answered in the Paycheck Setup system. Click **Record** when you're sure it's correct.

And that's it. You can record any number of paychecks through the Paycheck Setup, editing them anytime thereafter. (To manage your paychecks, start the Paycheck Setup as described earlier in this section.)

How Can I Track Paychecks I Receive for More Than One Job, or for Me and My Spouse?

The easiest way is to define a class for each job or person. Assign these separate copy numbers when you set up each class. Doing it in this way means that each paycheck can use the same income and expense categories, but when you generate your tax reports you can set it up so each individual or job works with only those transactions assigned to it.

If you receive a paycheck that is more or less than it would normally be, or contains a special one-time only deduction, don't edit the memorized paycheck. Instead, change it in the register using the Splits window. This saves you from editing the scheduled or memorized transaction when your pay reverts to its usual rate.

Tracking Your Income

In general, the IRS is interested in anything that increases your net worth. (And by that, I mean obsessively so.) For example, money that flows into your account through your earnings increases your total assets and thus your net worth, and, in most cases, causes the IRS to want its chop.

Assets that increase in value and are sold are similarly taxed through realized capital gains. However, money that you borrow escapes tax because those funds increase your liabilities just as they do your assets.

There are also certain expenses without which you could not earn your living. These are for the most part tax deductible, and at least in this sense the IRS treats the individual the same as it does any business—as cash cows ready for milking.

Bound up with this financial ebb and flow is a complex series of rules, exemptions, deductions, and conditions that have a direct bearing on the amount of tax you will pay.

This is where Quicken helps.

When you report the changes the year has wrought on your financial situation through the Form 1040 and its related schedules, you do so by dividing your income and expenses into certain categories. IRA distributions, alimony, pensions, and annuities must all go their own separate ways.

The Form W-2 you receive from each of your employers through the previous year further divides your income into gross pay, withholdings, actual income received, reported tips, Medicare and social security tax, and the like.

Obtaining Tax Forms

You can obtain all IRS forms and publications by calling 1-800-TAX-FORM. In numerals, that's 1-800-829-3676. You can also dial 1-703-487-4160 from your fax machine to transmit copies to your own fax. Alternatively, you can get the forms and publications at the IRS site on the World Wide Web. They're at http://www.irs.ustreas.gov/forms_pubs/top-forms.html. (You might want to obtain these early in the new year as the site can become extremely busy around March and April.) The easiest way to view these is using the PDF (Portable Document Format) files supported by Adobe Acrobat. The viewer is available from the Adobe Systems site at http://www.adobe.com.

Quicken's categories already track most of these tax-related items. Indeed, in many cases, specific categories are already attached to specific tax-form line items. This means you can print a report that shows you exactly what and where to enter data on your tax form.

Setting Up Tax-Related Categories

Quicken makes filing the 1040 as easy as it can be, but before it can give you much help, you need to do a little preparation.

You should check your list of categories to make sure you have all the categories you need. You should also check that you aren't using a tax-related category for non-tax-related transactions or vice versa. Otherwise, you could end up paying more tax than you need, or possibly not enough.

You can learn how to create categories in Chapter 4, "It's a Category and Class Thing." Rather than repeating the complete list of steps required to define a new category, just refer to Chapter 4 and then read on for more information on the tax-related aspects of those categories.

You have two options when setting up tax-related categories: you can define a category as tax-related and have it appear as part of Quicken's Tax Summary report; or you can define a category as tax-related but also link it to a tax-form line item. While this category continues to appear in the Tax Summary, it also appears in the Tax Schedule report. (It's the latter that links your data to parts of the 1040.)

The default Quicken installation includes a large number of categories that are both tax-related and linked to tax-form line items. These categories should cover most people's needs, but from time to time you might need to define additional categories that aren't already part of Quicken.

For instance, a private pilot who enjoys self-piloted, tax-deductible flights to business appointments and conventions isn't covered by the standard categories. Quicken simply doesn't have an "AvGas" (Aviation Fuel) category in its default installation. However, it's a legitimate and deductible business expense, and any transactions assigned to that account need to appear on the pilot's taxation reports. The easy solution is to define an AvGas category as tax-related and, for cream on the cake that isn't pie in the sky, link it to the appropriate tax-form line item.

A category can be marked as tax-related either when you first set it up or any time thereafter. Marking a category as tax-related does not change any of the transactions that have passed or will pass through that category. The tax-related information is only used when producing the Tax Summary and Tax Schedule reports.

Browsing Tax-Related Categories

The easiest way to see which categories have already been set up for tax-related functions is to open the **Finance** menu and select **Category & Transfer List**. A 'T' in the T column indicates the category is tax-related. To view the links to tax-form line items, pull down the **Options** menu and select **Show Tax Item**.

Using the Tax Link Assistant

Quicken's Tax Link Assistant is a handy utility designed especially to help you assign Form 1040 and Schedule items to particular categories within your accounts.

The Tax Link doesn't do your work for you, but it does make it easier to work out which categories are most applicable to certain 1040 and Schedule items.

To set up tax schedule categories with the Tax Link Assistant, first open the **Features** menu, select **Taxes**, and then **Set up for Taxes**. This opens the Tax Link Assistant shown in the following figure.

Use the list box headed **Category** to select the category in Quicken you want to adjust. The **Assigned Line Item** listing shows the currently assigned Form 1040 or Schedule item.

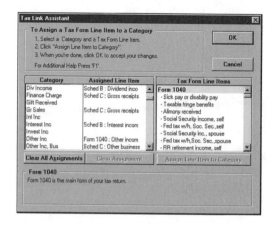

Use the Tax Link Assistant to assign categories to line items on the Form 1040 and its Schedules.

Double-click any category or assigned category line to display that category's Name, Description, and Type. Subcategories are displayed with the name of the parent category preceding the name of the subcategory. For example, the Fuel subcategory of Auto becomes Auto Fuel.

To change the assigned tax-related category, select from the list box headed **Tax Form Line Items**. Read the description provided in the lower panel and, when you're ready, click **Assign Line Item to Category**.

To delete an Assigned Line Item, click **Clear Assignment**. To delete all Assigned Line Items, click **Clear All Assignments**.

Click **OK** to confirm the changes or **Cancel** to exit the Tax Link Assistant.

The Least You Need to Know

➤ There's nothing easy about tax: it's onerous, it's painful, but it's also for the greater social good. At least with Quicken the mechanics of paying that tax are very well taken care of.

➤ Setting up your paycheck is a vital part of accurate tax preparation. Quicken needs to know about every component of your paycheck before it can build a complete financial picture.

➤ By using tax-related categories, you can prepare Quicken for printing your return, either in the Summary form which is useful for other tax professionals, or the Schedule form which is most useful for finalizing the return on your own.

➤ Many of Quicken's default categories are linked to tax form line items. If you add tax-related categories and you plan to print a Tax Schedule, don't forget that you should also link these to actual tax form line items. Just keep in mind that you may need to consult a tax professional to learn the exact links required.

Chapter 10

Deductions and Capital Gains

> **In This Chapter**
>
> ➤ Using the Tax Deduction Finder
>
> ➤ Estimating your capital gains

Tracking Your Deductions

Quicken's tax utilities can make you as expert at finding deductions as Sherlock Holmes was at making them, and you don't even need a Watson on hand.

Between the Capital Gains Estimator, the Tax Deduction Finder, and the Tax Planner (discussed in the next chapter), you'll find little need for guess work when finalizing your taxes. Quicken can even calculate your appropriate withholding and estimated tax payments.

Deductions fall into two broad categories: those that apply before your Adjusted Gross Income (AGI) are known as adjustments to income. Those that apply after are either itemized deductions, depending on which you choose. To arrive at your taxable income, you must apply both sets of deductions and then take into account any exemptions.

(Exemptions don't usually make an appearance until tax time, but you will see them in the Tax Planner.)

The Tax Deduction Finder included with Quicken Deluxe and Quicken Home and Business helps you explore ways you can lower your taxes. (Having said this, also speak to your taxation professional, because the finder might not find them all.)

Finding Tax Deductions

The Tax Deduction Finder is a powerful interrogative tool that helps you decide whether you are eligible for certain tax deductions.

It is built around a knowledge base that understands the requirements for various deductions and establishes your eligibility (or ineligibility) through a series of simple questions, mostly of the yes/no variety.

Knowledge Base?

A knowledge base is any system that stores factual information so that it can be easily retrieved, a bit like a specialized encyclopedia. Today's knowledge bases are most often cast in software, but they've been around since we first put pen to papyrus.

All in all, the Tax Deduction Finder is a remarkable piece of work—one well worth exploring. So, without further ado, let's get going.

To open the Finder, pull down the **Taxes** menu and select **Tax Deduction Finder**. The first time you run the Finder you see a small introductory screen. Just click **OK** to move on to the window shown in the following figure.

The four steps highlighted onscreen lead you through the process of finding your deductions. Start with **1.**, selecting a deduction type. You can change this as often as you like, moving from one set of deductions to another.

Now you need to choose a specific deduction. Go to **2.** and start with the most likely in the list. This list changes according to the deduction type previously specified. Again, there's no need to work through them all—just those most pertinent.

To establish whether you meet the basic criteria for any deduction, answer the questions shown in **3**, clicking **Y** or **N** as appropriate.

The Tax Deductions Finder's answer is displayed at the bottom of the third window. If it suggests you are or might be eligible, click **More Information** to learn more about the deduction.

Finally, to track any future transactions that might be eligible for that deduction, click **Create a Category**. Isn't that handy? The Create a Category dialog box opens, telling you exactly how you should apply that deduction to your tax forms.

Select the deduction type.

View a summary of your responses and possible deductions.

Clear all your responses so far.

View your action plan.

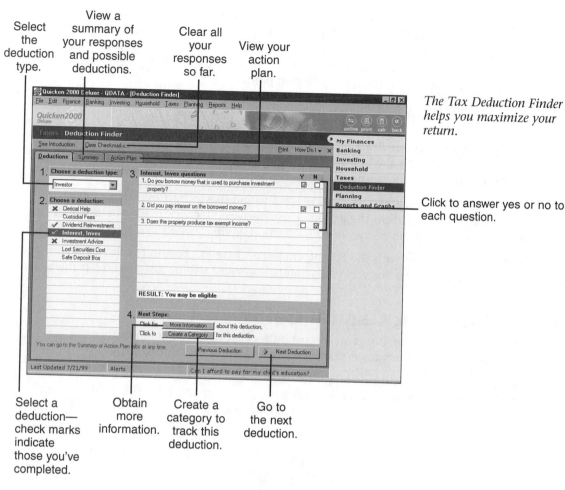

The Tax Deduction Finder helps you maximize your return.

Click to answer yes or no to each question.

Select a deduction—check marks indicate those you've completed.

Obtain more information.

Create a category to track this deduction.

Go to the next deduction.

Check This Out

Always Ask for More Information

Don't always trust the Deduction Finder! Quicken cannot know for certain whether you are eligible for a deduction, and it makes good sense to look under **More Information** if it suggests you are eligible. Although this tells you a little more about the deduction, you should also speak to your taxation advisor. The requirements for many deductions are complex, and if Quicken tried to establish the full set of circumstances, it would take you much longer to complete each question.

After you finish the current set of questions, you can move on to the next set by clicking **Next Deduction**. However, you don't need to complete these deductions in sequence or even complete them at all. If you aren't sure about one deduction, just leave it at whatever stage of completion it was and move on; when you return, Quicken remembers your answers up to that point.

When you finish answering all the deductions that interest you, click the **Summary** tab. This shows you how many deductions you might be eligible for in each category.

Finally, click the **Action Plan** tab to see what you should do to support your claim for this deduction with the IRS. You can also print yourself a copy of the plan using the **Print** button in the top-right corner of the window.

If you think you've made some mistakes and would like to start over, click **Clear Checkmarks** and confirm the action. This removes the check marks (or crosses, if you aren't eligible) from every previous question, giving you a clean slate.

When you've finished with the Finder, click the **Close** (**X**) button to exit. The next time you return, all the answers you've already entered will be just as you left them.

Estimating Your Capital Gains

The Capital Gains Estimator is an important tool for calculating in advance the tax you need to pay on gains from share trading and other investment activities.

Awareness of the implications of capital gains can make a big difference in regard to your tax bill. For example, you must pay a higher rate of capital gains for shares you have held short- or medium-term than for those you have held long-term.

Short-, Medium-, and Long-Term Gains?

Capital gains and losses fall into three categories: long-, medium- and short-term. For investments made on or prior to July 28, 1997, a long-term gain or loss is one in which you held those items longer than 12 months. For investments made after that date, a long-term gain is one where you have held the investment for more than 18 months. Short-term gains are those held for 12 months or less. Medium-term capital gains apply for investments made after July 28, 1997 and are held between 12 and 18 months.

When you use the Capital Gains Estimator, you only receive an estimate of the capital gains tax due. This might seem obvious from the function's name, but it's an important point. The rules for capital gains remain complex, despite efforts at simplification, and the Capital Gains Estimator in particular makes no effort to calculate a net tax based on both gains and losses. As you will see, it deals only with gains.

This means you should always consult a taxation professional before embarking on any major transaction, and especially one dealing with capital gains.

The figure below shows the Estimator at work. Notice how it uses a divided window? The lower one shows your holdings in all your investment accounts. It doesn't include asset accounts, even though some holdings in your asset accounts (for example, your home inventory) are considered susceptible to capital gains. The Estimator can only help you with your securities investments.

The upper section is your work area. You use this to log proposed sales and calculate their approximate taxes. The three tabs labeled Scenario A, B, and C are there to help you plan up to three different divestment strategies.

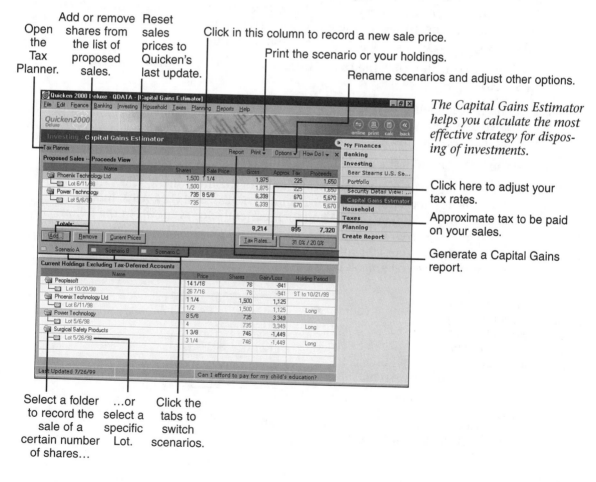

Open the Tax Planner.

Add or remove shares from the list of proposed sales.

Reset sales prices to Quicken's last update.

Click in this column to record a new sale price.

Print the scenario or your holdings.

Rename scenarios and adjust other options.

The Capital Gains Estimator helps you calculate the most effective strategy for disposing of investments.

Click here to adjust your tax rates.

Approximate tax to be paid on your sales.

Generate a Capital Gains report.

Select a folder to record the sale of a certain number of shares...

...or select a specific Lot.

Click the tabs to switch scenarios.

Sick of Your Scenarios?

You can rename your scenario tabs so they represent something more meaningful by clicking the scenario tab you want to rename, selecting the **Options** drop-down menu that resides at the top of the Capital Gains Estimator window, and selecting **Rename Scenario**. Enter the new name and click **OK**.

The Estimator's scenarios aren't linked to each other, so you can test the same sales in all three. However, keep in mind that you cannot turn your proposed sales into actual sales without creating and recording those transactions in your investment register (and, of course, selling them in the real world). Also, although you can't save your scenarios, Quicken retains them between sessions. Indeed, the only way to delete a scenario is by replacing its proposed sales with new ones.

To open the estimator, click the **Investing** menu and select **Capital Gains Estimator**.

Every investment you own is shown as a folder in the lower pane, with every lot purchased arranged hierarchically underneath. The folders are listed alphabetically, making them easy to find.

There are two ways to test a sale using the estimator:

➤ To sell a specific quantity of shares or units in the investment, select the investment folder (not the Lot entries underneath), and click **Add**. Indicate the number of **Shares to Sell** and their current price as shown in the following figure. (Quicken uses the most recent price available. If you change this, you can replace your edit with Quicken's price at any time by clicking the **Current Prices** command button.)

By clicking a security's folder, you can sell a specified number of shares at a set price rather than an entire lot all at once.

➤ To sell a specific lot of shares (for example, your oldest purchase), select it from under its folder and click **Add**.

Should You Sell FIFO or LIFO?

The most tax-effective method to sell securities is on a *FIFO*, or first-in, first-out, basis. This means the oldest shares are sold first. However, on rare occasions you might find selling shares on a *LIFO*, or a last-in, first-out, basis proves more effective—at least in the short-term.

For example, if you have been steadily buying shares over several years in a sleeper stock that suddenly finds market favor again, you would end up with more post-tax money in your pocket by selling the last shares first. Why? The capital gains tax on the short-term shares is a higher percentage applied to a smaller profit. It might well turn out the long-term shares cost you less in tax and put more in your pocket. If you can hold off from selling the more recent purchases until they too become long-term, you're that much further ahead.

The capital gains tax rate is linked to your marginal tax rate. Click **Tax Rates** to select your tax bracket or customize the tax rates as required. You can specify separate tax rates for each scenario. As you add to your list of proposed sales, Quicken re-calculates the **Approx. Tax** column. Again, keep in mind that this is only a guide, and it doesn't take into account your capital losses.

Click **Remove** to remove a security or lot from the list of proposed sales.

The three columns to the right of the Proposed Sales window are the important ones:

➤ **Gross** or **Gain/Loss**   The gross is the amount realized by the sale of those lots or a particular lot. To view your sales ordered by their gain or loss rather than their gross, click **Options** and select **View Sales by Gains**. (The default is to **View Sales by Proceeds**.)

➤ **Approx. Tax**   This is only an estimate. If you happen to lose money on a sale, all you see is zero here. Of course, this means that you might, in fact, come out better in these trades than you think.

➤ **Proceeds** or **Net Gain**   The amount left over after tax. This column changes according to the previously mentioned View Sales setting.

There are totals at the bottom of each column along with the tax rates applied.

After you have determined the best case for your capital gains, click the **Report** button at the top of Capital Gains Estimator's window (the button, not the Quicken

Printing Other Capital Gains Reports

Quicken provides a host of reports targeted at capital gains, tax, and investment matters. You can learn more about using and customizing reports in Chapter 8, "Powerful Reports and Great Graphs."

Reports menu). You can use this as a guide for when you record those transactions in your investment register and transact them through a broker.

As a final note, the **Tax Planner** link in the upper-left corner of the Estimator's window takes you to Quicken's Tax Planner discussed in Chapter 11, "Estimating and Finalizing Your Return." You should be aware that the Tax Planner doesn't copy any information from the Estimator's window. You need to take note of the estimated gains and manually plug them into Tax Planners' fields.

Also, one last reminder that this is only an estimator—any sales you've played with in your scenarios aren't recorded as actual sales. When you do send those instructions to your broker, you need to record the appropriate transactions in your investment register. You can learn about this in Chapter 14,"Creating and Managing Your Portfolio."

The Least You Need to Know

➤ The Tax Deduction Finder is a great way to open some of the loopholes that lie hidden in the bottom drawers of America's best tax lawyers. Make sure you explore all the questions; you never know what you'll find.

➤ In its way, the Capital Gains Estimator is equally useful, especially if you invest in a lot of stocks and other securities. Set up different scenarios and experiment with the effects of selling different lots from the one bundle of shares. It's another great way to minimize your liability.

EENIE, MEENIE
MINY, MO...

Chapter 11

Estimating and Finalizing Your Return

In This Chapter

➤ Calculating your estimated tax payments

➤ Preparing your tax return

Tax Planning

The IRS collects two forms of income tax: withholding and estimated.

Withholding tax is paid out of your earnings each pay period. It is taken from salaries and wages, tips, taxable fringe benefits, sick pay, pensions and annuities, gambling winnings, unemployment compensation, and some federal payments.

Although withholding tax is designed to account for the total income tax payable by many wage earners, it doesn't cover all possibilities. Estimated tax looks after the rest, making up the difference between the withholding removed and the amount you are expected to pay throughout the year.

Quicken's Tax Planner helps you decide if you need to pay estimated tax by calculating your potential tax liability and taking into account payments already or expected to be made.

The Tax Planner can do this using your Quicken data as a base, or you can use it in a standalone fashion, providing all the relevant data through a series of dialog boxes.

Tax Facts

When Federal income tax was introduced in 1913, the highest tax bracket (or marginal tax rate) was just 7 percent, and that remains the most favorable rate for the taxpayer ever recorded. Tax rates peaked during the second World War, where income tax in the top earnings bracket climbed as high as 94%!

In comparison, the highest tax bracket for the 1996 tax year was 39.6% on income over $271,663.

See, taxes don't always go up!

Do You Need to Pay Estimated Tax?

Estimated tax is used for both income and self-employment tax and is reported on Form 1040-ES, Estimated Tax for Individuals. It applies to all U.S. citizens and residents as well as nonresident aliens (dependent on the terms of a tax treaty, if one exists); essentially, it applies to anyone who earns an income in the U.S. or its territories.

Several conditions have to be met before you become liable for estimated tax.

If your estimate tax is less than $1,000, feel free to skip it. Furthermore, if the estimated tax is less than 10% of the total tax, there's no need to pay.

You also don't need to pay estimated tax if your withholding tax and credits for this year equal at least 100% of the total tax paid on your previous return.

There are some additional conditions as well, but the previously mentioned conditions apply to most U.S. citizens.

The easy way to avoid paying estimated tax is to increase the amount of withholding tax you already pay. To do this, use the Tax Planner to calculate the extra amount required and submit a new Form W-4 to your employer, requesting the extra deduction.

Why should you worry so much about meeting your estimated tax payments? In a word, penalties. If you fail to pay or do not pay enough, you almost certainly face a penalty. Furthermore, if you miss the estimated tax payment date, you might be penalized even if it turns out you are due a refund after you have filed your return.

Refunds and Estimated Payments

One of the easiest ways to reduce your estimated payments for the upcoming year is to apply your tax refund from the previous year to the current year's estimated payments. Enter the amount of the refund that you want to apply to your estimated tax on Form 1040 or Form 1040A.

This isn't a particularly fun thing to do with your return (Aspen can wait), but it's certainly sensible.

Calculating Your Estimated Tax Using the Tax Planner

Quicken's Tax Planner is more than a tool for the end of the year. You can use it at any time to not only determine your eligibility for estimated tax, but also to show you how key financial decisions might change those amounts.

In short, the Tax Planner helps you to

➤ Estimate the tax you will owe at the end of the year

➤ Calculate the appropriate level of withholding tax

➤ Develop different scenarios to establish the advantages or disadvantages of filing separately or jointly

➤ Show how major decisions, such as buying or selling a home, will affect your final tax bill

➤ Interface with Quicken to download your existing tax information

Tax Planner is like a smart spreadsheet; simply enter the values where required and it calculates your tax due. However, it does take some effort to complete. You should take the time before you start to use the Tax Planner to gather as much information about your financial affairs as possible, including all your banking records, paycheck stubs, receipts for taxes paid, dividend and annuity records, last year's return, and so on.

Is Tax Planner's Data Up to Date?

Congress has a nasty habit of changing the tax rules, standardized deductions, and other taxation parameters each financial year. Even though the Quicken you purchase might not include the latest information, that data should update to the latest information when you perform in Quicken what is called a One Step Update. You can learn more about this in Chapter 13, "Online Banking and Bill Paying."

If you file jointly, do the same for your partner.

The good news is that the Planner works directly with this or last year's Quicken data, and can even annualize or project it forward if your totals for the year are incomplete.

If you haven't been using Quicken long enough for Tax Planner to use your existing data, think of it more as an electronic slate that you can use to draw up and adjust different scenarios. You learn about this in "Using Tax Planner Without Existing Data," later in this chapter.

Using Tax Planner with Existing Data

To use Tax Planner to calculate your liability based on existing data, just follow the steps below. You can edit this data after it has been imported into the Tax Planner to update it with information that hasn't yet been recorded in Quicken.

To open the Tax Planner, open the **Taxes** menu and click **Tax Planner**. You'll see a window similar to the one shown in the following figure.

Specify your filing status using the **Status** drop-down list and select the appropriate **Year**. To use last year's data as the basis for the next financial year, select the previous financial year and import your previous Quicken data as described in the next step. After you've finished importing the data, move **Year** forward one notch so that it equals the next financial year.

Now for a wonderful shortcut. To copy all your existing financial information from Quicken, just click **Quicken Data**. Quicken imports data from the start of the current year through to the end of the previous month.

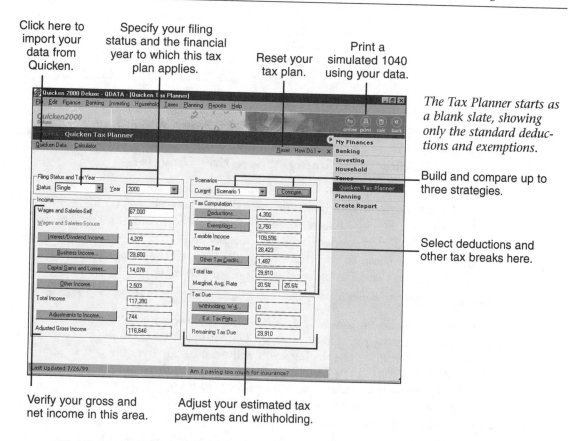

Click here to import your data from Quicken.

Specify your filing status and the financial year to which this tax plan applies.

Reset your tax plan.

Print a simulated 1040 using your data.

The Tax Planner starts as a blank slate, showing only the standard deductions and exemptions.

Build and compare up to three strategies.

Select deductions and other tax breaks here.

Verify your gross and net income in this area.

Adjust your estimated tax payments and withholding.

The Preview Quicken Tax Data dialog box is designed so you can select the items that are to be annualized through the year. When Quicken annualizes, it forecasts a total for the year according to the average already incurred by that account. Typically, you should annualize your wage or salary, medical expenses, and interest income. However, you probably don't want to annualize rarely occurring totals such as capital gain on the sale of your house. Double-click an item to toggle its annualization status. You should see the original Quicken Amount, as well as the Annualized Amount. Alternatively, **Annualize None** and **Annualize All** control a blanket annualization on the entire lot. When you're done, click **OK** to copy that data to the Tax Planner.

The Tax Planner is designed to cope with tax only as it relates to the Form 1040, so it's possible you might have recorded data in certain tax-related categories that isn't applicable. Tax Planner tries to import these items but fails, as it hasn't anywhere to put them. These are marked in the Preview Quicken Tax Data window as <Not imported; no corresponding item.> You can ignore these items.

After your financial information has been imported, start exploring the taxation implications in the Tax Planner window.

When I Click Quicken Data in the Tax Planner Window, I Receive a Message No Items Found, and the Tax Planner Window Stays Empty. Where Can They Be?

The Tax Planner takes its information solely from categories marked as tax-related and targeted at the appropriate tax-form line items. If you've been recording transactions to categories you haven't defined as tax-related or aren't set as tax-form line items, you'll find yourself faced with a sadly empty Tax Planner window. The easy way around this is to edit those categories through the category list. See Chapter 9, "Paychecks and Tax Categories," for more information.

Look to the groups of two buttons and three fields in the lower-right corner for a quick sum-up of your situation. The field called Remaining Tax Due shows the shortfall (if it exists) that Tax Planner calculates you will need to pay over the course of the year. A shortfall of more than $1,000 results in a penalty, therefore you should arrange either for additional withholding to be taken from your wages or pay an extra estimated tax. You can use each button in this section of the Tax Planner window to play with the amounts until your tax due equals zero.

Keep in mind that Congress can change the tax laws at any time. (Sometimes it seems by pure whimsy.) This means the Tax Planner might not always be working with the latest rules and regulations—or even the correct formula. For this reason, never rely solely on the Tax Planner results. Yes, it gives you an excellent general idea of how your tax situation is panning out, but you should always call on the services of a tax professional in order to verify the results.

Using Tax Planner Without Existing Data

Not everyone will use the Tax Planner the same way. For example, if you aren't self-employed, you won't need to go near Business Income.

Use the following descriptions to determine those parts of the Tax Planner window in which you need to record further data. When you're done, the Tax Due (or Refund Due) section of the window shows how your existing rate of withholding or estimated tax payments is bearing up.

To get started, open the **Taxes** menu and click **Tax Planner**.

Specify your filing status using the **Status** pull-down list and select the appropriate **Year**. Then work through each of the sections in this list:

➤ **Wages and Salaries—Self**   Enter or adjust the total wages and salary you expect to earn through this or the following year. The IRS considers your income in terms of total compensation, but there's plenty of room later on to enter any other employment benefits you might receive.

➤ **Wages and Salaries—Spouse**   Use this field for your spouse's wages or salary. This field is only available if you selected **Married-Joint** from the **Status** pull-down list.

➤ **Interest/Dividend Income**   Click this button to fill in the amounts required for your Schedule B. Your taxable interest income is noted on copies of the Form 1099-INT that is filed with the IRS by the organizations that pay you interest. Dividends come from banks, S-corporations, mutual funds, stocks and bonds, and so on, and are shown on Form 1099-DIV.

➤ **Business Income**   Click this button if you file a Schedule C with the rest of your tax return. If you are uncertain how to calculate your business income and expenses, talk to a tax professional.

➤ **Capital Gains and Losses**   Click this button if you expect to fill out a Schedule D. You must consult the current tax rules to determine investments that count as long-term or short-term. Although this window is used for simple capital gains and losses such as stocks and bonds, it is also used for more complex issues, such as the sale of real estate or business investments. Again, consult a tax professional. The IRS Publication 17 also makes a good starting point. It is available from any IRS office or across the Internet from their Web site at `http://www.irs.ustreas.gov`.

➤ **Other Income**   Click this button to specify income received through refunds on state tax, alimony received, rents, royalties, and more.

➤ **Adjustments to Income**   Adjustments to income include IRA deductions, alimony paid, Keogh/SEP deductions, moving expenses, and other IRS-specified items. After your total adjustments have been subtracted from Total Income, you end up with your Adjusted Gross Income.

Now you're about halfway there. Your AGI is the basic starting point for calculating the rest of your tax. It's like working out the net profit for a business.

The next step is to work out whether you should claim the itemized or standard deduction.

Claiming Itemized and Standard Deductions

When filing your return, you can choose between an itemized deduction and the standard deduction: choose whichever benefits you more.

Click **Deductions** in the Tax Planner main window to open the Itemized (Schedule A) and Standard Deductions dialog box.

Use the left side of the deductions window to list your Schedule A deductions, including State and Local Income Tax. Many of these deductions have other conditions associated with them, but Tax Planner includes all the pertinent rules. Use the right side of the window to calculate your standard deductions.

For help on the specific conditions associated with each deduction, click in that field and press your **F1** key.

When you're done, click **OK** to return to the Tax Planner window. Next to the Deductions button, Tax Planner displays whichever is the higher of your itemized or standard deductions.

Recording Exemptions

Think of an exemption as a gift from Congress, handed down to provide tax breaks where they are most needed. Historically, exemptions were supposed to cover the total food costs for one person through the year. Today, supermodels excepted, that isn't close to the case, but exemptions are still some of the most powerful tax deductions you will find.

Everyone is worth one exemption. In 1999 that was $2,750.

The trick to exemptions is determining just who gets to claim that deduction. For example, if you are single, have no dependents, and are not being claimed as a dependent, you may apply that exemption to yourself and claim the deduction.

However, if someone else claims you as a dependent, your exemption and subsequent deduction goes to them, and you may not claim that deduction for yourself. The IRS does not look upon your spouse as a dependent. You may only claim a spousal exemption if you both file jointly (in which case there is no net gain). If you file separately, you may only claim his or her exemption if he or she has no income and that exemption is not being claimed elsewhere. The IRS applies a five-part test to establish dependency. Potential dependents must satisfy each part. The test is not built-in to Tax Planner, but it is included in the Quicken Deluxe help system (bring this up by pressing **F1**) and is also included in the IRS Publication 17. Exemptions are phased out when your adjusted gross income exceeds a certain ceiling. Tax Planner takes this into account.

Recording Other Tax and Credits

The Other Tax, Credits dialog box provides a useful overview of your (and your spouse's) main sources of income.

Like the Other Income window discussed earlier, it is something of a catch-all for the bits and pieces that would turn the main window into an unmanageable, non-navigable mess.

The dialog box has two parts: Self-Employment Income Tax and Alternative Minimum Tax. These are discussed below.

Use the upper portion, Self-Employment Income Tax, to adjust your final income. The first line takes its total from the information you entered under Schedule C, Business Income and Schedule F, Farm Income.

Tax Planner assumes any amounts entered under Schedules C and F were earned by yourself. If they were earned by your spouse, you must enter a negative amount in **Other Income** and the identical, but positive, amount in your Spouse's **Other Income**. For example, if you and your spouse worked equally running a part-time market and it turned a profit of $4,000 for the year, *and* you are filing joint returns, you should enter $-2,000 in your **Other Income** and $2,000 in your spouse's. This balances the $4,000 entered into your return under Schedule C, Business Income.

Add any remaining income that wasn't reported on Schedules C and F to whatever amount is already summarized in **Other Income**.

When Should I File a Self-Employment Return?

The IRS regulations state that you must file Schedule SE (attached to Form 1040) if you were self-employed and your net earnings from self-employment were $400 or more, or if you received a church employee income of $108.28 or more.

Use **Other Wages** to record any other wages from which Medicare and social security tax have been withheld but which weren't reported elsewhere in Tax Planner.

Use the lower portion of the dialog box, Alternative Minimum Tax, to calculate whether or not you are liable for this additional tax. The field labeled Other Adjustments and Tax Preference Items increases the amount of AMT taxable income. Possibilities include claiming for accelerated depreciation of property acquired prior to 1987 and tax-exempt interest on nonessential private activity bonds. The use of these goes beyond the scope of this book. However, you can read all about them in the instructions for completing Form 6251. Notice that you also can indicate Medical Expense Adjustments. The parameters for these are explained in the IRS's Publication 17.

Enter any other taxes you have incurred in **Other Taxes**. These include tax on foreign income, tax attributable to early retirement plans, and tax on lump-sum distributions.

Alternative Minimum Tax?

The Alternative Minimum Tax increases your tax if you are receiving an unusual level of tax benefit through certain itemized deductions and other exemptions. (If the tax law was a computer program, AMT would be known as kludging a bug fix.) Basically, AMT works like this: it calculates the actual monetary benefit from those deductions or exemptions. Then, it adds that amount to your taxable income and calculates your new income tax. If that income tax is greater than your usual income tax, you have to pay a penalty. AMT is usually figured using Form 6251, but Tax Planner can also do it for you. Thank goodness.

Tax credits directly reduce the amount of tax you must pay. A tax credit is the most powerful form of tax deduction available. Use **Credits** to record the total amount. Typical credits include the following:

➤ **Child and Dependent Care Credit** Use Form 2441, Child and Dependent Care Expenses.

➤ **Credit for the Elderly or the Disabled** Use Schedule R along with Form 1040.

➤ **Earned Income Credit** Use Schedule EIC with Form 1040A or Form 1040.

➤ **Nonrefundable Credits** Credit for prior year minimum tax, mortgage interest credit, credit for electric vehicles, and foreign tax credit.

➤ **Refundable Credits** Credit for excess social security tax or railroad retirement tax withheld, credit from a regulated investment company, and credit on diesel-powered highway vehicles.

When you've finished, click **OK** to return to the main Tax Planner dialog box. The results are recorded in the field to the right of the **Other Tax, Credits** button.

Understanding the Results

It takes some time to complete the entry of data, but after you're done, Tax Planner delivers the results on a plate. The following figure shows a typical Tax Planner calculation. Take a look at the lower-right corner of the Tax Planner dialog box. You should see the following fields:

➤ **Total Tax**   This is the total tax you must pay throughout the year.

➤ **Marginal, Avg. Rate**   Your marginal tax rate is that rate applied to the final bracket of your income. It is shown as a percentage in the left box. The marginal rate is also referred to as your tax bracket. The average rate is that applied across your total income. This is the real percentage of the tax you pay. It is shown to the right of the marginal tax rate.

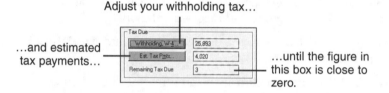

Adjust your withholding tax...

...and estimated tax payments...

...until the figure in this box is close to zero.

When your Remaining Tax Due or Refund Due equals $0.00, or just a few dollars off, you know Tax Planner has completed the job.

Calculating Tax Due

Use Tax Due to work out how much withholding tax you should remove from your paycheck or, alternatively, how much you should pay in estimated tax.

To calculate your optimal withholding click **Withholding, W-4**.

The Withholding and W-4 Allowances dialog box calculates the total annual withholding from the amount withheld to date, the amount removed each pay period, and the number of pay periods yet to come. In **Withholdings To Date**, record the total amount of Federal withholding tax removed from your paychecks so far. (Note: This is not the number of instances withholding tax has been withdrawn.)

Then enter your **Next Pay Date** and select your **Pay Period**.

What's the difference between every two weeks and twice each month? The correct choice depends on whether you earn a salary or a wage. Wages tend to accumulate every week or two and are calculated on the number of hours you work. For continuity, you almost certainly are paid on a specific day of the week or month. A salary runs through the year and tends to be paid on a calendar basis, for example the first and 15th day of each month, no matter which day of the week it falls upon.

Use **Withholding Per Pay Period** to enter the amount of Federal Tax that is being withheld every pay period. The lower-right corner of the dialog box displays either the Refund Due or the Remaining Tax Due calculated for the end of the financial year. Your goal is to try to reduce this to zero so that you neither pay too much nor too little.

If you would like Tax Planner to calculate the actual amount of tax that should be withheld from your wages or salary every paycheck in order to fully cover your estimated tax, select **Recalculate Withholding Allowance for Future**

Withholding and continue. Tax Planner takes into account the total already withheld and the number of pay periods remaining in the financial year.

In **Taxable Pay Per Period** enter your gross pay, less pre-tax deductions.

Enter the number of allowances you are claiming in **Allowances Claimed**. Click **Recommend** for the Tax Planner to calculate the ideal withholding tax you should pay from now on. The planner also considers any estimated tax payments already made or promised to be made. You might need to record these as described below and then jump back to this window for another recommendation.

To hold more than the recommended, enter the desired amount into **Additional Withholding Per Pay Period**.

Projected Total Withholding Per Period is the amount you should enter on Form W-4 and file with your employer.

Click **OK** when you're done to return to the main Tax Planner window.

Entering Your Estimated Tax Payments

Click **Est. Tax Pmts** if

➤ You have already made estimated payments

➤ You intend to make estimated payments

➤ You chose to have your previous year's refund applied to this year's estimated payments

If you need to proceed, use the **Estimated Taxes (1040-ES) Paid to Date** field to record the total estimated tax paid so far this year.

Use **Projected Future Estimated Tax Payments** to indicate the estimated taxes you expect to pay through to the end of the year. If you decide to increase your withholding tax and reduce your estimated tax payments to zero, leave this field at zero and re-work your withholding payments using the Withholding and W-4 Allowances dialog box as previously described.

In the third field, enter the refund from last year that you chose to apply to this year's estimated payments.

Click **OK** when you're done.

If all went well, you should now see a Refund Due of almost zero instead of Remaining Tax Due, as shown earlier in Figure 11.2. If not, click **Withholding, W-4** and let the planner calculate a new Recommended additional withholding rate for you or increase your estimated payments.

Creating Multiple Scenarios

The Tax Planner is useful not only for working out your end-of-year tax liability but also for playing around with various situations to see how you can reduce the amount of tax you pay.

For example, what would happen to your tax situation if you and your spouse jumped from separate to joint filing? For that matter, what will happen to your taxes in the next financial year?

Check This Out

How Do I Save Tax Planner's Data After I've Completed a Scenario?

There's no need. Like the rest of Quicken's data, the Tax Planner scenarios are part of your existing files.

By using multiple scenarios, you can compare up to three different situations, and then choose the most advantageous.

To start, just enter your base data as described through this chapter.

In the Scenarios area of the main Tax Planner window, open the Current list and select either of the three alternate scenarios.

If you want to use your current data in the new scenario, click **Yes** when asked. This copies the data from the current Tax Planner window to the new scenario. Otherwise, click **No** to start over with zero amounts.

Adjust that data as necessary. Click any of the scenario buttons to jump back and forth between scenarios. Tax Planner even remembers those scenarios between Quicken sessions.

To see how the scenarios stack up against each other, click **Compare**. This shows you how the base and two alternates stack up. When you're done, click **OK**.

To reset a scenario and start over, click the **Reset** button at the top of the Tax Planner window.

Finalizing Your Return

Everything you have achieved to date has been aimed at one task: making it easier to file an advantageous tax return. By defining tax-related categories, tracking your income and expenses, recording every transaction you make, and planning your tax payments, you have already achieved an enormous amount. In fact, you're way ahead of the vast majority of U.S. taxpayers.

You can, at this point, print a Tax Summary Report or a Tax Schedule Report (open the **Reports** menu and select either one under the **Taxes** sub-menu) and take those to your tax professional or use them to complete your returns by hand, but there's also a better way.

As far as tax preparation goes, it's the icing on the cake. It's name is "TurboTax". It can uncover deductions with alacrity, file complex returns in a single bound, and stop IRS audits with a...sorry, nothing stops an audit.

Whether you own TurboTax or plan to use the online version available through the Intuit Web site, Quicken can feed TurboTax all the information it needs. You can file your return electronically, online, or print a version that you can simply put in the mail.

Frankly, the only way taxes would be any easier is if you didn't have to pay any!

Linking Quicken to TurboTax

TurboTax comes in several different versions including the innovative Web TurboTax.

It is a complete, standalone product that interfaces perfectly with Quicken, stepping you through the creation of a tax return line-by-line using data you've already recorded. The Deluxe version of TurboTax is also filled with advice from taxation professionals and includes electronic copies of nearly all the IRS documentation.

Web TurboTax is accessible through Quicken's Web browsing window or an external browser. You can jump to it from Quicken by opening the **Taxes** menu and selecting **Web TurboTax**.

Should I Use Web TurboTax or Buy the TurboTax Product to Lodge My Return?

When Web TurboTax was introduced for the 1998 tax year, it was designed solely for California residents and, even then, only for those with very simple returns—that is, those who could get away with filing a 1040EZ. It's worth checking, however, on the Web TurboTax limitations when you prepare to file your next return. After all, it's cheaper than purchasing TurboTax, and it is being constantly improved by Intuit.

Because there are so many different versions of TurboTax, this isn't the place to look too closely at their different features. Suffice to say when you combine Quicken with these products you have a formidable tax partner. Some of the features and capabilities include

➤ A simple step-by-step interview that makes filling in the Form 1040 a piece of cake.

➤ A TaxLink that copies your data from Quicken, saving significant retyping.

➤ A Tax Advisor that jumps in with personalized money-saving advice.

➤ Tips to help you plan your taxes for the year ahead.

➤ Audit Alerts that let you know when an item on your return falls outside the norm, helping to stave off that audit.

➤ A U.S. Average Comparison that draws on previous IRS statistics to show you how the items on your return compare to others in the same income bracket.

➤ If you've purchased TurboTax Deluxe, a CD-ROM with numerous onscreen publications including most of the IRS's major efforts, several income tax handbooks, and video advice from taxation experts.

If that isn't enough, all CD-ROM versions of TurboTax include every major form and worksheet required by the IRS. These include the three versions of the Form 1040 (1040EZ, 1040A, and 1040 Standard), all of the associated schedules, and all of the forms required for specialized procedures, such as filing for an extension, selling property, foreign-earned income, and some 80 more! Each of the forms includes a "Guide Me" tutor that steps you through the completion of each.

In addition, Intuit also publishes TurboTax for Business and TurboTax State.

TurboTax works with your current data in several ways. You can, for instance, import last year's TurboTax data and use that as the basis for the current year. Alternatively, you might import tax return data that was prepared by your taxation professional. However, you will probably prefer to import your Quicken data.

When you do import your data, keep the following points in mind:

➤ TurboTax will find the file you've most recently used in Quicken—this is usually QDATA.QDB, but you can browse to a different file.

➤ Make sure you have completed recording all financial information for the year you are filing this return, but feel free to also treat TurboTax as a tax planner you can use any time during the year.

➤ You do not need Quicken running to perform the import. TurboTax launches Quicken if necessary while it copies the tax-related data. When it's finished, it closes Quicken down.

➤ If your Quicken data is password-protected, you must provide that password before the data can be imported.

➤ TurboTax works best importing data contained in Quicken categories marked as Tax Form Line Items. However, you can reassign any tax-related Quicken category from within TurboTax. You do this through TurboTax's TaxLink feature. This changes Quicken's category records so future transactions assigned to the same category automatically appear in the correct Tax Form Line Items in TurboTax the next time you import your data.

➤ TurboTax automatically looks for tax data pertaining to its version year. That means that TurboTax 99 will only look for and read data earmarked for the 1999 tax year. You cannot use TurboTax 99 for any other tax year unless you import data saved in the TXF format. To create a TXF file from Quicken, open the **Reports** menu, select **Taxes**, and then **Tax Schedule Report**. After the report appears, click **Export**. Assign a name to the file and click **OK**.

TurboTax is a very capable product, but you should always seek the advice of a tax professional. When you finish, you can print and mail your returns or file them electronically. The latter will attract a small additional fee but has the advantage that if a refund is due, you receive it far quicker than you would if you had sent in a printed return.

The Least You Need to Know

➤ The IRS knows more about your financial affairs that probably anyone else—and that can often include yourself. Quicken's tax tools don't help you to cheat on your tax, but they certainly help you to file the most advantageous return.

➤ If you are in the position that you have to pay estimated tax throughout the year, consider the Tax Planner an essential part of your tax-year preparation. It will help you pay enough to avoid penalties, and also help you to avoid overpaying.

➤ Set up different scenarios in the Tax Planner to work through different tax strategies. You can even use this to estimate the tax you and your spouse would pay filing separately as compared to the tax you pay filing jointly.

➤ TurboTax and Web TurboTax are a perfect match for your Quicken data. TurboTax in particular takes the Tax Planner several steps forward. There's an excellent chance you'll save its purchase price and a whole lot more in extra deductions and tax minimization.

Part 3
Online in No Time

Unlike the real world, the virtual world knows no bounds. Indeed, cyberspace already contains most of the world's financial knowledge, but it's now even showing an expanded girth.

There is such a wealth of information and assistance out there that you should consider a modem and an Internet account one of the most important additions you can make to your computer.

When combined with Quicken, you'll have a superbly capable tool that, with apologies to Buzz, can take your finances to infinity and beyond.

Chapter 12

Useful Connections

In This Chapter

➤ The online experience

➤ Connecting Quicken to the Internet

➤ Enabling your accounts for online transactions

Oh, What a Wonderful Web!

In just a few years, the Internet has moved from suspected evanescence to confirmed omnipresence. It has become as much a part of the way we use our computers as menus and mice, screens and sound.

Quicken 2000 includes many robust Internet features that enable you to receive stock updates, pay bills, manage your bank accounts online, and a whole lot more.

In fact, Quicken's online capabilities contribute an enormous amount to the software's total functionality.

With just a couple of copper wires and a modem, you can:

➤ Manage your banking and receive and pay bills

➤ Order Quicken-compatible stationery

➤ Perform great financial research in almost no time at all

➤ Update your security prices

➤ Download the latest financial headlines

➤ Quickly grab any improvements and bug fixes made to update your existing Quicken software

➤ Access Intuit's vast Quicken.com range of online resources (see the following figure)

➤ Record transactions on the World Wide Web and download them into Quicken

➤ Set Alerts that appear when you log into Quicken's site on the Web from any other computer, even if it's not the computer that holds your data

Quicken.com is the portal to an astonishing range of financial services and information.

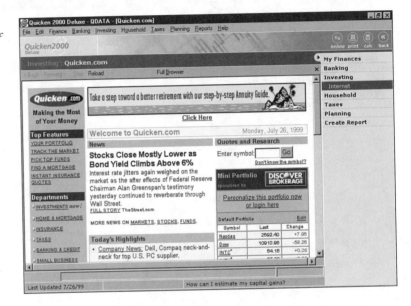

Quicken's online services crop up throughout Quicken, but nearly all appear under the Banking menu. If you open it now, you'll see the following menu entries scattered amongst the menus other offerings:

➤ **Online Banking**   This is the Online Financial Services Center from previous versions of Quicken. You can use this section of the software to manage online transactions, write to and receive email messages from your financial institutions, and download statements for your online accounts.

➤ **Online Bill Presentment**   Online billing enables you to receive your bills electronically rather than by mail. This is electronic commerce in all its glory with zero paperwork and zero hassle.

➤ **Checkfree**   An older bill-paying standard which, although superseded, continues to operate. Checkfree works with any U.S. checking account and enables you only to pay your bills online. To access other financial services, use the list of Financial Institutions to select a provider compatible with Open Financial Exchange. The Checkfree menu enables you to set up your software to use Checkfree. After you have set up Checkfree, several extra options appear under this menu.

Open Financial Exchange?

Known as OFX, this is the standard that has replaced Checkfree. Organized as a joint venture between Checkfree, Intuit, and Microsoft, it now has a huge number of participating institutions able to offer online payments, statement downloads, and a variety of other services such as online bill presentment.

➤ **Online Banking Setup**   This menu entry helps you enable your online accounts by accessing configuration data from participating financial institutions.

➤ **Online Payees List**   View a list of all the creditors you have set up for electronic bill payment.

Checkfree

The online facilities and procedures described in this part of the book are, for the most part, not applicable to Checkfree accounts, with the exception of online bill payments. If you do use Checkfree, you might like to consider moving to a financial institution that supports Open Financial Exchange—the replacement for Checkfree that is much more widely supported by the financial services industry.

The previous list doesn't include all of the aspects of Quicken's online prowess, but it's a start. These and many more online features are discussed in the chapters to come.

Before You Begin

Quicken transmits all its financial data over the Internet. So long as you are also connected to the Internet (or connected with one of the special deals included with your Quicken package), you've got everything you need to start setting up your accounts for online access.

Of course, financial data and the Internet is not the sort of combination that bodes a good night's sleep. Indeed, it's more likely to lead to midnight visions of folks you've never heard of taking a holiday in Bermuda courtesy of your American Express.

The good news is that every scrap of financial information Quicken transmits across the Internet is totally secure. Oh, sure, 50 hackers with the power of a supercomputer might be able to break the encryption if they go for it night and day for four months—and that assumes they even notice your little nugget of stealth-cloaked data slipping by amongst the flotsam and jetsam that already clog the Internet's grid-locked arteries—but neither of those events is particularly likely.

The encryption technology of today is such that it costs more in time and resources to crack the code than any benefit derived from cracking that code might be worth.

So what about someone who tries to crack into your online accounts?

Well, just as is the case with your ATM card, your accounts are protected by PINs, or Personal Identification Numbers.

If you keep your PINs secret, no one else should be able to access your accounts.

Indeed, unless you use the PIN Vault (which in turn has its own PIN to protect the other PINs—it's almost a PIN cushion) Quicken doesn't even store your PINs on your computer. This means that should someone break into your computer onsite or remove it from your premises altogether, he or she still won't be able to access your accounts.

And don't forget that you can also assign a password to your Quicken files. This prevents anyone but you from accessing your accounts and online services. (This is far more secure than the Windows password, which only controls personalized settings and has nothing to do with security.)

How Do I Use the PIN Vault, and Is It Secure?

When you setup your PIN Vault, assign the existing PINs to each of your accounts and then create an overall PIN. Make it secure and fairly random, or use something you already know, such as the PIN to your ATM card. Quicken stores an encrypted version of your PINs. Whenever you perform an update for all your online accounts at once, just supply the overall PIN when it's requested. Quicken then automatically sends the PINs you've recorded in the PIN Vault to each account as they are requested. Yes, it's secure, and it also can save a heck of a lot of time.

You'll find a command to set up your PIN Vault under the File menu, but you can only do this if you have two or more online accounts.

Connecting Quicken to the Internet

So, are you ready to continue? Getting Quicken connected to the Internet is quite simple.

To begin, open the **Edit** menu and select **Internet Connection Setup**.

Use this dialog box to specify the method you want to use to connect to the Internet.

For instance, select **I have an existing dial-up Internet connection** if you use Windows' Dial-Up Networking or AOL.

Select **I have a direct Internet connection** if you connect via a LAN, cable modem, or some other system that isn't based on a modem. (ADSL and satellite spring to mind, but pigeon probably doesn't qualify.)

If you don't have an existing connection, now's your chance to take the giant leap into cyberspace: Select **Tell me how to sign up for an Internet connection** instead.

After you've made your choice, click **Next>>** and follow the instructions onscreen.

The final screen summarizes your choices so far. Click **Finish** to complete the setup. Quicken runs through a few configuration issues and stores your settings.

Using the Internet

Quicken's Internet facilities are divided into two major services: financial transactions and information. The financial side requires at least one account with a participating financial institution. (You learn about obtaining and configuring these accounts later in this chapter.) You can use the financial side to perform online banking, payments, and billing.

Quicken's other Internet capabilities are scattered innocuously around its major menus and in the major centers for Banking, Household, Investing, and Taxes.

Here you find a host of links for such items as Web TurboTax, Credit Research, and Professional Planning Resources. You should also explore the Quicken.com online resources. Most of these are collected under the **Finance** menu in the submenu called **Quicken on the Web**. You can use this menu as a launch point to several financial services sites operated by Intuit. As long as you have a working Internet connection, you can use these essentially free, very useful, and extremely informative facilities. They are accessed through the Web browser you chose when setting up your Internet connection. However, instead of opening in a separate browser window, Quicken makes the browser a subset of its own window, as shown in the following figure.

Click to move back or forward one page.

Refresh this page.

Display page in actual browser.

Print this page.

Use Quicken on the Web windows as you would any page in your usual browser.

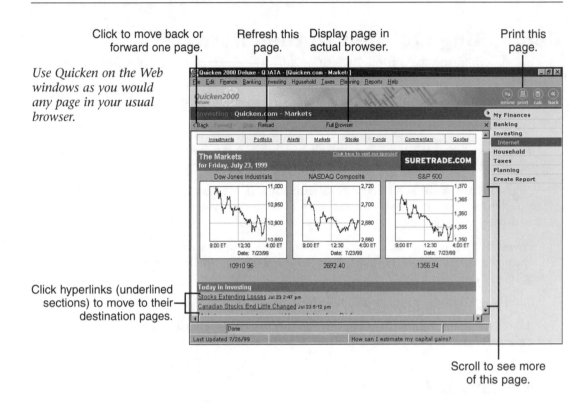

Click hyperlinks (underlined sections) to move to their destination pages.

Scroll to see more of this page.

Even though it appears to be part of Quicken, the browser works just as it would outside of Quicken. For example, the **< Back** and **Forward >** buttons move through pages you have already downloaded, and **Stop** prematurely halts downloading the current page. **Reload** refreshes the display and **Full Browser** opens the page in a standard browser window. (Click **Return to Quicken** when you're finished with the Full Browser mode.) **Print** obviously prints out a copy of the current page.

If you right-click in the browser window, you see exactly the same menu as you would right-clicking with your standard browser open. This menu doesn't actually have anything to do with Quicken and is entirely outside its control.

When you're finished browsing, click the **Close** button. If you are using a dial-up connection, you might need to manually shut down your Internet connection using the Windows Dial-Up Networking tool. (See your Windows documentation for details.) However, depending on your settings, you might also find that Windows prompts you to do just that.

The browser window is only a small part of Quicken's online capabilities. All of your electronic transactions take place through the Online Center.

Getting Started with Online Accounts

Online accounts provide access to Quicken's online banking, online payments, online investing, and online billing facilities. Together, these provide a very impressive set of features.

For instance, using online banking you can

➤ Download up-to-the-minute statements and account balances

➤ Easily reconcile your accounts

➤ Transfer money between accounts

➤ Communicate with your financial institution using email—even if you don't have an Internet email address

➤ Save time by copying your account or credit card transactions from the electronic statement straight into Quicken

By using online payments, you're able to

➤ Electronically pay your bills to anyone within the U.S., regardless of whether they have a computer

➤ Do away with handwritten checks, envelopes, and stamps

➤ Schedule your bill payments in advance so that the bills will be paid on time, every time, even if you've taken a six-month holiday

➤ Stop payments online

How Much Does It Cost to Write Electronic Transactions?

You should speak to your financial institution. Generally, however, an online payment usually costs in the order of 50 cents and is usually charged in blocks of 10. Even though this isn't cheaper than a stamped envelope, the prices might fall as these services become more popular.

With online investing you can

➤ Record the latest price movements, providing you with an up-to-date value of your investment holdings

➤ Download the latest cleared transactions, balances, and positions

➤ Automatically record commissions and other costs associated with your investment account

➤ Update the cash balance in your investment account

➤ Automatically register stock splits and other transactions that adjust the level of your holdings

Finally, with online billing, you can receive your bills electronically; but this is an option only if your biller has chosen to participate. When you pay your bills online, the transaction is automatically entered into your register.

To use any of these facilities, you must first set up your Online Center. This is easy and will take you only a few minutes. To start, open the **Banking** menu and select **Online Banking Setup**.

Use the first step in the Online Account Setup dialog box to select an existing account to which you want to add online capabilities, or to create a new account. If you do change an existing account, you are still able to write checks, perform a paper-based reconciliation, and carry out all the other activities you're already used to doing. The only difference is that you also have the option of completing many of these through the online center.

All of the information you record from now on is also available simply by selecting and editing the account through the Account List. If you create a new account, you must provide all the usual information for creating an account (see Chapter 5, "Accounting for Accounts") and then provide the online information.

Can I Shift My Old Checkfree Account to OFX?

There's no simple way to do the transfer, mainly because each standard works on very different principles. You remember when you set up your Checkfree account that you had to, in effect, give permission to Checkfree Corporation to write checks against your account on your behalf? With OFX, you are the one creating the transactions, in effect accessing your account directly. However, if the financial institution against which you were writing Checkfree transactions supports OFX, you should be able to cancel Checkfree and switch to OFX simply by applying for online access through that institution.

Click **Next** to work your way through each step. At one point Quicken needs to go online to download information about your financial institution including the types of services supported by your account. Make sure you only select those services for which you have applied.

When it is requested, provide the routing and account numbers and your Customer ID. All of this information is included on the information sheet provided by your financial institution for each of your online accounts.

When you've finished, click **OK** to conclude the setup.

Canceling Online Accounts

If you ever need to cancel an account's online capabilities, open the **Finance** menu and select **Account List** (**Ctrl+A**). Select the online account and click **Edit**. Deselect those online options you wish to cancel and click **OK** to save the changes.

And that's it! Chapter 13, "Online Banking and Bill Paying," tells you how you can use your accounts to make electronic payments, download bills and statements, and perform an online reconciliation.

Banking online is hip, it's connected, and it saves you time. What more endorsement should one need?

The Least You Need to Know

➤ It's difficult these days to find a computer program that doesn't boast some amazing capability brought about solely because of the Internet. Quicken is no exception. To connect Quicken to the Net, you need nothing more than a modem, a phone jack, and an account with an Internet provider. (Things you probably already have.) After you've done that, its capabilities double!

➤ One of the brightest aspects of the online revolution is the ability to do all your banking from your own computer. If you have an account with a participating financial institution, there should be no barriers left to inhibit you from writing checks, transferring funds, and even receiving bills online, all via your computer.

Online Banking and Bill Paying

Using the Online Banking Center

The Online Banking Center acts as a clearing-house for all your electronic transactions. You can use it to create and check on those you are waiting to send, as well as to write email to your financial institution, download your most recent transactions, and more.

You can start to use the Center as soon as you have complete setting up a single online account. To access it, open the **Banking** menu and select **Online Banking**. A screen similar to that shown in the following figure appears. (If you see some other dialog boxes instead, just ignore them by clicking **Cancel** to remove each from your screen.)

The Online Banking Center enables you to work with all your online accounts in one convenient window.

Select your financial institution.

Click the tabs to move between different online activities.

Choose an account held with the selected institution.

View the transactions current for that account.

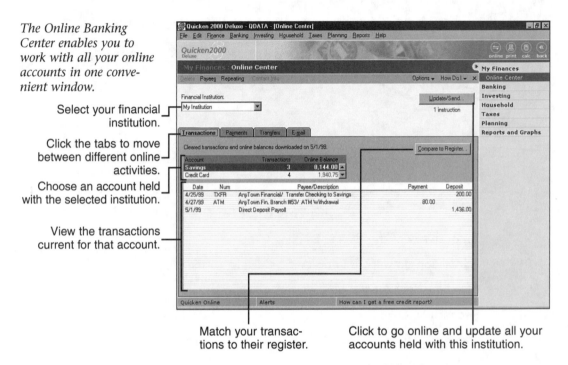

Match your transactions to their register.

Click to go online and update all your accounts held with this institution.

The tabs in the Online Banking Center change according to the type of services that are provided by your financial institutions. You might see any or all of the following:

➤ **Transactions**   This tab shows all the downloaded transactions for each account.

➤ **Transfers**   This tab is used to record transfers between accounts held at the same financial institution. Unfortunately, you can't make transfers between accounts held at different institutions.

➤ **Payments**   Use this tab to record online payments. These can be recurring and scheduled in advance.

➤ **Balances**   This tab shows the balance of cash held in your online investment accounts.

➤ **Holdings**   This tab is linked to the Balances tab. It shows the value of stocks held in each investment account.

➤ **Email**   Use this tab to create and send or receive and read email exchanged between you and your financial institution.

The format of the information presented in each tab also changes from one to the next, but you have ample opportunity to explore them in this chapter.

Doing the Transaction Download

One of your first tasks after enabling an online account is to download that account's transaction data. Performing this action provides you with a list of the transactions your financial institution has applied to your account; just as if you downloaded an online statement.

Quicken performs several tasks when you download or update your financial data:

➤ First, it connects to the Internet through the default settings you specified in Chapter 12, "Useful Connections."

➤ The Online Center then downloads the most recent transaction data for all your financial institutions or, if you prefer, for only the one you selected to update.

➤ The minimum payment and date due information stored with credit card statements is also copied to the financial calendar. This saves you the embarrassment of missing your credit card payment when it falls due.

➤ Any account transfers or other instructions are communicated back to the institution.

➤ Outgoing email is sent and incoming email is received.

Your financial institution supplies up to 90 days of account information the first time you connect to its online service. This torrent of transactions takes some working through, especially if you have already been using Quicken. Why? Because you need to match the transactions you download to those you've already recorded.

Are you ready? Great. Let's grab that first bunch of data. Keep in mind that this is the account data held by your institution. For checking accounts it shows cleared checks but it doesn't show checks which are yet to be presented. This data may also show banking fees, taxes deducted, and other transactions you might not know about but which the institutions take great delight in applying.

You can update your online accounts in two ways. If you just want to update a single financial institution (which updates all the accounts held by you in that institution), you can do so from the Online Banking Center by selecting that institution from the **Financial Institution** drop-down list and clicking **Update/Send**.

This is how easy it is. Click **Update/Send** right now. A dialog box offers to perform one or more tasks, such as downloading your latest cleared transactions and account balances, and updating your online payments data.

Click in the left column of this dialog box to deselect all those except "Download latest cleared transactions and account balances" and click **Send** to continue. The first time you go online, you need to change the PIN from the one assigned by your bank to one you choose yourself. Make the changes to your PIN numbers in the Change Assigned PIN dialog box, if shown, and click **OK**. After that, it should take just a few moments for Quicken to start your Internet connection and download your transaction data.

If you prefer to update all of your financial institution accounts at once and add to that any investment-related data such as security prices and news, you should perform a One Step Update instead. In the future you'll find it easier to perform a One Step Update than updating individual institutions one at a time. You can read how later in this chapter, under the heading "Steps to a One Step Update".

For now, though, you should reconcile the online transaction data you just downloaded. Here's how.

Comparing Downloaded Transactions

After you have downloaded the latest transactions, you need to update your register by comparing the transactions downloaded to those you have already recorded, adding and editing as required. This isn't the same as reconciling your account. In fact, that's a whole different process that you need to undertake later.

The good news is that Quicken is very good at automatically matching downloaded transactions to those you've already recorded in your register—with certain exceptions.

To start, make sure you have your Online Banking Center open. If not, click the **Banking** menu and select **Online Banking**. Then choose the Financial Institution you just updated from the **Financial Institution** drop-down list.

Click the **Transactions** tab and select the account (if you have more than one) from the **Account** list in the lower part of the Center's window. The Account List summarizes each of your accounts, showing you how many transactions have been downloaded along with the closing online balance.

With the account selected, click **Compare to Register**. (This button isn't active unless you see entries in that account's transactions list.) A window similar to that shown in the following figure appears.

This split window shows your current register transactions in the upper section and your downloaded transactions underneath. The buttons to the right of the downloaded transactions are used to compare your downloaded transactions to those in the register.

Now here's where Quicken's auto-matching shortcuts come into play.

If Quicken believes it has matched a downloaded transaction with one already recorded in your register, you see the word Match in the Status column to the left of that downloaded transaction.

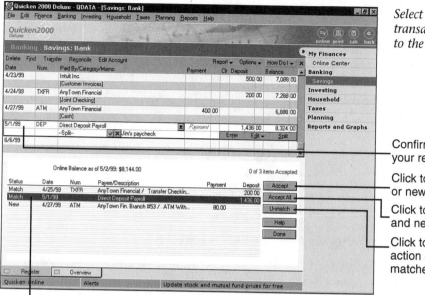

Select each downloaded transaction to compare it to the register.

Confirm that it matches your register's transaction.

Click to accept a matched or new transaction.

Click to accept all matched and new transactions.

Click to delete a new transaction or unmatch a matched transaction.

Select a downloaded transaction.

How does it do it? It starts by attempting to match your transactions by the order in which they occurred, looking back to transactions in your register that took place 90 days ago. That is, if two transactions fall near the same date and are for the same amount, they're likely candidates. It then searches throughout your register for any transactions that have the same value. If the amounts don't match, it tries to match on check numbers, comparing the digits in the downloaded transaction to the same number of digits falling at the end of any check numbers recorded in your register. Therefore, if the downloaded transaction's check number is 101, this could be matched in your register against check numbers 53101, 1102101, or just 101.

Edit the details on any matched transaction by clicking the downloaded transaction. Quicken takes you to the matched transaction in the register.

Matching Transactions Without Check Numbers

If a downloaded transaction lacks a check number, Quicken compares the amount to any non-numeric entry in the Num/Ref field recorded over the previous 30 days. For example, a downloaded transaction marked as TXFR for $60 could be matched to a transaction for $60 marked in the Num field as ATM.

Downloaded transactions that couldn't be matched are marked with the word New in the Status column. Click bona fide new transactions to copy them to your register and adjust their details. Typically, you need to record a payee and add a category or memo. Just record these in the register as you would when recording or editing any other transaction. You can also remove downloaded transactions from the list by clicking the **Delete** button to the right of the downloaded transaction, whether they have been matched or not. You would only do this if you knew those transactions were incorrectly downloaded, at which point you should also get in contact with your financial institution to have the error corrected.

Where's the Unmatch Button?

When you select a downloaded transaction whose status is set to New, you see a Delete button in the middle of the group of five buttons down the right side of the transaction list. When you select a downloaded transaction whose status is recognized as a Match, the **Delete** button is replaced by an **Unmatch** button.

If a transaction has been matched incorrectly, select it in the list of downloaded transactions and click **Unmatch**. Quicken tries to match the downloaded transaction with a more recent entry. If it doesn't succeed, it marks that transaction as New, in which case you can record it as described in the box above, "Where's the Unmatch Button?".

What About Online Credit Card Accounts?

Online Credit Card accounts present a slightly special issue. When you download the transactions for credit card accounts, you see the name of the payee as well as a description, which Quicken automatically copies from the last transaction flagged to that payee. This saves you from typing when you copy those transactions to your register, but other than that, updating online credit card accounts is identical to doing the same to any other bank accounts. By the way, you might not be able to download your credit card statement until one month has passed since your last paper-based statement was mailed.

If you know that the transaction should match an existing register transaction but doesn't, select the register transaction and click **Edit** so that its details match the downloaded transaction. (This assumes your original register entry is incorrect. If the downloaded transaction is incorrect, you should contact your financial institution as soon as possible.) Adjust the check number, date, and amount until the register and downloaded transactions correspond. The new transaction is now marked as a match against your existing transaction.

What's Happened to IntelliCharge?

IntelliCharge is the name of Quicken's now superseded online credit card system. If you've been using a previous version of Quicken with an IntelliCharge account, that account is automatically upgraded to an Online Credit Card.

To approve a transaction's match, click **Accept**. Quicken marks the register transaction as cleared, placing a "c" in the Clr column. A cleared transaction is a transaction that has been presented and passed through the bank. It is not the same as a reconciled transaction. You learn how to reconcile your online accounts next.

If all of the transactions marked as a Match are correct and you are also satisfied with those marked as New, click **Accept All** to copy all your new transactions to your register and to mark all your matched and new transactions as cleared. You will return to the Compare to Register window, but with Accepted showing in the Status column of your downloaded transactions.

Click **Done** to leave the Compare to Register window.

If not all of your downloaded transactions have been accepted, Quicken will display a dialog box warning that you haven't finished matching those transactions. Click **Finish Later** to return to the Online Center.

Duplicate Check Number Found

If you see a dialog box with this title after clicking **Accept All**, you are trying to import a new transaction with a check number identical to a previous transaction. Click **Accept** to add this new transaction to your register, duplicate check number and all, or click **Skip** if the transactions are one and the same. Skipping rejects the new transaction, retaining the one already recorded.

Now that Quicken has all of the transactions your bank believes it should have, you're ready to reconcile that account. Fortunately, although the steps are almost identical to a paper-based reconciliation, your list of transactions should be perfectly up-to-date, making online reconciling an almost automatic process. You can read about online reconciling later in this chapter.

Performing an Online Account Reconciliation

Each time Quicken downloads the most recent transactions, it also takes note of the ending account balance. The next time you reconcile that account, Quicken uses the ending balance data as the basis for that reconciliation.

Reconciling an online account is easier than reconciling a paper-based account simply because you don't need to enter those odd account transactions made by your bank for fees, taxes, and so on.

To reconcile your online account, update your account as previously described and match and accept the transactions. You must perform this step for the reconciliation to be up-to-date with the latest data. However, if you have already performed an online update once today, don't worry about doing so again.

To begin, open the **Banking** menu and select **Reconcile**. Choose your account from the drop-down list and click **OK**.

If you have never downloaded data for this account or you haven't downloaded data in the last two days, you are asked to do so now. If you have, you move straight to the Reconcile Online Account dialog box.

Select **Online Balance** and click **OK**.

Now you should see the Reconciliation window. This window is identical to that used to reconcile paper-based accounts. However, all of the transactions already accepted into your register through the Online Center are already marked with a "c" for Cleared. (That is, cleared through the bank.) Look at the **Difference** in the lower-right corner of the Reconciliation window. This is based on your Quicken account's cleared balance. That's the balance of your account's cleared and reconciled transactions. The **Cleared Balance** should match your **Online Balance**, giving a **Difference** of zero.

If the Difference does equal zero, click **Finished** to complete the reconciliation. Wasn't that just too easy?

Otherwise, check the list for duplicated transactions or transactions mistakenly marked as cleared or reconciled. To edit any transaction, select it and click **Edit** in the upper-left corner of the Reconciliation pane. You can also add **New** transactions or **Delete** existing transactions, or read more about reconciling in Chapter 5, "Accounting for Accounts." When you have the difference down to zero, click **Finished** to move on.

And that's it! Now that you know how to download the latest transactions and perform a reconciliation, you're ready to tackle the more interesting side of online banking: electronic transactions. This is the part that saves you from making those pesky trips to the bank.

Paying Off Your Credit Card Balance

If your credit card account and your online checking accounts are held with the same financial institution, you could theoretically transfer the funds from one to the other, thus paying off your credit card. However, online credit card accounts also include a payments system that is designed to work with their special requirements.

To pay your credit card balance, make sure you have downloaded the latest credit card transactions. This ensures your register is up-to-date but, more importantly, provides Quicken with the most recent closing balances for your credit card account and the account from which you will be making the payment.

From the Online Center, select your credit card's financial institution and click the **Transactions** tab. Then select your credit card account in the account list and click **Payment Information**. This button appears only when a credit card account is selected, but you won't be able to select it until you have downloaded your first monthly statement.

In the Credit Card Payment Information dialog box, click **Make Payment**. From the Make Credit Card Payment window use the **Amount to Pay** drop-down list to choose from:

➤ **Minimum Amount** Select this if you want to pay the minimum required, as indicated on your most recent downloaded statement.

173

➤ **Full Amount**　Select this if you want to pay the full amount owed on the credit card account.

➤ **Other**　Select this to specify any other amount to pay.

Open the **Payment Will Be** drop-down list and select the payment method:

➤ **Printed Check**　Select this for Quicken to print the check for you. If you are using windowed envelopes, make sure you enter the payee's address.

➤ **Handwritten Check**　Select this to record the payment in your Quicken register as a handwritten check.

➤ **Online Payment**　Choose this option if you will be making the payment from an account that is set up for online payments.

Finally, use the **Pay From** drop-down list to select the account from which you want to make this payment.

Transferring Funds Between Accounts

It isn't yet possible to transfer funds between accounts held with two different financial institutions—unless you write a check or make an online payment—however, you can easily do so between two accounts held with the same institution.

Why would you use this facility? It's handy for mortgage or loan repayments where you can set up a scheduled transaction. You might also use it to transfer regular amounts to an investment or retirement savings account.

Either is very easy to do. As long as you have two accounts with a single financial institution, here's how you can start transferring funds.

From the Online Banking Center choose your **Financial Institution** and click the **Transfers** tab. The window shown in the following figure appears.

Select your originating account using the **Transfer Money From** drop-down list. Then select the destination account using the **To** drop-down list.

Type in the **Amount** or click the **Calculator** icon to use Quicken's built-in calculator and click **Enter** to record the transfer. The transfer instruction is added to the Transfer tab along with a Status message showing that it has not yet been sent.

To send the transfer, immediately click **Update/Send**. (It won't happen until the close of the business day.) Another dialog box helps you to record the transfer in your account registers before it is sent. You can click **Yes** to do so now, or leave the recording until later by selecting **No**. In the latter case, you should see the transfer appear on the next statement you download. I find recording the transfer immediately more convenient because both sides of the transfer are automatically matched when the statements come through.

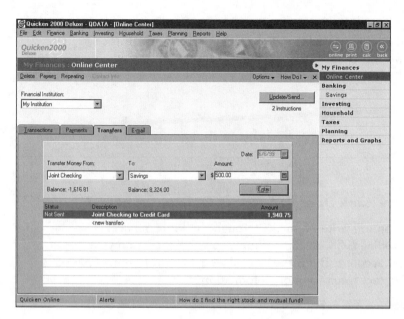

Online transfers are the easiest way to move money between your accounts.

Correcting a Failed Transfer

If the transfer doesn't take place due to insufficient funds, banking errors, or some other reason, you receive notification via email or the phone. So that your Quicken accounts continue to balance, you should delete the transfer from either register. Deleting one side of a transfer automatically deletes the other.

If you would rather not immediately record the transfer, continue with your other Quicken activities. The next time you update that financial institution, instructions to execute the transfer head down the wires.

Online Payments

Online payments are to checks what email is to mail: They're very "how the heck did I get along without them" convenient.

The online payments system beautifully dovetails with the rest of Quicken, meaning you only have to record those transactions in one place at one time. Furthermore, after you have sent the payment, you can keep track of its status as it proceeds through the financial channels. You can also create payments in advance so that while you are away, on vacation or whatever, bills continue to be paid according to your pre-arranged schedule.

What If My Bank Doesn't Support Online Payments?

All is not lost. You can still write payments through the Intuit Services Corporation by providing ISC with the authority to write checks on your behalf through your regular account. This is the CheckFree system. It is under Quicken's **Banking** menu. Contact Intuit for more information.

Creating an Online Payment

To make an online payment you need the following:

➤ An account set up for online payments

➤ The payee's name, address, and telephone number. You cannot proceed without all three!

Online payments are supported by Quicken's checking, savings, money market, and credit card accounts. You can also make online payments from a checking account that is linked to an investment account. These accounts must, of course, be set up for online payments as was described in Chapter 12, "Useful Connections."

Any payment you make from any of these accounts—and from just about anywhere within Quicken—can be flagged as an online payment. For example, the Write Checks window for online accounts includes an Online Payment option. In other places, for example, when creating a scheduled transaction, you should be able to select **Online Pmt** from the **Type of Transaction** pull-down list.

However, the central place to make online payments is the Online Banking Center. It makes a good starting point, and after you can create online payments through here, you should have no problems creating them elsewhere.

To start, open the **Banking** menu and select **Online Banking**.

Choose the **Financial Institution** where your online payments account is kept and click the **Payments** tab. The following figure shows the Payments tabs with an online payment already complete.

Select the account from which to draw the funds.

If displayed, this date tells you when the payment should be processed by your financial institution.

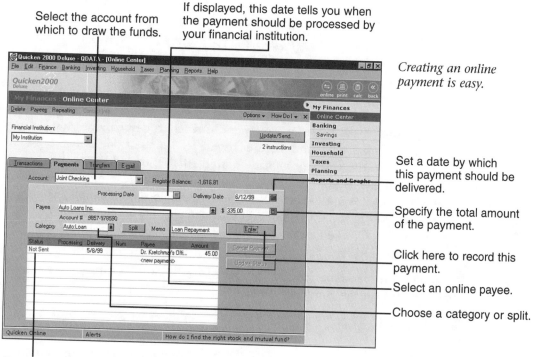

Creating an online payment is easy.

Set a date by which this payment should be delivered.

Specify the total amount of the payment.

Click here to record this payment.

Select an online payee.

Choose a category or split.

Previous payments are listed here.

Fill out the online payment as you would any check, with a couple of minor differences. Let's go through them field by field:

➤ Use the **Account** field to select the account you want to use to make this payment. The current balance is displayed to its right.

➤ If you can change the **Processing Date**, set it to the date the payment is to be processed by your financial institution. Even if you transmit it today, it won't be acted upon until the processing date.

➤ By default, the payment's **Delivery Date** field is set so that it is delivered as soon as possible; that is ASAP. However, there is a certain lead time associated with each payee, so Quicken sets the delivery date to the date you specify here, minus each payee's lead time. You can set this field to the date a bill falls due so that it is automatically paid neither too soon nor too late.

➤ Unlike handwritten or printed checks, each of your online payees must be added to a special Online Payees database. Simply type in the payee's full name in the Payee field and press **Tab**. Quicken responds with the Set Up Online Payee dialog box. For further information, see the section "Creating Online Payees," later in this chapter.

Lead Time

The lead time is the time it takes for a payment to reach its destination. Most payees that support electronic funds transfer have a lead time of one or two business days. However, if the payment must be posted—that is, they don't accept direct electronic payments from your financial institution—that lead time grows to four business days. Quicken looks after the lead time for you. For example, when you create a new payee, the lead time is set to a default of four business days. When you go online, Quicken establishes if the payee supports electronic payments and cuts the lead time accordingly.

You can also set the lead time for each of your payees from the **Online Payee List**, available through the **Banking** menu.

The remaining fields are the same as any payment transaction, save that you should treat the **Memo** field with a little caution, for the contents of that field might be transmitted to your financial institution and your payee.

Click **Enter** to record the payment and add it to the payments list.

You can send payments immediately using **Update/Send** or send them later with **One Step Update**. Either way, you're also able to choose whether or not you want to record the transaction immediately or leave it until you can match it to a statement.

Inquiring About a Payment

Until you have seen several electronic payments successfully processed, you might begin to wonder if everything's happening as it should. To set your mind at ease, you can inquire on the status of a payment. There is a built-in system for inquiring about the status of electronic payments you have already sent, although the response you get back does depend on your financial institution.

To send an inquiry, select the **Payments** tab of the Online Banking Center, choose the transaction about which you want to inquire from the transaction list, and click **Update Status**. This opens the **Payment Inquiry** dialog box.

Oops! Canceling an Online Payment

You've recorded an online payment and now you don't want to send it. What to do?

Canceling the payment is as easy as selecting it from the list contained within the Payments tab of the Online Center and clicking **Delete**. (It's in the upper-left corner of the window.)

Canceling a payment you have already sent is just as easy.

Simply select it and click **Cancel Payment**. After you confirm the cancellation, Quicken places a *Stop Sign* symbol next to the original payment. Click **Update/Send** to go online and forward the cancellation before your payment instruction is processed.

To send a request for an update on its status, leave **Update Status** selected and click **OK**. If you would like to create a longer text message, select **E-mail Message**, click **OK**, and complete the email message.

The next time you update that account, you also send the payment inquiry. How long the reply takes depends on your financial institution, but if they have an automatic system in place, it should take just a couple of minutes.

Creating a Repeating Online Payment

Repeating online payments are perfect for bills you receive regularly or payments you regularly make. For instance, cable connection fees, online service subscriptions, regular deposits in an investment account, loan repayments, garden maintenance, and more.

These payments might seem identical to repeating scheduled payments, but there's one important difference.

When you create the instruction for a repeating online payment, it is sent and stored at Intuit Services Corporation. Thirty days before each scheduled payment is due, ISC sends you a special note letting you know that it has created and postdated that payment. The payment is automatically recorded in your register.

In this way, whether you go online regularly or not, your payments are still made. (In fact, you should be careful that if you cancel your service, you should also cancel the repeating payments. To cancel individual online payments you must delete them from your repeating payments list. This generates another instruction that cancels the payments stored at ISC.)

Now, there's no need to dwell on the specifics of repeating online payments; they're very similar to the scheduled payments detailed in Chapter 6, "Memorized Transactions Are Made of This."

However, there are some important differences.

To create a repeating payment, open the **Banking** menu and select **Scheduled Transaction List (Ctrl+J)**.

Select the **Repeating Online** tab and then click **New**.

A dialog box similar to the one shown in the following figure appears.

Recording an online payment is a simple matter.

Fill out the top of the dialog box using these fields:

➤ **First Payment** This is the date that you want the first payment made. The actual payment will be generated according to the payee's lead time but post-dated so that it can't be banked until the first payment is due. If a monthly or other regular payment is overdue, use the date it was due. This ensures future payments are paid on time.

➤ **Account** Use the drop-down arrow to select the account from which the funds are to be paid.

➤ **Payee** Select from your list of online payees. To create a new online payee, type in the name and press **Tab**. Fill in the Set Up Online Payee dialog box as described below under the heading "Creating Online Payees."

➤ **Memo** Depending on your financial institution, the contents of this memo might or might not be visible to the institution or payee. Don't use it for sensitive information.

➤ **Category** Type in a category or account transfer, or select the category from the drop-down list. Otherwise, click **Splits** to divide the payment as required.

➤ **Amount** Record the total amount for a single payment.

The Scheduling part of the dialog box provides the following fields:

➤ **Frequency** Select how often you want this payment to occur. For example, you would probably pay a cable subscription once a month.

➤ **Duration** Setting this field to **Unlimited** keeps the payment running indefinitely. However, you can also limit the payments to a certain number, such as 12 monthly payments. Quicken calculates and displays the due date of the final payment.

Temporarily Disabling Online Transactions

To disable a repeating online transaction that you believe you might need in the future, just edit it so that the Duration is set to stop after 0 payments. When you need to get it going again, either enter a figure greater than zero or change it to Unlimited.

Finally, specify how much forewarning you want using **Prompt To Connect**. Just set the number of days' notice you need. When you're finished, click **Authorize** to save the transaction.

After you have entered your repeating online payments, return to the Online Center and click **Update/Send** or do a **One Step Update**. You might see a dialog box that asks whether Quicken should enter the payment (into the register) before going online. Click **Yes** to record those transactions before the instruction is sent to your financial institution. Click **No** to record those transactions later.

Emailing Your Financial Institution

Email is popular because it is essentially free, blazingly fast, and wonderfully flexible.

Quicken supports email, but not to the same extent as you are probably used to with your usual email account. However, you can use it to communicate with your financial institution, and you don't even need to remember a complex email address.

To begin, open the **Online Banking Center**, select your **Financial Institution**, and click the **E-mail** tab.

The lower part of the window lists all of your email messages waiting to be sent, already sent, or already received.

To write an email message just click **Create**. Use the next dialog box to select the type of email you want to create. Is it about online banking or online payments? If it is about the latter, click **E-mail about an online payment** and select the appropriate account. (You cannot select this unless you have already sent an online payment.) This creates a list of all payments made using that account. Select the payment from the list. If you haven't made any payments, you can only create an email about online banking. Click **OK** to continue.

Create your message in the Message To dialog box. The **To** address is filled out for you by Quicken, although you can also change it if required. This isn't an address in the sense of a traditional email address, so don't worry about "@" symbols or domain names. However, you should enter your name in the **From** field and type in a **Subject**. Select the account this message is about and create the message in the message pane.

After you're finished with the message, click **OK**. Quicken sends the message the next time you update your accounts with that financial institution.

To read a received email message or any message you have previously created, select it from the list and click **Read**. You can **Print** a copy of the message or click **Close** to return to the Online Center. To print the entire list of email messages, return to the list and click **Print** any time the **E-mail** tab is open. Finally, to delete any message, select it within the list and click **Delete**.

Creating Online Payees

Online payees are a little different to those stored in Quicken's address book, but only a little. Every payee who receives an electronic payment must first be set up as an online payee. You can create online payees from several areas within Quicken. For instance, this can be achieved by typing a new payee in the payee drop-down list in the online payments window. You can also view a list of all your online payees by clicking the **Payees** button at the top of the Online Center window or by opening the **Banking** menu and selecting **Online Payees List**. From this list, click **New** to add a new online payee.

However you go about it, you end up at the Set Up Online Payee window shown in the following figure.

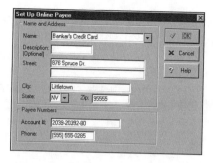

All of the fields (except Description) in the Set Up Online Payee dialog box must be filled for an online payee to work.

Most of the fields in this list are self-explanatory. Besides Description, which is optional, make sure you fill in them all.

In the **Account #** field, type the number the payee uses to identify your account. That is, the account number or reference number that the payee has used to identify *your* previous payments. This might be a telephone number, customer number, loan number, or similar. If you are sure you don't have an account number, record your surname instead. However, contact your payee a few days after the payment is made to make sure it went through the system and was correctly credited to your account.

In the **Phone** field type the number you would usually use if you had a question about your billing. If there are any problems processing the online payment, Intuit Services Corporation will call that number to follow your payment through.

And that's it! When you've finished, click **OK** to save the new or edited Payee. Check the details in the Confirm Online Payee Information dialog box and click **Accept** to add the payee to your list of online payees. From now on, that online payee is available from the drop-down list in the Payments tab of the Online Center.

Steps to a One Step Update

You can perform a One Step Update from anywhere within Quicken; you do not need to be in the Online Center. The One Step Update is convenient because it can perform all your online tasks at once, even to the point of uploading your portfolio to the Web so that you can view it from remote locations, sending and receiving transactions for your online accounts, updating stocks and other security prices, and downloading transactions you have recorded elsewhere through Quicken's innovative Web Transaction feature.

That's a lot of work, but doing the update is easy.

To start, either click the **Online** button in the top-right corner of Quicken's window, or open the **Finance** menu and select **One Step Update**. If you have set up a PIN Vault, you see an additional dialog box for entering the vault's PIN.

Use the One Step Download Selection dialog box shown in the following figure to select those items you want to update. In general, it works best to leave everything selected. However, if you want to update just a single financial institution, remove the red check mark from beside every financial institution except for the one you want to update.

Click the items you want to update, and don't forget to provide the PINs.

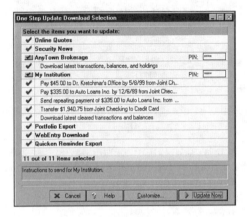

If you don't want to use the PIN Vault, also make sure you type the access PIN into the field provided to the right of each institution you plan to update.

What's My PIN?

Your PIN is included in the online account access information kit sent to you by your financial institution. Some people call it a PIN number, but given its acronym, that's like saying *Personal Identification Number number*, which makes you very uncool in certain banking circles. The easiest way to track your PINs is through Quicken's PIN Vault, described later in this chapter. After you record your PINs and are assigned a password, you can automatically plug all of your PINs into your account updates simply by providing that password. However, you can't use the PIN Vault until you have two or more online accounts.

Click **Update Now** to start. You could see several dialog boxes, depending on the specific items you choose to update:

184

➤ **Online Quotes**   If you choose to download online quotes and some of your securities are lacking ticker symbols, you see a warning dialog box. Simply click **Update Now** again to ignore it. (See Part 4, "Investing: Making Dollars with Sense," to learn more about investing and ticker symbols.) You can also place a check mark in the box **Don't show this warning anymore** to bypass it from now on.

➤ **Security News**   Download financial news relating to the securities in your investment portfolio. The securities must have ticker symbols or you'll see the same ticker warning as when downloading Online Quotes.

➤ **Financial Institution**   You'll also see an entry named for every financial institution in which you hold online accounts and any instructions due to be transmitted listed underneath. These entries update the Online Center. Enter your PIN in the field provided. (You can find the PIN in the information packet you received when applying for online access to those accounts.) The first time you access any of these accounts, Quicken forces you to change your PIN through an additional dialog box. Make sure you write down the new PIN and keep it somewhere safe. If you forget it, there's no easy way to generate another without your financial institution posting you replacement details.

➤ **Portfolio Export**   You have to log in with Quicken.com before you can export your portfolio or carry out the next two options shown below. Follow the dialog boxes to register or provide your login name and password.

➤ **Web Entry Download**   You can record transactions away from your computer by going to the www.quicken.com Web site and clicking the link **Quicken Web Entry**. Log in and record your transactions. When you return to your main Quicken computer, use this feature to download those transactions. Review and copy them to your register by opening the Banking Center and clicking the link **Accept Transactions**.

➤ **Quicken Reminder Export**   This option enables you to place your reminders on the Web. This means you can view your reminders from any computer with Internet access simply by logging into Quicken.com.

After you have worked your way through the various dialog boxes associated with your update, click the final **Update Now**. If you are not online, Quicken takes you there, displaying a progress dialog box. (If you haven't yet registered with Quicken.com, you aren't able to export your current investment portfolio to the Web or use Web-based transactions. An extra dialog box that you can use to register appears. Follow the onscreen directions. When you've finished, Quicken returns you to the One Step Update.) Although most updates usually take less than half a minute, you can ignore the process if you like and keep working in Quicken. To do so, simply click the **Minimize** button shown in the lower-left corner of the Download Status dialog box.

Canceling a Download

Click **Cancel** in the Download Selection dialog box to abort the download before you actually go online. To cancel a download in progress, click the **Stop Download** button shown in the lower-right corner of the Download Status dialog box. Don't worry about losing any data because any process that wasn't finished is completed the next time you go online.

After the update is complete, you see the Download Summary dialog box. As the prompt says, just double-click any underlined item to jump to the updated data in Quicken. (This is a great way to quickly jump to the Online Center after updating your online accounts.) Otherwise, simply continue from where you started the update, and click **Done**.

Keeping Your PINs in the PIN Vault

The PIN Vault is the best way to keep track of your PINs. By storing them in one place and then locking that place with a password of your choosing, you can control access to those PINs while reducing their inherent security risk.

To use your PIN Vault, open the **File** menu, select **PIN Vault**, and choose **Setup**.

Click **Next** to move past the introductory screen, select your financial institution in the next dialog box, and click **Next**.

Type your PIN, re-entering to ensure you didn't make a mistake, and click **Next**.

Click **Yes** to record additional PINs (you will repeat steps 2 to 4) or **No** to move on. Then click **Next** to continue.

Enter a password to protect your PINs. Again, re-enter it to confirm and click **Next**. The best passwords are those that combine numbers and letters in random patterns. Using your pet names, special dates, nicknames, common words, or letter patterns is the worst idea because they're the first things hackers try—with a frightening rate of success. Therefore, rather than "Woozycat," go for something odd like "AC89PQ". Avoid well-known combinations of letters and numbers such as "R2D2."

Are PINs Really a Security Hazard?

Anyone who knows your PIN can access your online accounts. All they need is your account number and the name of your bank—information readily available through non-secured means.

By keeping your PINs in the PIN Vault, you avoid the inconvenience of working out exactly where to store your PINs. Instead, you can put them in a safe-deposit box or similar and be done with it. The real problem is that anyone without the convenience of a safe-deposit box has to find somewhere else to keep those little scraps of paper that list each PIN. The first time I ever received a PIN, I ended up unscrewing the back of a speaker, hiding it in there, and then forgetting about it. I sold the speaker to someone who lives in another city, and the scrap of paper with my old PIN is probably still there.

After all that you see a Summary Screen that shows all your institutions, indicating those accounts with PINs in the vault. Click **Done** to save your setup.

The next time you perform a One Step Update, you're able to indicate the vault's password to automatically enter the appropriate PIN beside each institution's Download Statement command.

To add new PINs to your vault, or edit or delete existing entries, open the **Online** menu, select **PIN Vault**, and choose **Edit** or **Delete** as required.

Changing the PIN Vault Password

It's a good idea to change your PIN Vault's password once in a while, especially if you feel you have reason to be concerned about the password's integrity. You might change the password several times each year, once each year, or possibly never. It really just depends on your level of concern.

To change the password, pull down Quicken's **Online** menu, select **PIN Vault**, and choose **Edit**.

Type the original password into the **PIN Vault Password** field and click **OK**. Click the **Change Vault Password** button at the top of the Edit PIN Vault dialog box, type the new password into the **Password** field, repeat it in the **Re-enter** field, and click **Add**. Then click **Done** to close the Edit PIN Vault dialog box.

Receiving Bills Online

Quicken's Online Billing is a quick and easy way to receive your bills from participating creditors, pay those bills through the Quicken Online Billing Web site, and automatically record those payment transactions in the appropriate Quicken register.

It isn't available in all geographic regions, and the number of billers supporting the service, while impressive, is chiefly comprised of utility companies, but online bill payments are handy if for no other reason than that they turn your bill payments into an entirely electronic procedure. Think of the trees, if nothing else.

Online Billing is subject to constant revision, so it isn't really possible to provide step-by-step instructions. However, the sign-up procedure is quite easy to work through.

To get started, open the **Banking** menu and select **Online Bill Presentment**.

A screen with three buttons and a Web-link called "log in here" appears.

Click **Biller List** to see if any of your regular payees support online billing. (If you don't mind going online, select the **click here** link to update the list.) If you do pay bills to an online biller, click **< Back** to return to the Welcome page and select **Apply Now**.

Read the terms of agreement and, if you decide to proceed, click **Yes**. Fill in every field included in the Personal Information form and click the right arrow at the bottom of the pane to move forward.

At the Online Biller List, select the business type and select the online billers from whom you want to receive electronic bills. Click **Add** to copy them to the **My Online Billers** list.

When you've finished, click the right arrow to provide your account number with each online biller. Click the right arrow twice more and submit your application.

After you receive your password, go back to Online Bill Presentment but click the link **log in here**.

Provide your name and password to go to the Online Bill Presentment page.

The upper-left pane shows any bills you have received. The right pane displays any messages received from your online billers. Use the left pane to select those bills you want to pay, selecting them to view more detail.

Click **Enter Payments** to open the Pay Online Bills dialog box. Select the account you will use to pay the checked bills as well as the payment method. You can choose between **Online Payment**, **Printed Check**, or **Hand-Written Check**. When you're finished, click **OK**. Each of the payments appears in your Quicken register as a completed transaction.

To actually pay your bills, either print the checks, write the checks, or transmit the online payments through a One Step Update.

The Least You Need to Know

➤ The range of online facilities built into Quicken is second to none. While each transaction costs a small amount, they are a great timesaver. Add to that the ability to schedule regular transactions, transfer money between funds, and even receive bills electronically from a limited but growing number of companies, and this is very good stuff indeed.

➤ If you don't already have online access to your accounts, talk to your financial institution. Even if you do nothing more than download your statement every so often, that still makes your reconciliations a great deal easier.

➤ It is important to match downloaded transactions to those already recorded in your register. However, you'll find that if you keep Quicken's records up to date, this process should take no more than a minute or two each time.

➤ Setting up a scheduled online transfer is a great way to ensure you never miss an important payment again. Use this facility to pay mortgages, loans, and to make regular deposits to retirement, savings, and investment accounts.

➤ e-Payments isn't particularly widely supported just yet, but keep a close eye on online billing for your own utility company; it makes payments even easier.

➤ The PIN Vault is the best place to store PINs if you have more than one online account. However, make sure you keep your original PINs in a safe place just in case you lose the keys to the vault.

Part 4

Investing: Making Dollars with Sense

There's no secret to a cashed-up retirement: Invest in the long-term and don't jump out of the market at the first or even the last hint of a crash.

In this section you'll learn how to manage your existing investments and record new ones. If you do these within the scope of a cohesive investment strategy, you'll all but guarantee a delightfully rosy future.

Creating and Managing Your Portfolio

Shares and Profits Alike

Shares are responsible for more wealth creation in recent times than any other identifiable factor. Whether you own shares your sweet Auntie May left you, earn stock options through your employment, play the market as a day trader, or just buy and hold shares for years at a time, you'll find Quicken's securities investment and portfolio management features second to none. They are, quite simply, the best.

You can set up any number of accounts.

Quicken's approach to investing is a very logical one: Just as your Quicken checking account perfectly follows the ebb and flow of the balance in the bank, so too, each of your investment accounts rises and falls with the value of the securities you hold.

Buying, selling, and other transactions are recorded in a register attached to each of your investment accounts. If your brokerage account includes a linked cash management account, you can work with this as you do any other checking or bank account.

For best results, you should create one investment account for every real-world account you hold with a broker or trading house. However, you can also follow the value of all your securities through Quicken's Portfolio View.

You can use several forms of investment accounts in Quicken, as was described in Chapter 5, "Accounting for Accounts." These help you to manage your share trading, 401(k), IRA, and a DRIP.

Creating an Investment Account

Using Quicken, you can easily set up and maintain one or more investment accounts or registers. Each register may contain one or more securities, and all of the registers combined form your investment portfolio.

Just as diversification is good for any portfolio, it is also good for Quicken. By arranging your brokerage and other funds in separate Quicken investment registers, you're in a better position to keep track of each.

To create an investment register, open the **Finance** menu and select **Account List** (**Ctrl+A**). Click the **New** button that resides just below the Account List window title.

Let's start with a brokerage account. This is the one you should use for all share trading accounts.

Select **Brokerage** in the Create New Account dialog box and click **Next**.

Creating Other Investment Accounts

The steps for creating a brokerage account are also the same as for the IRA/Keogh, Dividend Reinvestment Plan, and Other Investment account types. Only the 401(k) significantly differs. You can learn more about it in the section named "Creating and Managing a 401(k) Account" later in this chapter.

Now, let's take a shortcut. Rather than working through a myriad of dialog boxes, click the **Summary** tab at the top of the Investment Account Setup dialog box. This takes you to the Summary box shown in the following figure (although not with the sample data).

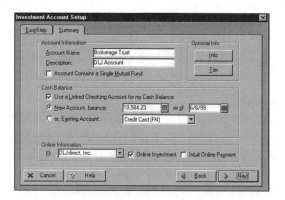

This account has been set up for online brokering, with a new cash management account.

Provide an **Account Name**, optional **Description**, select your broker using **Financial Institution** to use online services, and, if applicable, select **Account Contains a Single Mutual Fund**.

Techno Talk

Single Mutual Fund?

This is an account that doesn't have a cash balance. In other words, the account statement you receive simply lists the total value of the units you hold. Mutual funds are typically wholly managed portfolio or unit trusts. Although it is easy to track the value of mutual fund units you hold through an ordinary investment account, you might find it simpler to also track certain mutual funds in their own separate account, especially if that account is tax-deferred. Instead of tracking a cash balance, Quicken only concerns itself with the share balance, and the various transactions that can be applied to the account are correspondingly simplified. You can convert a single fund account to a multiple fund account, but you cannot covert a multiple fund account to a single fund account.

(Optional) If this investment account provides a check-writing facility, you need to tell Quicken about the CMA, or Cash Management Account. Select **Use a Linked Checking Account for my Cash Balance**. You can create a **New Account**, entering the **New Account balance** and **as of** date as shown on your last statement or link the investment account to an **Existing Account**. The existing account must be an account you've already set up to track this account's cash balance. Do not link this account to your standard checking account unless that account is the CMA for your investment account.

Changing a Linked Account's Name

Quicken names a new cash account linked to an investment account by suffixing the latter's name with "-Cash". For example, the linked checking account for an investment account called Five Star Funds would become Five Star Funds-Cash. You can change the linked account's name by editing that account. Open the **Banking** menu, select **Account List**, select the cash account, click the **Edit** button—not the menu—click in the **Account Name** field, and make the change. Quicken continues to maintain the link between the checking and investment accounts, even though you've changed its name.

(Optional) Click the **Info** button to enter any additional information such as the financial institution's contact details and the account's interest rate.

(Optional) Click **Tax** to set the tax status of this account. When setting up an IRA, 401(k), or similar, Quicken looks after this setting for you. You learn more about tax-deferred accounts in the section called "Creating and Managing a 401(k) Account" later in this chapter.

(Optional) Click **Enable Online Investment** to link this account to an online financial institution. If you haven't done so already, you need to provide your online account and access details when you complete this dialog box. You should select this and the next option only if you have already applied for online services with your financial institution and received from them your online access information pack.

(Optional) Click **Enable Online Payment** (or **Enable Intuit Online Payment**) to tie this account to Quicken's electronic bill-paying system. You can't select this unless your account has a linked CMA or checking facility.

When you finish, review the information and click **Done** to create the investment account and, if specified, a new linked checking account.

At this point you might need to provide your online investment details, but you'll probably just find yourself at Quicken's Security Setup dialog box, which is described next.

Deleting a Linked Cash Account

If you do create a linked checking account and decide that it was the wrong thing to do, don't try to delete it because you will also delete the investment account. Instead, edit the investment account. (Open the **Banking** menu, select **Account List**, select the cash account, and click the **Edit** button.) Click in the **Linked Cash Account** field and select **(none)**. Return to the Account List, select the cash or checking account, and click the **Delete** button at the top of the list window. Type **yes** to confirm you want to delete this account and click **OK**. Quicken deletes the checking account but retains your investment account.

Setting Up Stocks, Mutual Funds, and Other Securities

Quicken's capabilities with regard to securities have been massively upgraded in Quicken 2000, making it easier than ever to record a range of investment types that go far beyond shares alone.

If you have the Set Up New Security dialog box open on your screen, skip to the next paragraph. Otherwise, open your **Investing** menu, select **Security List** (**Ctrl+Y**), and click the **New** button at the top of the screen.

Security?

A security is a general term that covers interests in corporations and authorities. For example, stocks, shares, debentures, bonds, Treasury Bills, units in a mutual fund, option contracts, Treasury Notes, and CDs are all securities in one sense or another. Curiously, one of the few investment vehicles not generally considered a security is a futures contract. Well, that and the blanket you were dragging around when you were three.

Quicken can track six distinct types of investments, with a catch-all "Other" to handle the rest. Most of the securities require the same information: typically the name and optional ticker, your total holdings and the price you paid, the date you purchased the security, and the account for which they are destined. However, there are extra steps in some.

Let's start with the one you probably use most often.

Creating Stocks

Select **Stock** from the list of securities and click **Next**.

Type in the full name of the security as you know it, and provide an optional ticker symbol.

Type in the **Name** and provide a **Ticker** symbol. The ticker is optional, but it is mandatory if you want to update your portfolio with historical and current security prices. When you've finished, click **Next**.

Finding Ticker Symbols

Click **Look Up** to find a particular ticker symbol using the Internet. Quicken copies the contents of the Name field to seed the search. If you see the correct corporation listed in the Company Name column, take note of the ticker in the Symbol column. Click the **Back to Quicken** button to return, and type the ticker into the **Ticker Symbol** field provided in the security set up dialog box.

Select an **Asset Class** and **Investment Goal**. Investors use asset classes to ensure they aren't putting all their eggs into the one basket. One instance is stocks with a small capitalization. You can specify a specific asset class—or for mutual funds, a mix of asset classes—to match the structure of the fund itself, or you can leave **Download Asset Class Information** selected for Quicken to set the asset class for you.

Asset classes are particularly useful for showing how market segments have performed. For example, how have your investments in small cap, volatile stocks compared to those in the large cap, blue-chip areas?

Investment goals help you match your stocks to investment strategies and then compare those strategies to see how well they are doing. For example, say you decide to invest in some high-growth stocks on the chance that they will keep growing and provide you with a fast, effective return. By specifying a **Growth** investment goal, you can sort and subtotal these stocks in certain investment reports and graphs, helping you see how well all your stocks have performed on their own and compared to, say, stocks marked with other investment goals.

Click **Next** to continue.

Click **Next** again, and choose a cost basis for this security. You only need to worry about this if you have or think you will purchase more than one bundle of shares or units. Select **Lot Identification** if you want to be able to specify which bundle you sell when you make a trade. You can use this to sell the long-term bundles first, realizing lower capital gains. Or, if the profit is small enough on the most recent purchases, realize lower capital gains that way. Select **Average Cost** if you don't need to fine-tune your capital gains.

You should talk to your tax professional about which method is most advantageous to your situation, or simply use the method you have previously submitted to the IRS; but in general, although the average cost method is simpler, lot identification provides greater control and the potential for lesser capital gains.

Select the method and click **Next**.

Now you're almost home. At this point you need to decide how you want to track this stock. Select **Track my holdings** if you have actually traded in this stock, or **Put it on the watch list** if you just want to follow its share price for a while.

Who Watches the Watch List?

Everyone should watch Watch Lists. Really. Not only are they a great place to create a dummy portfolio through which you can test your investment prowess or the latest theories on trading, they're also useful for following the price of a stock, waiting for it to hit the lows before you swoop in for the purchase.

There are a three other choices in this dialog box that define for how long Quicken should track your holdings in this security. They are:

➤ **Today** This is the easiest starting point, but if you already own this security, you need to manually calculate any capital gains for taxation purposes. Note, however, that you can download historical stock prices for any stock going back five years, even if you only track it from today.

➤ **The end of last year** This option helps you prepare your Schedule B taxation return for the current financial year, but you must record any transactions or splits that have occurred along the way. Quicken still doesn't have sufficient information with this option to calculate your capital gains. That takes...

➤ **The date you purchased this stock** For most people, this option makes the most sense because it enables you to see how your stock and your net worth have changed over time. If you select this option, Quicken can also calculate capital gains and prepare your Schedule B at tax time. The date field uses today's date as the default. Adjust this to the date you purchased this stock.

Click **Next** to select the account through which you purchased the stock, and **Next** once more to indicate the number of shares, the price you paid for each, and the commission or fee that was paid to your broker for this purchase. Record the purchase price as the price you paid. Don't adjust it for stock splits; there's plenty of opportunity to do that later.

Fracturing Costs

You can record fractional prices as easily as you do decimal prices in Quicken. This means you can type in a purchase price of 81 5/16 or the decimal equivalent at 81.315. Quicken happily converts between the two.

Click **Next** again. Are you done, or would you like to keep adding securities? Select **Yes** and **Next** to record further stocks, mutual funds, or, as detailed in the following section, bonds. Click **No** and **Next** to move on to a summary of your activities so far.

Use the summary dialog box shown in the following figure to confirm the details of this security. If something isn't correct, click **Back** to return to that section, correct the problem, and then click **Next** to wend your way back.

Select whether you want to set up another security in the final dialog box, or click **Done** to finish.

Recording Other Securities

After you've recorded stocks, you've completed nearly all the steps required to record any other form of security in Quicken.

Let's look at some of the differences between stocks and the other options in that first screen of the Set Up a New Security dialog box:

➤ **Bond** Several additional pieces of information are required to record bond purchases. These begin with an optional Maturity Date—that is, the date the bonds expire and are paid out. On top of that, you also need to provide the Annual Yield (the interest rate attached to the bond), the Face Value (the value actually printed on the bond), and the Accrued Interest (any unpaid interest already earned by the bond).

At last, a new security defined!

Recording Other Types of Bonds

Quicken assumes standard bonds have a price factor of 10 built in for the difference between the quoted price of the bond and the face value. That is, 1 bond really equals 10 shares. Not all bonds work like this. In fact, some operate on factors of 100. You can record these manually, calculating the price per share on the total cost of the transaction minus accrued interest divided by 100, or you can try recording them as a standard bond and then editing the results in your investment account's register.

➤ **CD**   Certificates of Deposit also have a Maturity Date, but other than that they're identical to Stocks.

➤ **Employee Stock Option**   The famous stock option. Breeder of loyalty, filler of high-tech company car parks with Porches and Mercedes, maker of millionaires. Stock options are the most complex type of security, but Quicken steps you through them. First, choose an existing stock or create a new one as required. (This is the stock against which the option can be exercised.) I'd also advise you take advantage of the offer to create a new account to track the option's value, as they probably don't belong in your standard investment account. What else do you need to know? The Exercise Price is the purchase price specified on your options. Provide details for the vesting schedule—that is if you don't already have a 100% right to the options—and set the expiration date, if applicable.

➤ **Market Index** Setting up a Market Index is easy. Just select all the indices you want to track and click **Next** one final time. Market Indices are new to Quicken 2000, and are a great way to keep a close eye on the Dow Jones or the S&P 500, among others.

➤ **Mutual Fund** These are identical to stocks, the chief difference being that if you like to track asset classes, you should make sure you select the appropriate ones when recording your holdings in the fund. If your fund's prospectus specifies a mixture of holdings—for instance 50% Large Cap Stocks, 25% Small Cap Stocks, and 25% Domestic Bond—click **Specify Mixture** in the Asset Class dialog box, and provide those percentages.

➤ **Other** This security type provides the same steps as those for setting up a Stock. There is no discernible difference between the two security types, but you might want to use it to track stocks that aren't part of your daily portfolio. For instance, that curious parcel of several thousand shares in the Computing-Tabulating-Recording Company left to you by your grandmother.

After you have finished recording new securities, you can either go online when prompted and update their prices immediately with current and historical data, or return to the Security List.

Managing Your Portfolio

The Portfolio View provides an integrated and highly customizable system for viewing all of your securities, accounts, goals, and investment types. To open it, click the **Investing** menu and select **Portfolio View** (**Ctrl+U**). You should see a window similar to that shown in the following figure.

The Portfolio View is amazingly flexible, summarizing your portfolio by a host of factors including price, gain, performance, valuation, and more. You can even customize any view to display precisely the information you require.

For instance, click the folder icon for any major group (shown as a yellow folder) to collapse it, or click once more to expand it. You can do the same with individual securities, switching between viewing, say, the total gain for that security to individual gains made by each lot you hold in that security.

At the top of the Portfolio View window click the **Group by** pull-down list to change the major groupings for your securities and the **View** pull-down list to change the columns displayed.

Quicken provides a multitude of columns that you can display in the Portfolio View. They're hidden under the **Customize** button. However, make sure you first select the **View** you want to change. If you really feel like just playing around (and there's no better way to get a feel for it), select the views **Custom1** or **Custom2**.

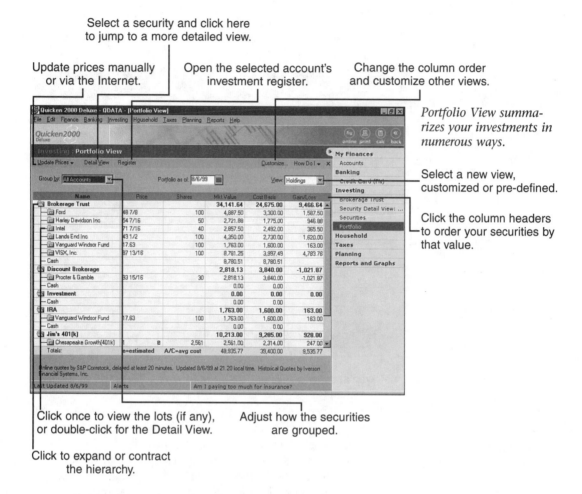

Select a security and click here
to jump to a more detailed view.

Update prices manually
or via the Internet.

Open the selected account's
investment register.

Change the column order
and customize other views.

Portfolio View summarizes your investments in numerous ways.

Select a new view, customized or pre-defined.

Click the column headers to order your securities by that value.

Click once to view the lots (if any),
or double-click for the Detail View.

Adjust how the securities
are grouped.

Click to expand or contract
the hierarchy.

Using the Security Detail View

The Detail View is one of Quicken's best features. You can use it to view a host of information pertinent to a particular security, including:

➤ Viewing those transactions that relate to a particular security.

➤ Studying that security's price history in a graphical format.

➤ Reading the latest news and linking to further online research.

To open the Detail View, either double-click any security in the Portfolio View, click the **Detail View** button at the top of the Portfolio View window, or open the **Investing** menu and select **Security Detail and News**.

The figure below provides a visual guide to this window.

203

Select a different
security to view.

All transactions relating to this security—
double-click to jump to the investment register.

*Detail View is ideal for
studying most of the
information you have
downloaded for a
particular security.*

Summary of your holdings
and investment value.

Switch to a market
value graph.

Change the time
frame for this graph.

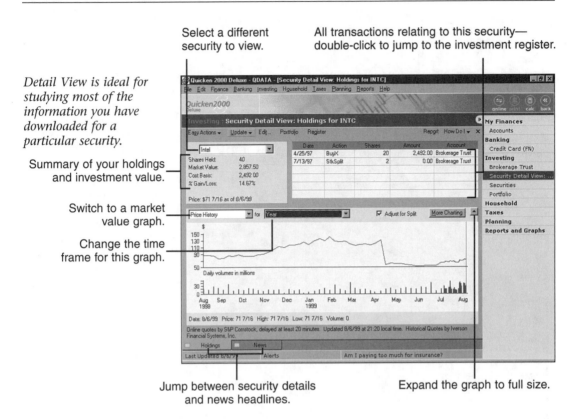

Jump between security details
and news headlines.

Expand the graph to full size.

Change securities using the drop-down menu located in the top-left corner of the Security Detail View window. The area underneath this menu provides key information on the security and your investment success so far, whereas the small register to the right shows all transactions recorded for that security. Double-click any transaction to edit it onscreen. The changes you make are made to the original transaction in the investment register.

The lower pane displays a price history graph, along with several menus that change the details displayed therein.

Two wide drop-down menus are located at the top of the lower pane. The one on the left provides two options:

➤ **Price History** This is the default setting. It sets the graph to plot the share price in the upper half and the volume of shares traded each day in the lower half. If you click a point on the graph where an entry has been plotted, you see the date, closing price, high for the day, low for the day, and volume enumerated in the small area at the foot of the graph.

➤ **Market Value** Select this setting to view the value of your holdings rather than the share price. If you sell shares, this value drops; when you buy, it increases. However, it also moves up and down according to the share price. If you pause the mouse pointer near the plotting point for a particular day, it changes to an hourglass and displays the actual market value for that day in a small pop-up window. Personally, I find the market value of less interest than the share price because it fluctuates according to your quantity of holdings, and this isn't as pure an indication of a securities movements as a pure, clean price chart.

The second drop-down menu is to the right at the top of the lower pane. It sets the term over which you want to view this graph. You can view the price changes or market value over almost any term. Select the preset Week to 5 Year values, or scroll to the bottom of the menu and choose any range by selecting **Custom**. Provide the **Start Date** and **End Date** in the Date Range dialog box that subsequently appears and click **OK** to apply those changes to the graph.

You have two more options in that top section of the lower graph pane. If any splits have occurred in the stock price, the **Adjust for Split** check box corrects the historical pricing data so you don't see any dramatic jumps in the stock price (market value graphs don't require adjusting because market value isn't affected by a split).

Splits?

Splits are used to increase the volume of shares available for trading with the advantage that the stock price also comes down to what appears to be enticing levels. (They aren't any cheaper in reality, but that doesn't seem to have much to do with trading.) Adjusting for a split works as follows: a stock trading at $150 undergoes a 2 for 1 split that brings it down to $75. That is, an extra share for every previous share is issued, so they are now "2 for 1". With **Adjust for Split** selected, all prices prior to that split are halved so the graph continues to provide a historically accurate picture of the stock price. If **Adjust for Split** wasn't selected, you would see a sharp drop from $150 to $75, an apparent 50% collapse in the price, when the actual value hadn't changed. Some evidence even suggests that splits encourage the performance of stocks and so lead to an improvement in real value, if only in the short term.

Click the up arrow next to the **Adjust for Split** check box to expand the graph in a new window so that it fills the entire center of the screen. If you are connected to the Internet, click **More Charting** to go online and explore further resources.

Eyewitness News

The Security Detail View has one more very impressive feature up its virtual sleeve. It's the capability to download the latest news headlines relating to your securities. Many of these aren't headlines of the six o'clock news fashion. They are company press releases; media stories where the security might have been mentioned in passing; copies of important SEC documents recently filed; earning reports; stock offerings, and more.

Check This Out

Change the Amount of News Downloaded

Quicken usually only downloads the previous week's news for any particular stock. To increase or decrease this, start One Step Update (just click the **Online** button in the top-right corner of Quicken's screen), then click the **Customize** button, and, with the **Quotes & News** tab selected, use the pull-down list beside **Get news for the last** to choose how newsworthy you want Quicken's news downloads.

Viewing news is easy. Just click the **News** tab at the bottom of the detail window. A window similar to the one shown in the following figure appears. (If there aren't any news headlines, either no news was available for that security, or you need to do another One Step Update.)

If you have downloaded news headlines for the selected security (see Chapter 20, "Program Options: Doing It Your Way," for more information), you see a window similar to that shown in the next figure. (If not, you see the same window without any of the links or headlines depicted.)

Click the underlined items in the News window to launch the internal Web browser and load that item. Alternatively, use the **Quote**, **Chart**, **Snapshot**, **Analysis**, and **Earnings** links to perform further research. You must be online to read the news and access the other links displayed in this window. If you aren't, Quicken starts your Internet connection for you.

Click the **Holdings** tab to return to main Security Detail View.

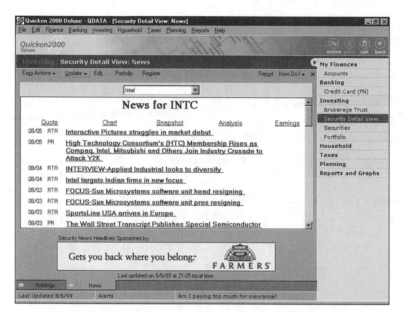

Not all news is good news, but with this Quicken feature you receive it all.

Downloading Security Price History

Updating security prices across the Internet takes mere seconds and is cheaper, easier, and more current than looking up those prices in the share listings of a newspaper.

You can also grab the latest news headlines and, through a Quicken Alert, learn when a stock reaches a high or low you previously specified. Incidentally, setting alerts this way is a great way to make sure you don't overlook a limit to buy or sell.

Security Price Alerts

There's nothing worse than learning that the stock you've been following has made that move you were waiting for while your back was turned. The solution is to set an alarm for when a security rises above a certain level or falls below another level. Open the **Finance** menu and select **Alerts**. Then click the **Investments** tab and choose **Stock Price Limits**. Click in the **High** or **Low** columns for every security for which you want to set an alert and click **OK** to save your changes. Alerts appear, well, just about all over the place in Quicken. They're in the Billminder window and the Reminders window, and in time you will even be able to upload them to Quicken's Web site. One way or another, Quicken makes sure you know about it.

Even though Quicken provides a system for updating your security prices manually (just change the prices in the Mkt Price column of your Portfolio View, or from Security Detail View open the **Update Prices** menu and select **Edit Price History**), it's hardly elegant. Instead, consider the Internet *de rigeur*.

It's incredibly easy to download up to five years of historical data for each and every one of your securities. Here's how.

First, open the **Investing** menu and select **Portfolio View**.

The Portfolio view's **Update Prices** menu provides four ways to update your security prices online:

➤ **Get Online Quotes Only**   Download the latest prices for all your securities. This is the fastest method because it does so without any intervening dialog boxes, although you might be requested to give permission to connect to the Internet. After viewing the Download Summary, click **Done** to return to Portfolio View.

Skipping the Download Confirmation

Quicken likes to check with you before it goes online. If you're happy to let it run free, you can bypass the download confirmation screen the next time you see it by selecting the check box **Skip this screen in the future**.

➤ **Get Online Quotes & News**   This is the same as performing a **One Step Update**. Click **Customize** to more precisely define the data you download.

➤ **Portfolio Export**   Select this to send your portfolio to Quicken's Web site. You should use this feature if you want to be able to view your portfolio on a Web page from any computer other than your primary Quicken computer. Just go to www.quicken.com and look for the Portfolio links.

➤ **Get Asset Classes**   Select the securities for which you want to download asset class information and click **OK**. When it's finished downloading, click **Done** to return to the Portfolio View.

➤ **Get Historical Prices**   This is the one in which we're interested. Select this to download historical pricing data for all the securities you specify. Choose exactly how much data you want using the **Get prices for the last** pull-down list. There is one caveat: daily data is downloaded for the past month only, while weekly prices are downloaded for all periods prior to the past month. This means you need to update your data at least once a month in order to maintain a record of constant daily prices. However, you can do that via the One Step Update rather than through the Historical Prices feature. Click **Done** to return to the Portfolio View when Quicken has completed its download.

The latest prices are used for calculating the value of your portfolio. This is live data, fed straight from the securities exchanges, although it is delayed by at least 20 minutes. Although a lot can happen in 20 minutes, the availability of this data means you can see how your portfolio changes throughout the day.

In addition, by exporting your data to the Web, you can jump to the Quicken.com Web site from any computer connected to the Internet and, after entering your registration name and password, view and even make changes to your portfolio. Now that's what I call connectivity!

Creating and Managing a 401(k) Account

If you use Quicken Deluxe or Quicken Home & Business, you have access to another account type designed specifically to help you track one or more 401(k) investments.

Setting up your 401(k) takes just a few minutes, but you should make sure you have your most recent 401(k) statement handy before you begin. When you're ready, follow these steps.

From the **Finance** menu select **Account List** (**Ctrl+A**). Click **New**, choose **401(k)**, and click **Next**.

Skip past the introductory screen by clicking **Next** once more. (Unlike the investment accounts where you can take a shortcut to a summary, you must proceed through this account setup interview step by step.)

Provide an account name and optional description and click **Next**.

Record the ending date shown on your 401(k) statement in the **Ending Date** field. This helps synchronize your Quicken and real 401(k) accounts. Also indicate the number of securities you hold in the account using the **Number of Securities** field. You can hold from 1 to 20 securities in any 401(k). Selecting one security sets this account to account like a single mutual fund; Quicken tracks the account balance instead of the value of securities with an additional cash balance. Click **Next** to continue.

Quicken can adjust itself to ask only pertinent questions about this 401(k) in the future. If your employer contributes to your 401(k), select **Yes**. If your statement tells you how many shares your 401(k) holds in each of its securities, indicate so here and click **Next** to continue.

Now you move into a loop based on your previous answers. You have to provide the security name, total shares (if known—this is blank if you answered **No** to the second question above), and ending balance for that security in the **Security Name**, **Total Shares**, and **Ending Balance** fields. All of this information should be provided on your 401(k) statement. Click **Next** to record the same details for the next security held.

Use the Summary screen to review the 401(k) information you just recorded. If you have any problems, click **Back** to navigate to the source of the troubles.

Click **Done** when you've finished. Quicken immediately creates the 401(k) account and records the transactions you just defined. To view your 401(k), open the **Investing** menu, select **Investing Accounts**, and pick your 401(k) from the list. This throws you straight into the 401(k) register. Click **401(k) View** at the top of the screen to open the new window shown in the following figure.

Update when you receive
a statement for this 401(k).

Display another
401(k).

Print this page or generate a report.

The 401(k) View provides a summary of your 401(k)'s most pertinent data.

Current securities held

Changing value over
past updates

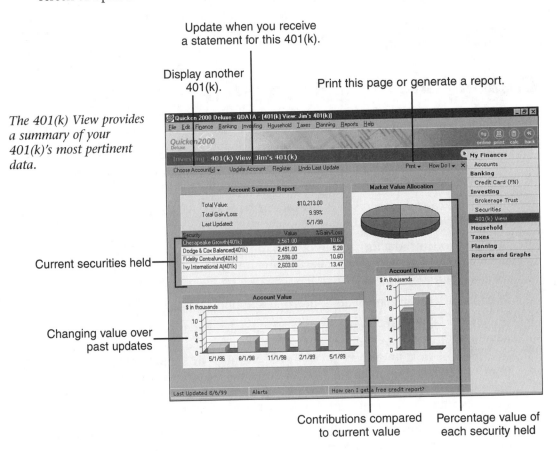

Contributions compared
to current value

Percentage value of
each security held

You can return to this view in the future by double-clicking your 401(k) account in the account list.

Updating 401(k) Accounts

The 401(k) is a special type of account. You can open the 401(k) register as you would any investment register and record the full range of transactions described in the next chapter, but that isn't the best way to go about it.

If you use Quicken Deluxe or Quicken Home & Business, the special 401(k) account type makes managing this important side of your finances very easy.

In short, whenever you receive your 401(k) statement, you should follow these steps.

First go to your **401(k) View** as described previously and click **Update Account**.

Select the Account Name of the 401(k) you want to update (if you have more than one) and click **OK**.

Type in the date shown on the statement most recently received and click **Next**.

You should now see a dialog box that displays the securities you currently hold. If any of these holdings have been sold, remove the check mark. If any holdings have been added, click **Add new Security**, provide a name, and click **OK**. Click **Next** to continue.

For each security held in the 401(k), record your and your employer's contribution, dividends, or interest earned and security's ending balance. Click **Next** to repeat these questions for all the securities in your account.

When you arrive at the Transfers dialog box, click **Yes** only if there have been transfers between the securities held in your 401(k). In other words, do this if the mix of the investment was adjusted to favor one security over another. If so, provide the number of transfers in the **Number of Transfers** field and click **Next**. For every transfer, indicate the **Transfer Amount** and the **From** and **To Securities**. Click **Next** to move through each transfer until you reach the summary dialog box.

Check the amounts shown in the Update Summary carefully. If any require editing, simply click on them in their column and insert the new amounts as required. (You can also use the Calculator icon that appears next to each field.) After you're finished, click **Done** to record the changes to your 401(k).

The Least You Need to Know

➤ Wealth through personal investment has replaced the dream of success as measured by a steady job, rising to the top, and owning one's home...for better or worse. With Quicken, the future's in your pocket.

➤ Quicken doesn't skimp on the personal investment tools. In fact, make sure you take every opportunity to wring the most from its prowess in this field. Set up your investment accounts, go online to download the latest share prices, investigate statement downloads through your broker, and take a more active role in the management of your 401(k) and IRA accounts.

➤ Creating an investment account is a little different than creating Quicken's other accounts, but it isn't any more difficult. Just follow the procedure and you shouldn't have any trouble.

➤ The easiest way to record transactions in a portfolio is to use the forms provided by the Easy Actions.

➤ Take advantage of Quicken's provision for downloading historical prices; they're a great way to get more from your investment dollar.

➤ The 401(k) account is one of Quicken's most difficult to create, but it's an essential part of tracking your wealth. You should endeavour to record all your retirement accounts. Then use Quicken's financial planning tools to ensure you have made adequate provision for that Florida mansion.

Chapter 15

Recording and Reporting Your Investments

In This Chapter

➤ Recording several types of investment transactions

➤ Putting a value on your investments...and yourself

Buying, Selling, and Other Transactions

One of the great things about Quicken in comparison to traditional accounting packages is its understanding of the complexities of modern life. For instance, categories are used in all accounting systems, although they might come under the heading of income and expense accounts, but only Quicken and QuickBooks, its small business colleague, offer classes.

But this is minor when compared to the inclusion of a complete investment portfolio management system.

Your investment register is *the* place to record all your investment transactions. Using the screen shown in the following figure you can buy and sell shares, record investment income, reinvest dividends, split stocks, and a great deal more. All of these events are stored under a special pull-down menu called Easy Actions.

The investment register has a similar appearance to other registers, but with some important differences.

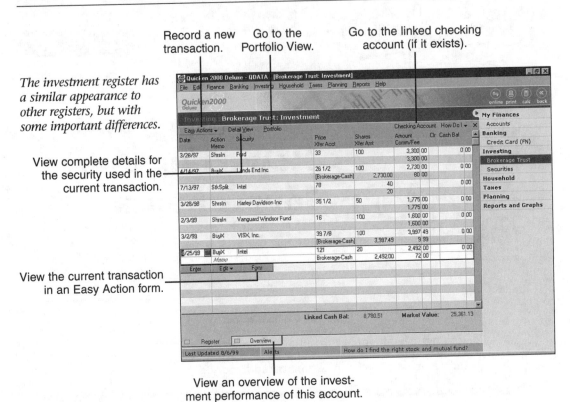

Record a new transaction.

Go to the Portfolio View.

Go to the linked checking account (if it exists).

View complete details for the security used in the current transaction.

View the current transaction in an Easy Action form.

View an overview of the investment performance of this account.

You should look to Easy Actions before you do anything else, for although there is no particular difficulty in recording transactions directly into your register, the Easy Actions menu makes things much easier and ensures you put the right information in the right place every time.

The forms built into Easy Actions help you with:

➤ Buying and selling shares

➤ Transferring funds between your checking and investment accounts

➤ Recording and reinvesting stock dividends

➤ Recording and reinvesting interest earned

➤ Recording stock splits

➤ Recording margin interest

These are the most common transactions you need to record, so I've covered them each in detail in the following sections.

Before getting started, make sure you have your investment register open. Open the **Investing** menu, select **Investing Accounts**, and choose the register you need from the list.

Buying or Depositing Shares

To buy or add shares or mutual fund units to your portfolio, open the **Easy Actions** menu in your investment register and select **Buy/Add Shares**. Ignore the first dialog box. Instead, click the **Summary** tab to jump to the dialog box shown in the figure below and fill out the top three fields as follows:

➤ **Date**   This is the date the transaction took place. Type it in or use Quicken's Calendar tool to select it.

➤ **Security**   Select a security from the list, or type in a new security's name. If this security isn't known to Quicken, you need to set it up. Quicken takes you to the Set Up a New Security series of dialog boxes described in Chapter 14, "Creating and Managing Your Portfolio." After you define the security, you can use it in any future transaction.

➤ **Account**   This defaults to the name of the current register and usually cannot be changed.

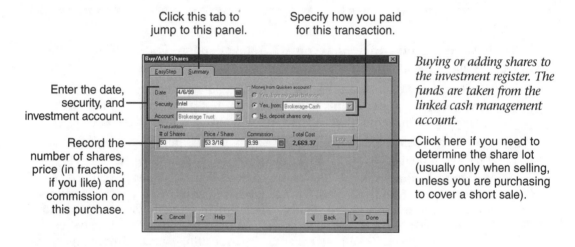

Click this tab to jump to this panel.

Specify how you paid for this transaction.

Enter the date, security, and investment account.

Record the number of shares, price (in fractions, if you like) and commission on this purchase.

Buying or adding shares to the investment register. The funds are taken from the linked cash management account.

Click here if you need to determine the share lot (usually only when selling, unless you are purchasing to cover a short sale).

Fill in the **Transaction** section of the tab as follows:

➤ **# of Shares**   This is the total number of shares purchased or deposited.

➤ **Price / Share**   Price paid per share.

➤ **Commission**   Amount paid to your broker for this purchase. Note that if you are only depositing shares without withdrawing cash from an account, you cannot pay a commission. This is because the commission would have been paid when the shares were first purchased.

➤ **Lots**   If you have recorded several short sales on this security, you can choose which bundles of short sales are to be covered by this purchase. You can learn how to use the Specify Lots dialog box under "Working with Lots," later in this chapter.

Short Sales

When you sell short, you sell stocks that are borrowed, not owned. If the price of those stocks goes down, you can repurchase the same number of stocks for less and return them to their owner. You get to keep the difference between the original sale price and the subsequent re-purchase cost. Of course, if the stocks go up, you still have to purchase the same number of shares, but this time for more than they were sold. Selling short is a great way to make money in a market that's trending down, but make sure it doesn't bounce back on you because then you just end up short-sheeted.

Use the **Money from Quicken account?** group of options to describe where the money to make the purchase came from:

➤ **Yes, from my cash balance**   Select this if you want to pay for the shares using the cash balance of this account. You cannot select this if you have a linked cash management account attached to this investment account.

➤ **Yes, from**   Select a different account to pay for this purchase. If you have a linked cash management account, you are not able to select any other account.

➤ **No, deposit shares only**   Select this to deposit these shares in your investment register without transferring their cost from another account. You can use this to "fund" a newly created Quicken investment account with shares already held in an existing account. Why would you need to do this? It's ideal when you first set up your investment register. By depositing shares without an associated monetary transfer, you can add them to your portfolio without affecting your finances.

When you've finished, click **Done** to record the share purchase.

Selling or Removing Shares

Selling or removing shares takes place through a dialog box that is almost identical to the Buy/Add Shares Easy Action. To sell or remove shares or mutual fund units from your portfolio, open the **Easy Actions** menu in your investment register and select **Sell/Remove Shares**. Click the **Summary** tab in the Sell/Remove Shares dialog box and fill out the top three fields as follows:

➤ **Date**   Provide the date the sale or transfer took place.

➤ **Security**   Select a security from the list, or type in a new security's name.

➤ **Account**   This defaults to the name of the current register.

In the **Transaction** group, indicate the following:

➤ **# of Shares**   Number of shares sold or removed.

➤ **Price / Share**   Sale price per share.

➤ **Commission**   Amount paid to your broker for enacting this sale. If you are only removing shares without depositing cash, you cannot pay a commission on the sale.

After you purchase more than one lot of any one security, you see a section in this dialog box called Cost Basis Method. For capital gains purposes you need to specify whether this security should use the average cost or lots-based method of calculating capital gains. You can select a basis for each security, but after you have used that basis, you must continue to use it for future returns unless you get permission from the IRS to do otherwise. Select a **Cost Basis Method**:

➤ **Average Cost**   Average out the costs of all the shares held in different lots and use this figure as the purchase price.

➤ **Lot Identification**   If you have purchased more than one lot, select this option. To use other than Quicken's "oldest lots sold first" ordering methodology, click **Specify Lots** and see the following section, "Working with Lots."

Use the **Record proceeds?** group as follows:

➤ **Yes, to my cash balance**   Select this if you want to deposit the money received for this sale into the cash balance of this account. You cannot select this if you have a linked cash management account attached to this investment account.

➤ **Yes, to**   Select a different account to deposit the proceeds received from this sale. If you have a linked cash management account, you are not able to select any other account.

➤ **No, withdraw shares only**   Select this to remove these shares from your investment register without creating a sale transaction. You can use this to record securities you've received as gifts or acquired in some other way. Don't use this to record shares you receive as the result of a split. You learn how to record these later in this chapter.

When you're finished, click **Done** to record the sale.

Working with Lots

What's a lot? How long's a piece of string?

Seriously, every bundle of shares you purchase is recorded as a lot. When you sell shares, you can determine which lots or parts thereof are included in that sale. This is important for capital gains purposes as you might want to maximize or minimize your long- or short-term gains, or you might prefer to use an average purchase price based on the cost of the shares across all your lots.

If you choose to sell by lots rather than on an average cost, you still don't need to specify certain lots. Quicken can assume that any selling activity runs through the lots in numerical order from the oldest transactions to the most recent. This is known as a FIFO, or a first-in, first-out cost basis.

However, you can also adjust this in almost any way, specifying which shares out of each lot should be sold (or covered by a purchase, if you had previously sold short). To do so, click the **Lots** button in the **Transaction** group of the Add/Deposit Shares dialog box or click **Lot Identification** and then **Specify Lots** in the Sell/Remove Shares dialog box.

The Lots dialog box is shown in the following figure. The upper scrolling list shows each lot or group of shares purchased, their purchase date, date of expiry of their current capital gains status (ST = short-term; MT = medium-term; LT = long-term), purchase price, and quantity available to sell.

The Lots window helps you to determine which shares you should sell out of several holdings.

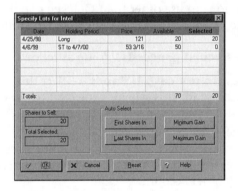

Click in the **Selected** column beside each lot to indicate the quantity of that lot you want to sell.

Use the four command buttons to specify how to call on Quicken's help in selecting lots for the current transaction. You can use the buttons to maximize or minimize your capital gain. Each button makes the following adjustments:

➤ **First Shares In**   Selects shares from the oldest lot moving forward.

➤ **Last Shares In**   Selects shares from the most recently purchased lot moving backward.

➤ **Minimum Gain**   Selects the shares on which you have made the least profit.

➤ **Maximum Gain**   Selects the shares on which you have made the most profit.

Click **OK** when you're finished to return to the Add/Deposit or Sell/Remove dialog boxes.

Transferring Funds Between Accounts

Quicken handles the cash in your investment account in three ways. If your account was set up to hold a single mutual fund, there is no associated cash balance. Instead, when units are purchased, the purchase price is taken from the account you used to make that purchase.

If your account has a linked checking or cash management account, be that a checkbook or online banking facility, you cannot transfer cash directly into your investment account. Instead, it must go through the linked account. In line with this philosophy, Quicken also assumes the linked account is used for the expenses and proceeds from all the purchases and sales you make on behalf of the investment account. You can transfer funds into or out of the linked checking account as often as you like just as you would transfer funds to any ordinary account or register, but you can't do it through the Easy Actions menu of the investment account.

The third type of account does have a cash balance built in. This is an investment account set up to track multiple securities, but it doesn't have a linked checking account.

Although you can't use the cash balance to write checks or make payments for things not related to the purchase of securities in that account's name, you can certainly transfer funds into or out of this account.

To transfer funds into this last type of investment account, make sure your investment register is open, and select the **Transfer Cash In** dialog box. (If you don't see this menu item, your account has been set up with a linked checking account and you should follow the previous steps.)

To transfer funds out of your investment account, open your investment register and select **Easy Actions**, **Transfer Cash from Account**.

Recording and Reinvesting Your Dividends

For high growth stocks, the payment of a dividend is a rare event indeed. Those companies prefer to hang onto their profits to fund future growth.

However, there are many other stocks that do pay dividends, and for many of the holders of that stock, that's the sole reason they invested.

There are two ways you can treat a dividend. The first is to take that income and deposit it into your bank account. This leaves you free to spend that income on whatever you want, be it to support your lifestyle or to transfer to some other form of investment.

The second is to compound your investment by using that income to purchase more units in that fund or shares in that stock. This can be enormously advantageous if you don't require that income to maintain your standard of living. By reinvesting in that security, the next income event generates even more money, giving you more to invest, and thus generates an even greater sum the next time around, sitting you squarely on that rocket ride up the exponential curve.

No matter whether you cash in your dividends or reinvest them, you'll find it easy to manage these income events through the Easy Actions menu.

Recording an Income Event

If you decide to not reinvest the dividend income you have received, you might prefer instead to transfer it to your account's cash balance. Quicken calls this an "income event." I call it manna from heaven.

To transfer dividend income to your account's cash balance, open your investment register, click **Easy Actions**, and select **Record an Income Event**. You should see the Record Income dialog box shown in the following figure.

Use this dialog box to record a variety of investment income types. The quickest way is to enter the details straight from a Form 1099-DIV or Form 1099-INC.

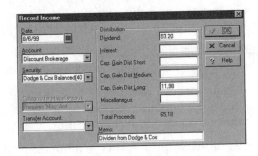

Enter the **Date** the dividend was recorded, select the **Account**, and choose the **Security** that generated the dividend.

Reporting on Investment Income

The best way to record dividends and interest earned is through the Form 1099-DIV or Form 1099-INC you receive from your brokerage or fund manager. Even if you hear a dividend has been generated by one of your investments, wait until you receive official notification. This helps you to match your accounts to your broker's accounts and also keep the income you report in line with that reported on your behalf to the IRS.

Under the **Distribution** group, specify how the dividend is comprised. Most shares generate straight dividends (the uppermost field in the list), but you might also receive income comprised of interest or capital gains distributions. Here are the options (the fields you can access are dependent on the investment account type):

➤ **Dividend**   Use this field to record dividends received. Most stock dividends are tax-free or "franked" because the tax has already been paid by the corporation. If you are unsure whether the dividends you have received are taxable or not, contact the Investor Relations department of the company involved, or speak to your tax professional.

➤ **Interest**   Interest is generated through money market investments, bonds, and certain mutual funds. Most interest income is taxable. If you have received tax-free interest, record it under **Miscellaneous**.

➤ **Cap. Gain Dist Short**   Record the short-term capital gain distribution.

Techno Talk

Capital Gains Income?

This isn't related to any capital gain you have made on your ownership of the security. For that, you need to sell it. Rather, it is the distribution of a capital gain made by the fund managing your money. Funds—just like you—can make short-, medium- and long-term capital gains.

Capital gains should be reported on your annual return using Schedule D. The IRS will match your information with that recorded on their own copies of the Form 1099s.

➤ **Cap. Gain Dist Medium**   Record the medium-term capital gain distribution.

➤ **Cap. Gain Dist Long**   Record the long-term capital gain distribution.

➤ **Miscellaneous**   Consider this field ideal for everything else. If you enter an amount here, you can choose the target income category under **Category for Miscellaneous**. If this is tax-free income, make sure it is recorded with a tax-free category so that your Tax Summary and Tax Schedule reports accurately reflect your true taxable income.

Select a **Transfer Account**. This is the account into which you deposit this income. It might be your investment account, a linked investment checking account, an IRA fund that you are maintaining through Quicken, or just your plain, everyday savings/checking account. You are limited in your account selection by the strictures of the type of investment account this is. For example, does it have its own cash balance, a linked checking account, or no cash balance at all?

When you're finished, type in an optional **Memo** and click **OK**.

Reinvesting Your Income

Reinvesting is a powerful way to boost your investment. Some securities don't allow the reinvestment of income, but most do. The reinvestment of income is usually something you can set up with your fund manager or stockbroker. You will receive details of the reinvestment in your monthly statement. These tell you how many extra shares, units, or other discrete chunks of the investment you have received. The Reinvest Income dialog box assumes all of the income entered is converted to shares. For this reason, it also supports the notion of fractional shares for those times (the majority) when the share price does not neatly divide into the income received. If your brokerage or fund doesn't support fractional shares, a certain amount is left over. You should record the amount remaining using the same steps as recording any other income event, as previously described.

To reinvest your income, open your investment register, click **Easy Actions**, and select **Reinvest Income**.

Enter the date in the **Date** field, select the **Account**, and choose the **Security** to which this income event applies. Again, depending on the type of investment account this is, some of your choices might be limited.

Under **Distribution**, apply the income to each form of distribution as described for the "Record an Income Event" Easy Action above. Beside each, enter the number of shares you are purchasing out of each distribution's income type. Refer to your statement for the precise numbers. Quicken displays the average share price in **Price per Share**. If this matches the share price shown on your statement, you've filled in this dialog box correctly. Any funds remaining should be recorded using the **Record an Income Event** Easy Action.

Finally, type in a **Memo** and click **OK**.

Note that you shouldn't record stock splits as reinvestments. Stock splits are tax-free because although your shares have increased, their total value remains the same. Speak to a professional tax consultant if you are in any doubt about how to record certain dividends, bonus stocks, or income received.

Recording Stock Splits

Stock splits occur when the share price climbs higher or falls lower than the corporation's vision of the ideal share price. Often a stock is split to dilute the number of shares, making the shares more plentiful in the marketplace and promoting increased trade. Stocks might also be split to increase the number of shares still held by the company. These are often used as employee or customer incentives to promote loyalty in employment and trade.

When a stock splits, the value of your holdings doesn't necessarily increase, although news of a split is often greeted with enthusiasm. Instead, you receive a certain number of shares for every share you currently hold. The market price of the shares is correspondingly adjusted so that no one's holdings are adversely affected.

The most common split is a 2 for 1 split. This means that for every old share you currently hold you receive one more share, leaving you with two shares in total. The share price is halved so that everything else remains equal. However, shares aren't always split 2 for 1. You might receive 1.5 for one, giving you 50% more shares than you previously held. If you owned an odd number of shares in a 1.5 for 1 split, you'd also receive a divestment equal to the value of the odd share out, giving you 1.5 times your current holdings, minus one.

Splits are shown on your brokerage statement, but you can record them any time they have been confirmed.

With your investment register open, select **Easy Actions**, and choose **Stock Split**.

Type in the **Date** of the split, select the investment **Account**, and choose the **Security** that was split. Some of these options might be grayed out on your screen.

Use the **Split Ratio** group to record the ratio of old shares to new. For example, if the split was 2-for-1, enter **2** into **New Shares** and **1** into **Old Shares**. Alternatively, just record your old and new shareholding. For example, if you had 300 shares and now own 450 shares (a 1.5-for-1 split), simply type **450** into new shares and **300** into old shares.

Quicken doesn't calculate the new share price according to the ratio provided here. Instead, enter the new price in the **Price after Split** field. Also, update your portfolio's prices as soon as possible.

Type in a **Memo** and click **OK** to record the transaction.

Recording Margin Interest

A margin purchase is one where some or all of the funds sufficient for the purchase are borrowed from your broker or another margin lender. You usually need some funds to back up the amount you borrow, but most brokers and lenders offer up to a 50% margin on most stocks (enabling you to double your purchasing power), 75% on some, and 100% on a rare few. By borrowing the purchase price, you increase the amount you can lose if the price falls, but also increase the amount you can make if the price rises.

When you trade on margin, you need to record your monthly marginal interest expenses.

To record margin interest expense, open your investment register, select **Easy Actions**, choose **Advanced**, and then click **Margin Interest Expense**.

Type in the **Date**, select an investment **Account** if you are able, and enter the margin interest into the **Amount** field.

Next select the **Transfer Account**. This is the account from which the margin interest expense is paid. If your stockbroker has deducted this automatically, select the account that stores your investment account's cash balance, whether it is the investment account itself or a linked checking account. Quicken might also determine this account for you.

Finally, enter a **Memo** and click **OK**.

In most cases, margin interest expenses are tax deductible. Even though there doesn't appear to be any entry made in a tax-deductible expense account, Quicken records the margin interest transaction as an investment interest expense. You see it when you prepare reports for the end of the tax year.

Valuing Your Investments

So how much are your investments actually worth?

As you've probably guessed, Quicken provides a surfeit of methods with which you can view and calculate the market value and performance of your investments. Some of the most handy include:

- ➤ **The total market value field in Portfolio View**   Open the Portfolio View and look for the total at the bottom of the Mkt Value column. This shows the value for all the investments displayed, including any cash stored in those accounts. It doesn't include cash held in a linked checking account.

- ➤ **Through a Portfolio Value Report**   This is a printed version of the Portfolio View window with several enhancements. Read about it in the next section, "Creating a Portfolio Value Report."

- ➤ **With an Asset Allocation Graph**   This shows your investments broken down by sectors, market capitalization, or other aspects you specified when defining those securities (or downloaded at a later stage). See the section titled "Creating an Asset Allocation Graph" to learn about this graph.

- ➤ **Using an Investment Performance Graph**   View your investment performance on a monthly basis, subtotaled in several useful ways. See "Creating an Investment Performance Graph" later in this chapter to learn more about the Investment Performance graph.

- ➤ **By creating a Net Worth Report or Graph**   The Net Worth report and graph view your assets as a whole and are discussed later in a section titled, " What Are You Worth...Net?"

Creating a Portfolio Value Report

To create a Portfolio Value Report, open the **Reports** menu, select **Investing**, and choose **Portfolio Value**.

At first glance, the report looks like a printable version of the Portfolio View. After all, both offer cost basis, current price, gain or loss, and the balance. However, the Portfolio Value Report improves on the Portfolio View because it enables you to subtotal by investment goal, asset class, or security type.

Use the drop-down menus and fields at the top of the report pane to adjust the dates bracketed by the report as well as the facet of your portfolio used to generate subtotals. Don't forget to click **Update** to generate a new report reflecting those changes.

Creating an Asset Allocation Graph

Asset Allocation Graphs are useful because they show you at a glance how well you have spread your investment portfolio.

To create an Asset Allocation Graph, open the **Reports** menu, select **Investing**, and choose **Investment Asset Allocation Graph**. A graph similar to that shown in the following figure appears.

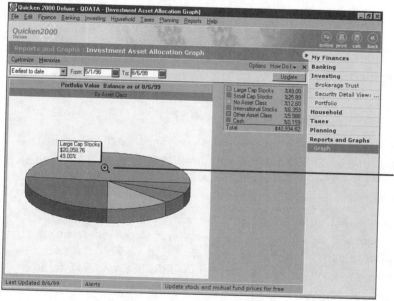

Want to see how your assets are divided? Use the Asset Allocation Graph to see this information at a glance.

Click once to view totals for each segment listed, or twice to zoom in on this piece of the pie.

This graph shows all securities that have had their Asset Class specified either when they were created or later through editing or downloading asset classes.

The first level of the pie chart shows a breakdown by all asset classes; by double-clicking on a segment of the pie you can zoom in to target the individual investments.

Creating an Investment Performance Graph

The Investment Performance Graph is made up of two panes. (Like the others, you find it under the **Reports**, **Investing** menu.) The uppermost pane shows your portfolio's dollar value either for all of your securities or those selected using the **Customize** function.

Try clicking the buttons that run across the top of the upper pane: **Type**, **Goal**, **Security**, **Account**, and **Asset Class**. Use these to compare the performance of accounts held with different stockbrokers or mutual fund managers, or set up a race comparing one investment goal to another. If you want to exclude certain accounts or securities from the graph, click **Customize** and use the listings under the **Accounts** and **Securities** tabs to deselect those you don't want to view in the graph.

This graph is enormously useful for seeing how your investments have performed, not only on their own but also as compared to the rest of your investments. As with all Quicken graphs, double-click any section to see a more detailed view of the makeup of each column.

The lower graph indicates your portfolio's Average Annual Total Return. This is shown as a heavy black horizontal line that runs in front of each column.

Pause the mouse over the colored block at either end of this line to view your Internal Rate of Return (IRR).

Internal Rate of Return?

The IRR is an important indicator of your portfolio's performance; it shows, in compounded percentage terms, exactly how your investments are doing, allowing you to make a direct comparison with bonds, bank savings rates, or some other fixed rate investment.

An IRR of 58.2% means that those investments have earned or grown (both factors are taken into account) at a rate equal to them being deposited in a bank account that happens to earn interest at 58.2%. During Bull markets, it is not uncommon to see highly aggressive investment earning IRRs between 50% to 80%.

The IRR is different to the growth rate figures you have already seen on other investment reports because it takes historical activity, compounding, and the investment period into account.

In doing so, the IRR formula looks at when the investments were purchased and when they were sold, adding in dividends, market value, reinvestments, and other factors.

Each column in the lower graph shows the IRR of the individual accounts, investments, goals, asset classes, or investment types, according to the button selected at the top of the graph. By comparing these to the annual average line, you can easily see which investments are not performing up to the market average and which are pulling more than their own weight.

The ability to adjust the timeline and the components that contribute to the graph makes it almost infinitely adaptable.

Improving the Graphing Accuracy

Although Quicken's 3D column graphs look wonderfully aesthetic, they're not as accurate as 2D graphs because their 3D depiction makes it more difficult to compare the top edge of one column to another. You can fix this by switching to 2D graphs. Simply click to pull down the **Options** menu in the upper-right corner of the graph window and select **Draw in 2D (faster)**. This also does wonders for estimating the comparative size of different segments of a pie chart.

What Are You Worth...Net?

Your net worth is the value of your assets minus your liabilities. In other words, your equity. With any luck, this is more than "nyet" worth.

From an investment point of view, the net worth is a very convenient means of seeing how your investments stack up. For example, if you buy stocks on margin, a slightly doctored Net Worth report or graph will help you to view your changing assets, liabilities, and what you would be worth if your investment assets were immediately liquidated and your investment liabilities immediately satisfied with the proceeds.

The following steps help you to create a New Worth Graph targeted only to your investment assets and liabilities.

First open the **Reports** menu, select **Own & Owe**, and choose **Net Worth Graph**.

The standard Net Worth Graph includes all of your assets and liabilities. For our means, that tends to cloud the picture. Instead, click **Customize** to open the Customize Graph dialog box and select the **Accounts** tab.

You should see a long list of ticks beside every type of Quicken account. Remove the ticks beside every account with the exception of your investment accounts and their linked checking or cash management accounts. You do not want to include your ordinary checking or liability accounts, but you might also like to include other major investments that have their own asset accounts—for instance, any mortgage and asset accounts that apply to your home.

When you've finished, click **OK** to produce a customized graph such as the one shown in the following figure.

This graph includes all the investment accounts, but excludes major asset accounts, providing a truer picture of portfolio performance as compared to overall net worth.

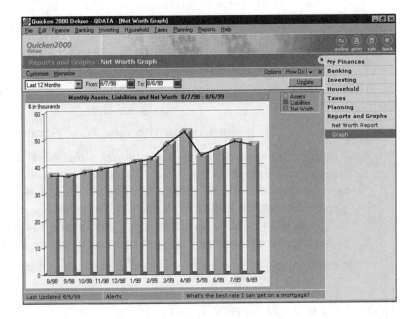

The Net Worth Report provides the same information as the graph, except that it displays that information as columns of figures instead of a single graph. Also, you may choose a time interval and period; for instance, weekly, monthly, or quarterly. This shows your changing net worth over that time at that interval.

To create a Net Worth Report, open the **Reports** menu, select **Own & Owe**, and choose **Net Worth Report**.

Use the **Interval** drop-down list at the top of the report window to select the cycle over which you want summations of your net worth. (The default setting of **None** generates an "as of now" report.)

To change the accounts contributing to this report, click **Customize** to open the Customize Graph dialog box, click the **Accounts** tab, and deselect all those not directly linked to your investments. Click **Create** to generate the report.

Memorizing Your Customized Reports or Graphs

If you find the customized report or graph you've just created particularly useful and feel almost certain you'll want to revisit it in the future, memorize it so you don't need to customize it each time. With it displayed onscreen, simply click the **Memorize** button that appears at the top of the report or graph's pane. Provide a title in the **Title** field, select an appropriate set of **Report Dates** (the Named Ranges fluctuate so they always display, say, the last 12 months from the date you next create the report), choose an optional **Description** and **Icon**, and click **OK**. Your memorized reports and graphs appear as an extra entry under the Reports menu. For more information on memorized reports or graphs, see Chapter 8, "Powerful Reports and Great Graphs."

After you have customized the report and graph, you can produce a useful hard copy by clicking the **Print** button at the top of the report or graph window.

The Least You Need to Know

➤ Some of the transactions that can be recorded by Quicken are mightily complex, but there's usually a shortcut or some form of assistance lurking around the screen that can make life that much easier.

➤ Using the Easy Actions built into each investment register is a perfect example. Yes, it is possible to construct almost every investment transaction through a complex series of register entries, but why would you bother?

➤ When you buy or sell shares, don't forget that you can also specify different "lots". These may have capital gains implications, but you can also estimate those as described in Chapter 10, "Deductions and Capital Gains."

➤ Use Quicken for all your investment-related transactions, including recording income events, stock dividends, stock splits, and margin interest. If you're a particularly active trader, look into an online brokerage who also allows you to download your statements. You'll save yourself loads of time.

➤ The investment-related reports and graphs are a great way to step back and admire the big picture or get right into the nitty-gritty of your investment performance. Visit them regularly through the Investment Center.

Part 5

Minding Your Business

Small business is big business to the economy. More than any 3M or IBM, small business pays the wages of millions of Americans. If you're not minding your own business, your own income, and your own future, you're probably overly busy with someone else's.

In this section you learn how to set up small business accounts and track your debtors and creditors. With Quicken Home and Business 2000, you'll find it easy to keep the cash flowing, the creditors credited, and the rest of your business running just as it should.

Chapter 16

An Instant MBA

In This Chapter

➤ How Quicken can help you with your business

➤ What you need to start

➤ Should you use cash- or accrual-based accounting

➤ Getting by with Quicken Basic or Quicken Deluxe

➤ Making it easier with Quicken Home & Business

➤ Using categories and classes to manage business transactions

---

Making Big of Small Business Accounting

Although Quicken is the perfect package to take care of your personal finances, it is equally adept at looking after your business. Just as you can use Quicken to track your income and expenses, you can also use it to track your business income and expense transactions. And just as you can use Quicken to track amounts you owe or are due, you can also use it to keep tabs on the business' receivables and payables.

Indeed, there's not much you can't achieve with Quicken: use classes to set up individual profit and loss centers, create an asset account to look after the petty cash, and, if you use Quicken Home & Business, build an inventory, generate invoices, track your creditors, print aged receivables and payables reports, and even more.

Getting Ready to Run

Before you begin, consider whether you want to combine your business and personal data, or keep them in separate files.

Combining your data has some advantages. For example:

➤ Easy transfer of funds between accounts.

➤ Simplified tax preparation.

➤ The ability to record splits so that one transaction can cover personal and business expenses.

➤ Fewer files to back up.

➤ When Quicken starts, it automatically loads the default file. With a single personal and business file, you never need to jump between the two.

➤ Corrections to transactions incorrectly assigned, as personal or business are more easily corrected.

➤ Net Worth reports which include both personal and business data.

You can also create a second Quicken data file devoted exclusively to your business. This method has some advantages and some disadvantages:

➤ Your data is separated, enabling you to assign different passwords to each file. This means you can assign someone else the task of recording your business transactions without worrying about that person being able to view your personal data.

➤ You won't need to resort to quite so many classes and subclasses trying to separate your business and personal transactions. This saves you some set-up time and also makes ongoing data entry a little more efficient.

➤ If you sell your business, you can turn over the business data without also turning over your personal information.

➤ This is the primary disadvantage: you might need to double-up on some of your data. For example, the transactions that record a transfer of funds from your business to personal bank account have to be recorded twice; once for each set of books.

➤ If you have a combined business and personal checking account, you'll find that attempting to manage it across two sets of books is completely unworkable.

The method you use is entirely up to you, and it depends to a certain extent on the nature of your business. For example, if your business runs under the auspices of a corporation, you're probably best setting it up as a separate file. This simplifies tax preparation and lends a certain propriety that keeps your personal finances and those of your company at arm's length. You should also keep in mind that if you feel your business is large enough to justify its own separate file, it might benefit even more from a small business accounting package such as Intuit's QuickBooks.

QuickBooks

Quicken can't match the numerous business accounting features built into QuickBooks and QuickBooks Pro—Intuit's dedicated small business accounting suites.

If you are connected to the Internet, you can learn more about QuickBooks at `http://www.quicken.com/quickbooks/`.

For Quicken-related small business tips and advice, go to `http://www.quicken.com/small_business/`.

A good rule of thumb is to combine your records if you run a micro business—you work for yourself, you don't employ anyone else, and you only have a few business transactions each week. Any business bigger than that should have its own file.

Setting Up for Cash- or Accrual-Based Accounting

However you go about it, you need to add some specialized accounts to your file to handle the unique financial needs of your business.

This might be no more complex than a checking register, but there's a very good chance you need to add accounts to track your business' bank accounts, payables, receivables, petty cash, payroll withholding, and, in some cases, inventory.

However, before you even begin doing so, decide whether your business uses cash or accrual-based accounting. This decision has numerous taxation ramifications. Indeed, the IRS requires that you nominate a method when you file your return, and it doesn't particularly like any business changing its tax basis thereafter.

Cash-based accounting is easier to manage than accrual-based accounting because expenses aren't recognized until the money actually changes hands, and income isn't taken into account until the money is in the bank.

When you use cash-based accounting, you record amounts you owe as checks post-dated to when they are due to be paid, or you can set those payments as scheduled transactions.

Amounts you are owed, your receivables, are recorded when you receive payment, not when you perform that service or sale unless, of course, those dates coincide. The amount you receive is recorded directly into the checking account and is usually credited to a gross sales income account.

Accrual-based accounting tracks accounts receivable and accounts payable as they are incurred, not when they eventually are settled. You do this by setting up asset and liability accounts in which to store your receivables and payables.

Now, you can do this in any version of Quicken. However, Quicken Home & Business makes it easier because it provides an invoicing framework that looks after the mechanics of customer payments, credit, returns, and so on, much as the Easy Actions menu in your investment registers looks after the mechanics of stock transactions, dividend reinvestments, and so on.

For that reason, this section of the book is mostly suited to Home & Business users. But just so users of Quicken Basic and Quicken Deluxe don't feel left out, here's your business management in a nutshell.

Managing a Business with Quicken Basic and Quicken Deluxe

You can't generate printable invoices in Quicken Basic or Quicken Deluxe, but if you use the accrual method of accounting, there's nothing to stop you from creating an asset account for your receivables and a liability account for your payables.

This has the advantage of providing you with a far more accurate financial picture. For instance, one glance at the accounts receivable register tells you precisely how much you are owed. A similar look at accounts payable tells you how much you owe. Use this information to create a balance sheet and you can see just how healthy your business really is.

But what transactions should you put in those accounts, and, for that matter, when?

Table 16.1 is provided to help you set up the appropriate accounts to track certain aspects of your business. I recommend that you don't jump in and create them all at once. Start with the receivables and payables accounts and, after you feel confident in how they work, move on to the rest.

Table 16.1 Account Types in Quicken Deluxe

Name	Type	Used For
Receivables	Asset	Storing the value of invoices awaiting payment.
Payables	Liability	Storing the value of bills that need to be paid.
Inventory	Asset	Tracking the value of your stock.
Petty Cash	Cash	Balancing the petty cash drawer.
Cash Float	Cash	Balancing the cash register.
Furn. and Fittings	Asset	Tracking the value of your office furniture and fittings.

Name	Type	Used For
Plant and Equip.	Asset	Tracking the value of your business equipment.
Motor Vehicles	Asset	Tracking the value of the business car fleet.
Sales Tax	Liability	Keeping track of any sales tax collected.
Loans	Liability	Storing the startup costs and other loans you or other people make to the business.

To record your receivables, type them directly into the receivables register, using the payee field to target the debtor, the increase column to show the total due, the category field to target a business income category, and the memo field to note the date this invoice is due.

When you receive payment, target the debtor using the payee field, the decrease column to show the total paid, and the category field to indicate a transfer to your business checking account.

You can view and print a report on each of your debtors by opening the **Reports** menu, selecting **Business**, and choosing **Accounts Receivable Report**. If things don't appear to work as you intended, make sure the appropriate accounts are selected through the **Accounts** tab of the **Customize** function.

You can track your payables in much the same way. When you incur the debt, type it directly into the payables register. This time use the payee field for the creditor, the increase column for the amount, and the category field to target a business expense category. You can also use the memo field to note when the payment is due.

When you pay the bill, again target the creditor with the payee field, use the decrease column to show the total paid, and use the category field to transfer the funds from your business checking account. If you use Quicken to print checks, do all of this from the Write Checks window, using the category field to show a transfer to your payables account. Either way, your debt is paid.

You can view and print a report on each of your creditors by opening the **Reports** menu, selecting **Business**, and clicking **Accounts Payable Report**.

Managing a Business with Quicken Home & Business

If you use Quicken Home & Business, you still need to create accounts to specifically handle your debtors and creditors, but with full invoice generation, receivables and payables management and more, this version of Quicken is infinitely more flexible than attempting the same with Quicken Basic or Quicken Deluxe.

To start, create two new small business accounts.

Open the **Banking** menu, select **Bank Accounts** and choose **Account List**. Look to the Home & Business section of the accounts you can create, and select **Invoices/Receivables** shown in the following figure. Follow the rest of the New Account Set Up as was described in Chapter 5, "Accounting for Accounts."

The Invoices and Payables accounts can only be found in Quicken Home & Business.

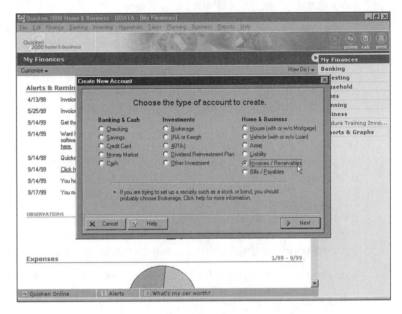

You can learn more about the receivables side of Quicken Home & Business in Chapter 17, "Managing Your Receivables."

When you need to handle your creditors, select and set up an account of the **Bills/Payables** type. Payables are covered in Chapter 18, "Paying the Pipers."

Creating your payables and receivables accounts satisfies only a small part of the requirements for a business bookkeeping system. You also need a range of categories that can track your business income and expenses. All versions of Quicken provide an extensive set of business-related categories, already linked to Schedule C, that simplify your business tax preparation.

Creating Categories for Small Business

First, a quick recap: Categories group related income and expense transactions. For instance, you might pay your telephone accounts to two or more telecommunications companies, but by noting those payments as a telephone expense, you can look over your books and see at any given time exactly how much has been spent on that utility, no matter to whom you made the payment.

Categories are important because they help you track your income and expenses, not only by the debtor or creditor, but also by how that money was used. At tax time, categories are also the perfect way to bundle up and claim your legitimate deductibles.

If you specified that you were using Quicken for your business when you installed the software, a complete set of small business categories is already built into your account books.

To view your existing categories, open the **Finance** menu and select **Category & Transfer List**.

If you don't see any business categories, you might want to try importing some from those Quicken holds in reserve.

Doing so is easy. With the Category & Transfer List displayed, click the **Options** button and select **Add Categories** from the drop-down menu. Select **Business** from the **Available Categories** menu as shown in the following figure. All Quicken's business categories should appear in the scrolling list on the left of the dialog box.

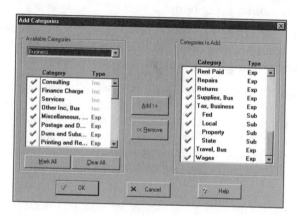

If you haven't already imported your business categories, please do so now; it makes your life easier.

Click **Mark All** to flag every business category, and then click **Add>>** to copy those categories to the scrolling list on the right.

Click **OK** to complete the import or **Cancel** to exit.

Business Classes and Categories

By assigning categories to your transactions, you help Quicken keep track of your books by using at least some of the principles of double-entry accounting.

Double-Entry Accounting

This accounting method maintains the integrity of a set of accounting books by ensuring that every transaction is documented in one or more ledgers that show exactly where it came from and where it went. The twin aspects to each transaction result in one entry in each of two registers, hence the term "double-entry."

Categories are useful, but they are also somewhat limited. For example, how would you normally go about separating a business payment from a personal payment if your books are built around a combination of both?

Assuming your business has its own checking account, the transactions are automatically separated. Just make sure you only ever assign business transactions to business categories, and personal transactions to personal categories.

What's the easiest way to keep your personal and business categories separated? Actually, it's very easy. Simply create Business Income and Business Expense categories and then set up subcategories under each to track your business transactions. For example, an architect might set up several categories under Business Income for Drafting, Consulting, 3D Modelling, and so on. Business Expense subcategories might include Computer Equipment, Rent, Electricity, Subcontracting, CAD Output, and My Wages.

If your business has its own separate file—in other words, you haven't decided to combine it with your existing data—your job's even easier. Don't worry about specific Business Income and Business Expense categories; just create all the appropriate income and expense subcategories as you would any other category.

You can also use classes to help keep business and personal transactions separate. Following are some ideas on how you might use classes in a business environment:

➤ **Personal**   Use this class to mark your personal transactions.

➤ **Business**   Use this one to mark your business transactions.

➤ **Client Name**   Assign a unique class name to each of your clients. This makes it easy to view every transaction ever applied to a particular client. In fact, Quicken Home & Business uses precisely this method to track its own invoices.

A Better Class System

It's most efficient, when using classes, if you set up class names of no more than two to three letters. For example, Rodgers and Hammerstein could become RH. Alternatively, create a client list and assign each client a numerical code. Although the numbers aren't easy to remember and can lead to typographical errors, you can lessen the likelihood by recording the full client name as the description for each class and then printing a copy of the class list. Stick it to the wall beside your computer for a handy reference.

➤ **Vendor Name**   Useful for quickly seeing just how much you've spent on paper clips and toner cartridges with Office Superworks, even if those expenses are normally stored in different categories.

➤ **Sales Staff**   Find out instantly exactly how much income each member of your sales staff generates.

➤ **Jobs/Projects**   Break down your income and expenses by job or project. Perfect for creating individual profit-and-loss reports. You can name them sequentially—for example, Job1, Job2, and so on—or by the actual job or project title.

➤ **Department**   Work out how much each department is receiving and spending by marking the transactions with a department class. As with jobs and projects, you might prefer a sequential numbering system or to just use each department's name.

Keep in mind that you can apply multiple classes to any transaction, thus a service sold by one of your team members for a particular project could combine the Business, Sales Staff, and Project classes and appear in reports that target any or all three.

Assuming this was applied to a category such as "Gross Income," the contents of the category field in that transaction would look something like: Gross Income/business:staff name:project name. (Classes are separated from one another using colons ":".)

Filtering Reports and Graphs with Classes

After you have started using classes, it's easy to filter Quicken's reports and graphs so they display only the segment of the data in which you're interested.

To do so, select the report or graph from Quicken's **Reports** menu.

Then click the **Customize** button in the Report or Graph window.

Click the **Include** tab and in the section titled **Select to Include**, click **Classes**. This causes all your classes to be listed in the box to the left of that option, as shown in the following figure.

Creating a job-based report through classes rather than categories. The classes ensure only relevant transactions appear in the report.

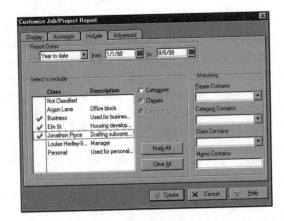

Indicate the classes you want to include in this report or graph by clicking beside each on the left side of the Class list. Quicken places an arrow beside those that will be included. This works on a toggle system, so just click again to deselect each class. From our example above, you could view a report or graph that considers transactions solely related to the staff member or the project itself. This is an easy way to create Profit and Loss reports on any staff member (what have they brought in compared to their wages), or to consider the profit and loss on a project itself, separating it from the rest of your books.

When you're finished selecting classes, just click **Create** to generate the new report or graph.

The Least You Need to Know

➤ Quicken's small business facilities aren't perfect (that's why Intuit made the inestimable QuickBooks), but they still are very darn good.

➤ If you use Quicken Home & Business and your business doesn't require stringent inventory or quoting control, make sure you consider the built-in Receivables and Payables accounts before looking to other software.

➤ Categories and classes can make a huge difference to the information you can extract from your financial data. By targeting transactions classified as business-related, and then further breaking them down by individual projects or a particular person's involvement, you can create an extraordinarily powerful data mining tool. Got the drill?

➤ If you look in the Quicken program group included in your Start, Programs menu, you'll see a link called "**Install QuickPayroll**." Click it and give it a go. You may be surprised at the difference it can make to your payroll management.

Chapter 17

Managing Your Receivables

In This Chapter

➤ Debtor management with Quicken Home & Business

➤ Creating invoices for your customers

➤ Handling payments and refunds

➤ Debt collection routines

➤ Giving your invoices that jazz

Getting Those Debtors Under Control!

I don't know anyone who has succeeded in business without really trying, but I do know that success in business is next to impossible to achieve without a solid system of debtor management. Out-of-control receivable accounts can spell disaster for any business's cash flow and stifle growth to the point of suffocation.

This, as I'm sure you've guessed, is where Quicken comes to the rescue, leaping tall buildings while rescuing poor debtor lists in distress. (Apparently the citizens of Metropolis have to put up with a mere substitute.)

All the releases of Quicken are great at managing your debtors, although Quicken Home & Business 2000 does boast features that enable you to more easily create invoices, record payments, note credits, and track a payroll. However, with the addition of a receivables account, both Quicken Basic and Quicken Deluxe can help you take control almost as effectively.

The techniques for managing receivables through Quicken Basic and Quicken Deluxe are quite different from those in Quicken Home & Business. This chapter considers only Home & Business. For a quick overview of debtor management with Quicken Basic and Quicken Deluxe, please turn to Chapter 16, "An Instant MBA."

What's Taking So Long!?

Although Home & Business makes it easy to record invoices, log payments, create credits, and so on (these options are simply entries you pull down from a menu), it also adds a great deal of functionality similar to that found in specialized small business management software. This makes it a little tricky to just jump in, light the burners, and start shooting out those invoices. The good news is that when you're up to speed, you have little trouble zipping through business transactions faster than the speed of light.

Invoicing Overview

The following figure shows the Home & Business version of the invoicing register. This window is based on the usual register pane, but it adds some extra features.

Each transaction recorded in this register represents an invoice, payment, credit, refund, finance charge, transfer, or any other transaction you elect to record if you ignore the Home & Business edition's built-in forms. (Invoices and most other common business transactions use forms to receive your data entry before storing that information in the register.)

Most of the transactions you need to create are available through the **Create New** drop-down menu at the top of the register window.

The forms use the category field, much as split transactions do, to store their data. After you have created one of the main transaction types, you can edit it by selecting that transaction in the register and either clicking the small green tick in the category field or the **Form** button in the transaction toolbar.

The register's remaining functions are designed to simplify tracking debtors or, in the case of the bills/payables register, creditors. For example, the **Report** drop-down menu at the top of the Register pane (not the **Report** menu that lives in the menu bar) helps you to create a report about the current payee, showing all transactions recorded for that payee between two dates. You can also print a similar report for the entire register or create a debt-collection report that shows all unpaid invoices.

Create a new transaction
using specialized forms.

Create a register report or
list of unpaid invoices.

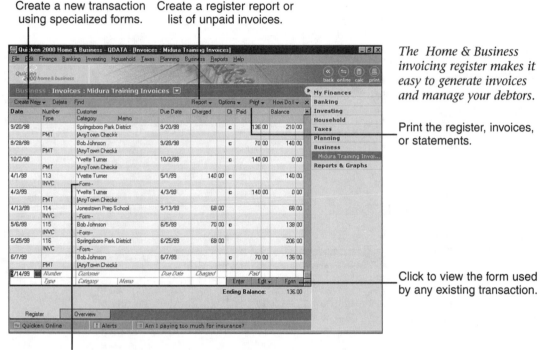

*The Home & Business
invoicing register makes it
easy to generate invoices
and manage your debtors.*

Print the register, invoices,
or statements.

Click to view the form used
by any existing transaction.

--Form-- shows this transaction uses one of the
Home & Business forms rather than a split.

The **Print** drop-down menu also enables you to create a register report. However, you also can print a copy of the current invoice, print all unprinted invoices, and print customer statements.

Before looking at those, let's cover the basics first. Before you can do anything else, you need to record some invoices.

Recording Invoices Made Easy

To record an invoice with Quicken Home & Business, first open the **Business** menu and select **Create Invoice**. If you already have your business register open, an easier way to create a new invoice is to pull down the **Create New** menu at the top of the register pane and select **Invoice**.

However you get there, you should end up at the Create Invoice dialog box shown in the following figure, although without my sample data.

The invoicing module in Quicken Home & Business is based on the same module in the QuickBooks accounting package.

Select or create a customer.

Choose an invoice template format.

Record this invoice and optionally print it later.

Provide basic invoice information here.

Apply payments to this invoice.

Record the items or services that make up the invoice here.

Enter an optional message to print on the invoice.

Immediately print this invoice.

Record an optional memo for the transaction register.

Select an account to track tax collected.

Indicate the tax component.

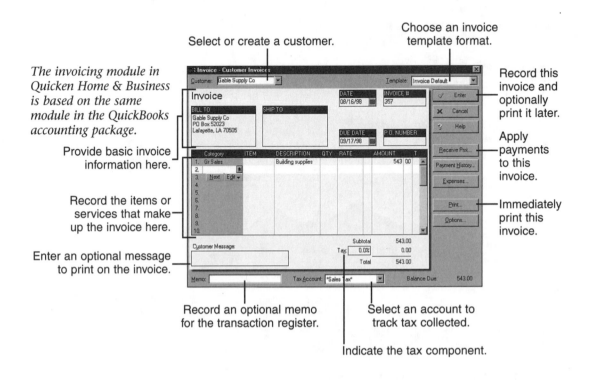

Enter the **Customer** name and fill in the **Bill To** and **Ship To** address blocks as required. Both addresses print on the invoice, but only the Bill To address appears in the window of Intuit's windowed envelopes. Depending on the number of lines you enter in the Bill To address, you might need to press your **Tab** key up to four times to work your way to the Ship To field, and then up to another four times to move on to the Date field.

Reusing Addresses

Each time you create an invoice for a previous customer, Quicken automatically fills in the Ship To and Bill To address blocks for you. Quicken also stores this information in the Financial Address Book and updates existing entries, if necessary. You can select the same customer and fill in the addresses either by entering the name into the Customer field or by selecting that customer from the pull-down list. Incidentally, you won't actually see the pull-down list until you have recorded at least one invoice.

Ship To Shortcut

There's a quick way to copy the Bill To address to the Ship To address with a single keystroke. Simply press **Tab** so that the entry cursor is in the Ship To address block and press the quote key (').

Record the **DATE, DUE DATE, INVOICE #** (Number), and customer's **P.O. NUMBER** (Purchase Order Number), if applicable. The invoice date is set to today's date and the due date is set for 30 days hence. The invoice number automatically increments after you have given it a starting point in your first invoice, so in the future you only need to confirm it rather than entering it.

Setting the Default Due Date Calculation

You can change the default setting for the due date by clicking the invoice dialog box's **Options** button and specifying a new **Default Due Date**. Click **OK** to return to the invoicing window.

Okay, at this point you have completed providing general information about this invoice. Now you need to get down to the specifics.

The lower half of the invoicing pane is used to record the items that make up the invoice. Quicken provides a basic inventory function you can use to define items with set characteristics, such as an associated income/expense category, sales or purchase price, sales tax tracking, and more. The next time you need to use that item, just type in the item code and all the other details are automatically inserted.

It also enables you to ignore the built-in inventory functions and to specify categories, descriptions, and prices on each line.

In general, most retail businesses use preset items because nearly everything they sell is based on a certain number of units of a particular product. What might not be so obvious is that service industries can also make excellent use of items to quickly fill invoices that deal with services often provided. For instance, an auto-mechanic might create an item for "Check and rotate tires".

To create an item invoice with a new invoice item, click the **ITEM** column of the first blank line you see in the list of invoice items. Ignore the **CATEGORY** column for now.

Enter the item code of the item you want to recall or select it from the list. (You only see the list after you have created items.) Press the **Tab** key. If Quicken can match your code, it fills in the rest of that item line for you. (If it can't, answer **Yes** in the next dialog box to create a new item and skip ahead to the next section, "Creating a New Invoice Item.")

After you have selected an item, use your **Tab** key to adjust the **DESCRIPTION**, **QTY**, and **RATE**. Click the **T** column to toggle the taxable status of this item. All items marked with the T are included in the tax calculation that contributes to the invoice's total.

Click **Next** to record this item and move to the next line. (Use the **Edit** menu to insert or delete items from the current position in the invoice.)

If you would prefer not to use the item inventory, simply ignore the ITEM column. Instead, use **CATEGORY** to select an income category that can be used to track sales of this item. Then set the quantity, rate, and taxable status of the item. Click **Next** to record this item and move to the next line. Feel free to combine both types of items into one invoice.

Tracking Reimbursable Expenses

A reimbursable expense is one that you incurred on behalf of your client. Reimbursable expenses are indicated as such in your checking register by clicking in the **Exp** column unique to Quicken Home & Business. After you have recorded reimbursable expenses, you can bill them to your client by clicking **Expenses**, which is available in the invoicing screen. Click in the **Use** column beside each expense you want to include in the current invoice.

Now you are ready to complete the invoice. Enter an optional **Customer Message** and **Memo**, and confirm the **Tax** percentage and the **Tax Account**. The tax account is the liability account used to track the sales tax you collect on invoices. Pull down the Tax Account menu to edit the account used or to even add an alternate one. Why would you need more than one? If you run more than one business, you need to file more than one return. In that situation, it's easier sending the tax to separate accounts.

If any amount has already been paid on this invoice, click **Receive Pmt** and fill out the Payment dialog box as described under the "When the Check Comes In" section that comes later in this chapter.

To immediately print this invoice, click **Print** and, in the next dialog box, **OK**. To add it to the to-be-printed list, just click **Enter**.

Creating a New Invoice Item

You can create new invoice items in two places: from the invoicing window when writing a new invoice and from the Manage Invoice Items dialog box. (Open this dialog box by clicking the **Business** menu and selecting **Manage Invoice Items**. Then click **New** to create a new invoice item, as shown in the following figure.)

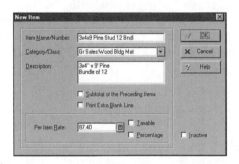

Long descriptions, and preset prices and categories make invoice items the easiest way to record sales of oft-provided goods and services.

Start with the Item Name/Number for the item you want to sell. You can use up to 30 characters in your code, including spaces, but I've always found it most useful to use a shorter, more efficient code. Use the large description field attached to every item for plain-English identification.

Useful Item Codes

How you use item codes is entirely up to you, but many retailers use the code assigned to that item by their suppliers. This makes it easier to memorize codes and also to match invoice items to items in your inventory. The next time you want to use an item, either select it from the list that appears in the ITEM column or type in sufficient letters of the code to uniquely identify that item. Quicken conveniently fills in the rest.

Enter or select a **Category** and **Class** and provide a Description. Quicken supports descriptions that run over more than one line, so feel free to be as explicit or terse as you need.

Click to select **Subtotal of the Preceding Items** if you want the price of this item to be based on all those recorded previously. You can use this to create items such as "Total for job," and then include more than one job on the invoice. The totaling of previous items runs from the first line in the invoice or the first line after a previous subtotal item.

Click to select **Print Extra Blank Line** if you would like to add a line after this item on the printed invoice. This is especially useful if you record items with lengthy descriptions.

Use the **Tab** key to navigate to the field **Per Item Rate**. This field displays the item's sale price. You can record a base standard here and edit it on the invoice if necessary. Selecting **Taxable** indicates this item should contribute to the Tax amount shown in the Customer Invoices dialog box. You can also change the tax status when creating the invoice. This type of tax is usually a sales tax and by default is set to be posted to a Sales Tax liability account.

Click **Percentage** to apply the figure recorded under the Per Item Rate to the preceding item in the invoice list. For example, if you created an invoice with a single item in it that summed $120 and you then added another item whose Per Item Rate was set to 20 and whose Percentage setting was also selected, the total for that additional invoice item would equal $24, or 20% of $120, making an invoice total of $144. This percentage adjustment only applies to the last item in the invoice. It does not apply to the total invoice. Therefore, if another line totaling $100 existed before the $120 item in the invoice, the total would still equal only $244.

Click **Inactive** to hide this item from the items list. You might do this if you only sell an item occasionally or during a particular time of the year and don't want it clogging up the items list at other times. Finally, click **OK** to save the item.

Making an Inactive Item Active

To make an item active again, open the **Business** menu and select **Invoice Items**, choose the item from the Customize Invoice Items dialog box, click **Edit**, deselect **Inactive** and click **OK**.

When the Money Starts Rolling In

Quicken Home & Business makes it easy to receive payments and apply them to specific invoices. The system enables you to indicate actual amounts received or to apply credits to existing invoices. All you need to do is select the customer, specify an account into which the payment has been deposited, enter the amount of the payment, and then choose how much and to what invoices it is applied.

To record a payment, open the **Business** menu and select **Receive Customer Payment** or, if you already have the Customer Invoices register open, click **Create New** and select **Customer Payment** from the menu. Either way, you see the dialog box shown in the following figure. The upper section is used to specify the payment details and the middle to apply existing credits. The lower section lists all open invoices (that is, those not yet paid in full).

Identify the customer, and record basic transaction information.

Select to use current credits in this payment.

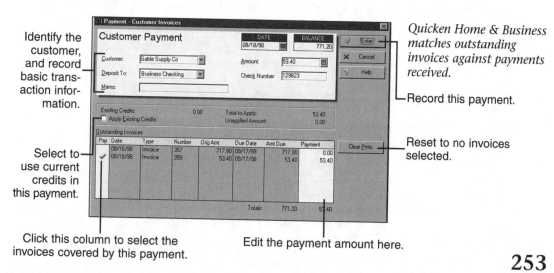

Quicken Home & Business matches outstanding invoices against payments received.

Record this payment.

Reset to no invoices selected.

Click this column to select the invoices covered by this payment.

Edit the payment amount here.

Click in the **Date** field and confirm the date that payment was received. Quicken sets the date to today's, but you can type in another date as required. Press **Tab**.

Click in the **Customer** field and either type in or use the drop-down list to select the **Customer** making the payment. Press **Tab**.

Use **Amount** to enter the total amount you received in payment. (Ignore this if you are recording credits. Instead, see the next paragraph.) Quicken automatically applies the payment to the oldest invoices first, working forward until all the payment has been allocated. If the payments exceed the debt, any remainder becomes a credit. If you need to apply the payment to another invoice, click **Clear Pmts** and continue with these steps.

Select the **Deposit To** account. This is the account into which you deposit the funds you have received. The funds are transferred from the receivables account to the deposit account. Press **Tab**.

(Optional) Use the **Check Number** field to record the last few digits of the check number shown on the check you received for payment. This is handy when you later need to match payments received with your bank statement (that is, when recording a reconciliation). You may also choose to press **Tab** and record a memo in the **Memo** field. Use this to enter any other information relating to this payment that you may want to record as part of your permanent records.

To use a current credit in this payment, click **Apply Existing Credits**. You can only apply credits stored in the name of the selected customer. Quicken applies credits to the oldest invoice working forward until the entire credit has been satisfied—or as much as possible. To apply the credit to other payments, click **Clear Pmts**.

The lower section of the Payments dialog box lists all outstanding invoices. Click the **Pay** column to include or remove invoices from this payment. Those included are indicated with a check mark. Click the **Payment** column to adjust the payment applied to each invoice. As you've already learned, Quicken marks invoices automatically, starting from the oldest and working forward. It also attempts to pay as many as possible in full. This matches the Balance Forward method of accounting. The open method can be simulated by matching invoices to their payments as those payments are received. After an invoice has been paid in full, it no longer appears in this list.

Click **Enter** when you've finished recording the payment.

Giving Credits Where They're Due

Crediting and refunding fully or partially paid invoices is almost automatic.

To create a credit, open the **Business** menu and select **Issue a Credit** or, if you already have the Customer Invoices register open, click **Create New** and select **Credit** from the menu. The dialog box that appears is almost identical to the Invoicing dialog box. In fact, they are identical. You can use it to indicate all those items returned for a credit the same way you originally recorded their sales, or you can simply type in a single line description, selecting an expense category such as Returns, describing the credit, and indicating the total in the Amount column.

Crediting Sales Tax

If you applied sales tax to the original invoice, make sure you indicate that in the credit. Do so the same way you recorded the tax. For example, by clicking the **T** column and specifying a percentage beside **Tax** at the bottom of the invoice. Also, make sure you are using the same tax account. This is the only way you can reduce the Sales Tax liability to take into account the canceled sale.

Complete the dialog box indicating those items for which you are providing a credit. Record the total and print the credit note, or click **Receive Pmt** to immediately apply this credit to a current invoice. You should give this to your customer.

After the transaction has been recorded as a credit you can apply it to other outstanding invoices through the Customer Payments function described previously in this chapter.

Recording Refunds

You can use credits to pay off the outstanding balance on other invoices, but you can't use it to actually pay back cash. For that you need to issue a refund.

The refund dialog box can be used to refund cash, record a handwritten refund check, record a printed refund check, or set up an online payment. You can also use this dialog box when you record a refund to a customer's credit card.

To record a refund, open the **Business** menu and select **Issue a Refund** or, if you already have the Customer Invoices register open, click **Create New** and select **Refund** from the menu.

Select the **Account to Pay From**. This is the account from which you are drawing to pay for the refund. Press **Tab**.

Choose the transaction type from the **Type of Transaction** field. Depending on the account you select, you can choose from a **Payment** (use for handwritten checks, cash, and credit card payments), **Print Check**, or **Online Pmt**. Press **Tab**.

Select the **Customer** and press **Tab**. If you are making the payment with a printed check or online payment, also click the **Address** button and provide the details requested.

Complete the dialog box by filling in the **Date**, **Amount**, **Memo**, and if you are handwriting the check, a check **Number**, pressing **Tab** to move between each field.

Click **Enter** to record the refund.

Printing a Hit List...Okay, a Debtor Report

Quicken Home & Business has a far more complete debtor management facility than Quicken Basic or Quicken Deluxe. To view outstanding invoices onscreen, open the **Business** menu and choose **Unpaid Invoices**. If you are already in the invoicing register, you can also click the **Report** pull-down menu (not Quicken's Reports menu) and select **Unpaid Invoices**.

After the Unpaid Invoices window appears, use the **Sort** pull-down menu to change the list so that it displays unpaid invoices arranged by Customer, Date, Amount, or other. Use the **Options** pull-down menu to view only those invoices past due and to hide other invoicing information.

Click **Print** and choose **List** to print the list of invoices currently displayed, select **Invoice** to print a copy of the current invoice, or **Statement** to generate statements for one or more of your customers. (See "Making a Statement" coming up next for more information.)

Viewing Unpaid Invoices

To view any of the invoices listed in the Unpaid Invoices window, simply double-click them with your mouse. Quicken moves to the Invoices register and opens the original invoice form. You can also open the form by double-clicking any invoice shown in the Invoices register.

Making a Statement

Statements are by far the easiest way to keep your debtors under control. They provide full account histories of your debtors much in the same way your bank statements do your own accounts, but they also list all outstanding invoices.

Quicken's statements begin with the opening balance for the selected period (usually a month) and end with the current balance due. In between, they list all transactions recorded for that customer in the register. These include invoices and payments, but also show how past credits were applied and when refunds were issued.

You can generate payments for one customer, selected customers, or all customers.

To print statements, open the **Business** menu and select **Create Statement**, or if you already have the Customer Invoices register open, click the **Print** pull-down menu at the top of the register window and select **Statement**. The dialog box shown in the following figure appears.

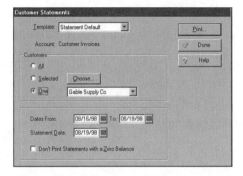

The Customer Statements dialog box helps you keep in touch with your debtors through regular postal reminders.

If you have created another statement template, click the **Template** drop-down list and select the alternative statement. Then press **Tab**. The default template should work fine in most situations. However, you can also create templates that might better suit your business. To do so, select **<New>** or **<Edit>** from the drop-down list. The options are similar to those provided when customizing an invoice, although you're able to turn on or off different columns and fields. You can learn more about this method of customization in "Customizing Home & Business Invoices" coming up later in this chapter.

Why Would I Customize Statements?

If you use pre-printed statements, you probably want to turn off the shading used behind column headers as well as the lines used between columns, as these are probably already built in to your pre-printed statements. You can also set up areas to print your company name, logo, and address information.

Select the groups of customers you want to include in this statement print run:

- ➤ **All**   Print statements for all customers with entries in the receivables register.
- ➤ **Selected**   Click **Choose** to select those customers you want to include. Hold the **Shift** key and click to select a range of customers, or hold the **Ctrl** key and click to pick them out one at a time.
- ➤ **One**   Select the customer from the list.

Click in the **Dates From** and **To** fields and enter the dates that determine the range of transactions you want to include in each statement. (You can also use the Calendar tool icons to the right of each field to select the dates you require.) Usually these encompass a set period such as the month just past. Also, specify a statement date. This is the date the statement was printed and, therefore, is usually today's date.

Finally, click to select **Don't Print Statements with a Zero Balance** to avoid printing statements where the customer is neither in debit or credit. This ensures you don't waste paper and postage printing statements for miscellaneous customers who paid cash or for those who have fallen inactive.

After you're finished selecting your statement options, click **Print** and **OK** to print the statements. Note that you also can use **Company Font** to change the look of your address details (if provided by customizing the statement template) and **Main Font** to change the typeface used throughout the rest of the statement.

Although it costs money to send out statements every month, they remain one of the most effective methods of debt collection. Use them in Quicken and your receivables register should remain remarkably up-to-date.

Hitting Them Where It Hurts: Finance Charges

Statements are a great reminder for your customers that certain bills are falling due, but it occasionally takes more than a gentle reminder to bring the message home to at least one or two of your clients that those bills actually need to be paid.

That's why the finance charge was invented. It's a penalty clause that, when enacted properly, not only helps ensure payment, but also recompenses you for opportunity lost, costs incurred through collection, and more.

The finance charge is recorded as an extra transaction in the register. However, it isn't usually printed as a separate item. Instead, it appears on the next statement you print for that customer.

With that in mind, let's take a look at what it takes to hit your more recalcitrant debtors where it hurts.

To apply a finance charge, go to your invoicing register, click the **Create New** menu, and select **Finance Charge**.

Click in the **Customer** field and either type in the customer's name or select the customer from the drop-down list. The customer is, of course, the original person or business to which this charge applies. Then press **Tab**.

Use the **Date** field to either confirm today's date or type in the date you want to use for the finance charge. (You can also use the Calendar tool icon to select the date from a pop-up monthly calendar display.) Press **Tab** to continue.

Type in a category or select the same using the **Category** drop-down list. It's usually a good idea to store finance charges in a special income category such as Other Income or even Finance Charges. Press **Tab**.

Record an optional number in the **Number** field for this finance charge (this is the number of the finance charge; you can ignore it if you don't record too many), press **Tab** and enter an optional memo in the **Memo** field. Both of these fields are optional. Press **Tab** to move on.

Select a due date for the charge using the **Due Date** field, either by typing in the date or by clicking the **Calendar tool** icon and selecting the date from the pop-up display. This date is the date by which time the charge is supposed to be paid.

The list of Unpaid Invoices doesn't contribute to the charge in any way. However, click in the **Use** column of any you believe should contribute to this charge (the column headed AGING is a good indicator because it provides the number of days the invoices are past due). Each selected invoice contributes to the Total shown at the bottom of the list.

Use the **Finance Charge** field to record the actual amount of this charge. Click the **Calculator** icon to use Quicken's built-in calculator to arrive at a percentage amount.

Click **OK** to save the charge, or **Cancel** to quit.

The finance charge appears on the next statement you print for this customer. You can remove it by locating and clicking on the charge in the receivables register and clicking **Delete** at the top of the register window.

Customizing Home & Business Invoices

Don't feel that you're stuck with Quicken's invoice design. There's a lot you can do to "get the look". With just a little customization you can:

➤ Adjust the information that appears on each invoice

➤ Select and change the column headers used for each item entry

➤ Create several different invoices, each ideal for a specific task

➤ Add your logo and other details to the invoice so that you can print the invoices as they are created

In Quicken it is possible to edit an existing invoice template or to create a new invoice template.

To edit an existing template, open the **Business** menu and select **Create Invoice**. Instead of filling in the invoice, pull down the **Template** drop-down list and choose **<Edit>**. (If you already have more than one invoice template, select the template you want to change in the Manage Templates dialog box and then click that dialog box's **Edit** button.)

You should eventually see the Edit Template dialog box shown in the following figure.

Edit your printable invoice templates from Quicken Home & Business.

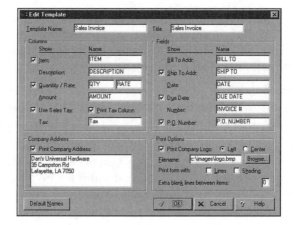

To create a new invoice template, select **<New>** from the Template drop-down list or Manage Templates dialog box instead.

As you can see, there's quite a comprehensive editing system built into Quicken. Indeed, you can change just about every aspect of the invoice to one degree or another.

When defining an invoice template, start with the **Template Name** text box. You can enter a new name for this invoice or edit an existing one. If you are creating invoices for different purposes, be quite specific. For example, Service Invoice, Professional Invoice, and Sales Invoice. Press **Tab** to move on.

Provide something descriptive in the **Title** text box. The title prints on the invoice generated by Quicken. In general, "Invoice" does just fine, but you might prefer to be more specific, perhaps using the same guidelines as for the Template Name. Press **Tab** to continue.

Use the Columns group to place or remove check marks from beside those columns you want to include on each invoice, and adjust the column heading of each to suit. If you work in the service industry, you probably prefer a more open invoice format by deselecting the **Item** check box to remove that column. If you also work on an hourly basis, you might like to change QTY to HOURS. In that situation, you probably won't require the Sales Tax column, so just click to remove **Use Sales Tax** and **Print Tax Column**. When you're finished setting these options, tab your way to the **Fields** group.

The fields print at the top and bottom of each invoice. As with the columns, you can click to place or remove check marks from beside each, and also edit the names of those fields. Keep tabbing until you reach the **Company Address** group.

Reverting to Form

If you make a mistake or change your mind about your column and field headers, click **Default Names** to revert back to Quicken's default entries.

If you aren't using pre-printed forms, click **Print Company Address** and enter your business's address details as required. Make the first line in the address block your company name. That's the only way you can include a business name on your invoices. You should also consider including your company or business registration number. When you're done, Tab to **Print options**.

To print a logo on your invoices, click **Print Company Logo**. Logos must be saved as a Windows Bitmap. (Nearly all painting packages, including Windows Paint, can do this.) Use the **Browse** button to find that logo on your hard drive and select whether you want it aligned to the **Left** or **Center** of the page.

Now you're almost done. If you aren't using pre-printed forms, select the **Lines** check box in the **Print Options** group. This draws lines around the fields such as the address block, as well as the column headers and between the columns. Without lines, your invoices can look very plain indeed. Click **Shading** to place a light gray stipple behind the field and column headers. Again, you should only do this if you aren't using pre-printed stationery because the default invoice format is compatible with the pre-printed business stationery available from Intuit. If you are using pre-printed stationery, the lines and shading are already there.

Finally, if you would like to open up your invoices by including a little extra spacing between each item, indicate the number of lines to add using the entry box to the right of **Extra blank lines between items**.

And that's it! Click **OK** to save your new invoice template.

The Least You Need to Know

➤ There are means and ways to manage debtors using Quicken Basic and Quicken Deluxe, but it's mighty difficult to beat the invoicing system built into Quicken Home & Business. Just remember, however, that any accounts receivable system is only as good as the operator. One of the quickest killers of any business is allowing the debtors to get out of control.

➤ The invoicing system built into Quicken Home & Business is based on that used in the best-selling QuickBooks business accounting suite. It's easy to learn and easy to use, and provides an easy way for any small business to present a professional face, even if you're working from the 10-foot attic above your parent's garage.

➤ The easiest way to track debtors is to generate invoices. However, the best way to stay on top of those debtors is to generate monthly statements. Print 'em, post 'em, and wait for the checks to come flying back.

➤ When a customer makes a payment, check first that it shouldn't be applied to an invoice. If you don't specifically apply payments to outstanding invoices (rather than, say, just recording a deposit in your trading account), Quicken will lose track of those that have and haven't been paid and, seemingly on its own, start generating rather terse reminders.

➤ Customize invoices to give them a flavor unique to your business. You can set up several unique customizations that are perfect for handling different services or jobs.

Chapter 18

Paying the Pipers

In This Chapter

➤ Becoming a credit to your creditors

➤ Paying the payables

Handling Your Business's Bills

Quicken Home & Business handles receivables and payables in very similar ways. If you've created invoices and recorded customer payments, you're going to feel right at home recording bills and your own payments.

The primary difference between the two systems is that billing doesn't support statements, finance charges, or reimbursable expenses. In addition, you cannot print the forms you use to record bills, so you can't use this system to generate purchase orders. This also means there is no forms customization facility.

You also won't find any mention of Invoice Items. This is a shame because it would be particularly handy for a retailer to be able to use the same product codes when recording the purchase of items and their subsequent sales.

Finally, you can't view unpaid invoices neatly sorted by their ages. However, the Accounts Payable report sorted by vendor provides almost as much information, so you don't miss out too much there. The good news is that these changes also simplify the steps we need to cover in this section. That not only saves trees, but a little bit of everyone's sanity. (And every bit helps.)

The following figure shows the Home & Business version of the billing register. This window is based on the usual register pane, but it adds some extra features.

Create a new transaction
using specialized forms.

Create a register report.

*The Home & Business
Payables register adds
several features beyond
those found in the other
Quicken editions.*

--Form-- shows this
transaction uses one of the
Home & Business forms
rather than a split.

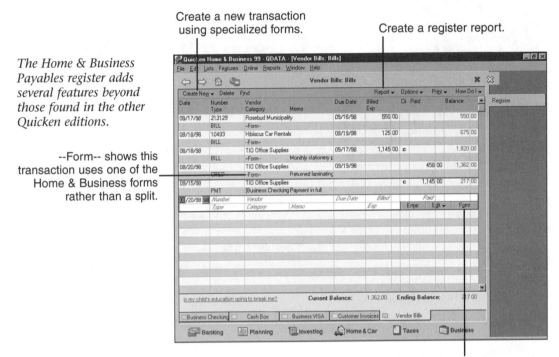

Click to view the form used
by any existing transaction.

Each transaction recorded in this register usually represents a bill, payment, credit, or refund.

The forms to record these are stored under the **Create New** drop-down menu at the top of the register window.

After you have created one of the main transaction types, you can edit it by selecting that transaction in the register and either clicking the small green tick in the category field or the **Form** button in the Transaction toolbar.

The register's remaining functions help you track the bills you need to pay. For example, the **Report** drop-down menu at the top of the Register pane (not Quicken's **Report** menu in the menu bar) can create a report about the current vendor that shows all transactions recorded between two dates. You can also print a similar report for the entire register, or create a creditor-payment report that shows all unpaid bills.

The **Print** drop-down menu also enables you to create a register report, including the complete billing information provided on each form. (In other words, you print all of the transactions included on each form, rather than a single line summary.)

So how do you record bills? Read on.

Recording Bills

To record a bill with Quicken Home & Business, open the **Business** menu and choose **Create Bill**. If you already have your payables register open, you can also create a new bill by pulling down the **Create New** menu at the top of the register pane and selecting **Bill**. However you get there, you should end up at the Bill - Vendor Bills dialog box shown in the following figure, although without the data already inserted.

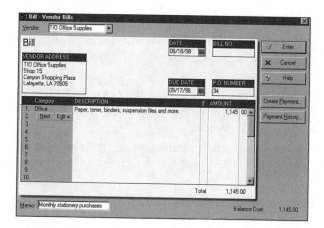

The billing module isn't as powerful as the invoicing module, but it does the job.

Use the field labeled **Vendor** to type in the creditor's name. Press **Tab** and use the **Vendor Address** area to record a new address or confirm the existing address. This is the creditor's address—not your own.

Click in the **Date** field and either confirm the date this bill was generated or type in a new date to change it. You can also use the Calendar icon to select the date from a pop-up calendar. Press **Tab** and indicate the **Bill No**. This is generally the vendor's invoice number, if known. Press **Tab** to proceed to **Due Date** and specify when payment for this bill falls due. The due date is automatically set 30 days forward, although you can edit this if required. Press **Tab** again and type in your own **P.O. Number** (Purchase Order Number), if applicable.

The lower half of the billing pane is used to specify the contents of the bill. You cannot use the invoice item inventory functions available in the invoicing window described in Chapter 17, "Managing Your Receivables." Instead, you are limited to providing a category, description, and amount for each line. You also can indicate any line as expensed—that is, to be used in the invoicing window as a reimbursable expense.

To begin, click in the **Category** column and select a business expense category. Alternatively, type in a new category name to create it as you go. Press **Tab** and provide a **DESCRIPTION**. Press **Tab** again and click in the **E** column to indicate if this item is a reimbursable expense. Press **Tab** again to move to the **AMOUNT** column and indicate the total amount of this billing item. Click **Next** in the Transaction toolbar to record this item and move to the next line.

After you have finished filling in the billed items, click in the **Memo** field and record an optional memo. You can use this to provide more descriptive information about this bill. For example, that the items were used for a certain purpose, job, or project.

If any amount has already been paid on this bill, click **Create Payment** and fill out the Payment to Vendor dialog box as described under "Making Payments," next.

If you haven't made a payment, click **Enter** to record this bill.

Making Payments

Quicken Home & Business makes it easy for you to pay your bills. All you need to do is select the vendor, specify an amount, and choose those bills to which that amount should be applied.

To record a payment, open the **Business** menu and choose **Make Payment to Vendor** or, if you already have the Bills/Payables register open, click **Create New** and select **Payment to Vendor** from the menu.

The upper section of the Payments dialog box is used to specify the payment details and the middle to apply existing credits. The lower section lists all outstanding bills (that is, those not yet paid in full).

Click in the **Date** field and confirm the date you are making this payment. Press **Tab** and select the vendor you are paying using the **Vendor** drop-down list. Press **Tab** again and use the **Amount** field to indicate the total amount you intend to pay. (Ignore this if you are paying using a previous credit. Instead, click **Apply Existing Credits**. You can only apply credits stored in the name of the selected vendor.)

Quicken automatically applies the payment to the oldest bills first, working forward until all the payment has been allocated. If the payments exceed your debt, any remainder becomes a credit. If you need to apply the payment to another bill, click **Clear Pmts** and continue with these steps. Press **Tab** to continue.

The **Withdraw From** field enables you to specify the account that provides the funds for this payment. Click within it and choose the account from the pull-down list. The funds are transferred from that account. Then press **Tab**.

Use **Check Number** as you would the Num column available in your checking register. You can use it to indicate a check that needs to be printed (select **Print Check**), a handwritten check (select **Next Check Num**), and several other types of payment. Also press **Tab** to move to the **Memo** field and record any other information you want to associate with this payment.

The lower section of the Payments dialog box lists all outstanding bills. Click in the **Pay** column to include or remove bills from this payment. Those included are indicated with a tick. Click in the **Payment** column to adjust the payment applied to each. As you've already learned, Quicken marks bills automatically, starting from the oldest and working forward. It also attempts to pay as many as possible in full. After a bill has been paid in full it disappears from this list.

Click **Enter** when you've finished to record the payment.

Handling Credits and Refunds You Receive

Looking after the credits or refunds you receive on paid bills is really quite easy.

First open the **Business** menu and choose **Receive a Credit** or, if you already have the Bills/Payables register open, click **Create New** and select **Credit** from the menu. You see a dialog box that appears to be almost identical to the Vendor Bills dialog box.

Select an income category such as Other, Inc, describe the return much as you did the original purchase, and indicate the total in the Amount column. Repeat for all the other credited goods or services applicable to this credit note.

Click **Enter** to record the credit or click **Create Payment** to immediately apply this credit to a current bill.

If you didn't immediately apply the credit to another bill, you can do so at any time when recording payments to the same vendor.

You can use credits to pay off the outstanding balance on other bills, but if the vendor pays you back in funds rather than credits, you need to record a refund.

To record a refund, open the **Business** menu and choose **Receive a Refund** or, if you already have the Bills/Payables register open, click **Create New** and select **Refund** from the menu.

Click **Account to Deposit To** and select any existing account using the drop-down list. You'll probably want to select your business checking account, but you can also choose a cash box account if, say, you've dropped the money into petty cash. Press **Tab** to continue.

Use the **Type of Transaction** drop-down list to select the nature of the transaction you are recording. This is generally a **Deposit**, but you might be able to select a different type of transaction, depending on the deposit account's capabilities. Press **Tab**.

Type the vendor's name into the **Vendor** field, or choose the vendor from the drop-down list; then press **Tab**.

Use the **Date** field to specify the date this transaction occurred, or select the date using the Calendar icon. Press **Tab** again.

Specify the total amount of this refund in the **Amount** field and press **Tab**.

Click inside the **Memo** field and type in any extra information you want to record with this refund and press **Tab**.

Use the final field, **Number**, to show the last few digits of the number of the check you received as a refund, if the refund was paid in that form.

Click **Enter** to record the refund.

And that's all there is to it.

Quicken Home & Business is small business management in a nutshell. Fortunately, that's not so tough a nut to crack.

The Least You Need to Know

➤ Although the Payables system built into Quicken Home & Business isn't quite so comprehensive as the receivables, it's still a great way to ensure you don't miss important payments.

➤ The Payables register helps you avoid over- or under-payments by providing a system where you can mark off your payments as you make them against specific invoices.

➤ Keep in mind that Quicken defaults to a "balance forward" method of marking off invoices. If you pay individual invoices rather than the balance, make sure you select the correct ones in the Payments dialog box.

Part 6

Extras, Extras: Read All About Them!

Quicken can do far more than look after your personal financial records, investments, tax planning, and small business. In fact, you'll find numerous handy extras scattered among its menus and windows. These include a program that can manage your home inventory, data back-up, and restore utilities, powerful search and replace tools, an emergency records organizer, and a financial address book.

In this section you'll also learn how to set Quicken's numerous customization options, and to transfer your data between Quicken files and other applications. This is an impressive feat, and it's also a fitting finale to what is by anyone's measure an extraordinary piece of software.

Chapter 19

Backing Up, Restoring, and Securing Your Data

In This Chapter

➤ Backing up data to file or floppy

➤ Restoring from a backup

➤ Securing with passwords

Backing Up Your Data

It's the sickening crunch of reason that does it. Why oh why didn't I back up my data?

It's not so much the resentment of redoing all that work, it's the tedium.

Survivors of a hard disk crash rarely let it happen again. They learn to back up their data before a single gremlin gets the chance to raise its big-eared head.

Regular backups are a vitally important part of safeguarding your data. After all, you can lose your Quicken information for all sorts of reasons ranging from accidentally deleting an important account, losing your computer to fire, theft, or some other catastrophe, to simply suffering a major or minor hard drive crash.

In fact, I've never known a hard drive to last more than five years without losing all its data, so be warned: the only way to beat the odds is by backing up.

Fortunately, backing up your Quicken data is easy. Quicken does it for you, storing it in the Backups folder of your Quicken directory every seven days. But there are also times you need to initiate a backup session yourself, especially after entering data for a lengthy period. (You wouldn't want to lose all that work, would you?)

Password Protection

Before you back up you might want to password-protect your data. This prevents someone else from recreating your Quicken file using the backed up data. You can learn about this extra security measure in "Securing Your Data," later in this chapter.

Quicken offers to back up your data every third time you exit the software. However, you can initiate a backup session at any time by opening the **File** menu and selecting **Backup** (**Ctrl+B**).

Read the introductory screen and, when you're ready, click **Yes**.

Select the **Backup Drive** you want to use, as shown in the following figure. You can back up to any compatible storage medium, including your hard disk drive, Iomega Zip disks, or floppy disks. To back up to a network drive you must first map that network connection to another drive letter. Your Windows manual tells you how to do this.

Back up your troubles? Quicken can archive your data to a floppy drive, hard disk drive, or any other Windows-compatible storage device.

Select **Current File** and click **OK** to begin. This backs up the file you were just using. To back up another Quicken file, click **Select from List** and then **OK**. You must choose the file you want to back up using the Back Up Quicken File dialog box. You should be familiar with this style of dialog box because it is based on the same file selection dialog box used throughout Windows.

Quicken stops if the backup needs to overflow to a second disk. Slide in a freshly formatted disk when prompted to continue.

How Do I Format a Disk?

You won't need much floppy disk space to complete your backup: one or two 1.4MB disks should prove sufficient. If you don't have any formatted disks, you can create them without exiting Quicken. Just wait for Quicken to prompt you for a new disk during the backup. Then use the Windows taskbar to open the list of **Programs** and select **Windows Explorer**. Insert the blank disk into the floppy drive, find its icon in the far-right pane, and right-click the icon using your mouse. Select **Format**, then **Start** from the menu. After the formatting is complete, use the taskbar to return to Quicken and continue backing up.

As a final word of warning (sorry to bear such ill tidings) don't leave those backups lying around. Label them clearly by file and date and store them in a safe place, preferably in a different building. A fireproof safe is always a good, if not guaranteed, storage facility, and a bank's safe-deposit box is even better. However, if you use Quicken at home, the simplest choice might be to store your disks in the office. If you use Quicken in the office, store your disks at home.

Restoring Your Data

If you ever need to use the data that was previously backed up, you must first restore that data to your hard drive.

This is really easy. To restore data, first open the **File** menu and then select **Restore Backup File**.

If you backed up to a floppy or Zip drive, insert the disk and select the appropriate drive letter using the Select Restore Drive dialog box. If you backed up to a hard disk drive or mapped network drive, simply select the drive letter using the same dialog box.

Select the correct backup using the Restore Quicken File dialog box and click **OK**.

Quicken tries to restore the file to its original location. If that file is a version of the one you are currently using, Quicken asks permission to overwrite your current data. If you approve, Quicken automatically closes your file and opens the restored data. If the restored file is different from the file you are currently using, Quicken saves the restored file to its original location.

Securing Your Data

Quicken can password-protect an entire file or just those transactions recorded before a certain date. The former is useful for preventing prying eyes from viewing your file; the latter is great for locking the previous year's transactions, protecting that information from an inadvertent change. You can apply both protection methods to a single Quicken file.

Password protection does not prevent someone from copying or deleting your entire Quicken file. However, even if someone copies that file to another computer, he or she is still unable to view its contents.

To set a password to protect your file, open the **File** menu, select **Passwords**, and choose **File**.

Use the Set Up Password dialog box to enter and confirm your password. Then click **OK**.

In the future you will need to supply this password before you can actually open the file.

You can also lock your file, protecting transactions that occurred before a certain date but leaving anything occurring thereafter open. You are not able to delete or edit transactions on or before that date without supplying the correct password. This is useful for preventing yourself—or someone else—from accidentally changing the previous year's financial data.

To set a transaction-based password, open the **File** menu, select **Passwords**, and choose **Transaction**.

Use the Modify Existing Transactions dialog box shown in the following figure to enter and confirm your password. Indicate the date through which you want to lock your transactions and click **OK**.

Use the date field to set a password for transactions prior to a selected date. In this case, everything prior to the start of the 1999 financial year.

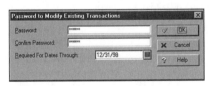

Changing or Removing Passwords

To change your password, select the same menu as you did previously (that is, either **File** for file or **Transaction** for transaction). Provide the **Old Password** and then the **New Password** followed with the new password repeated in **Confirm Password**. Click **OK** to save the new password.

To remove your password once again, select the same menu as you did previously. This time provide the **Old Password** but leave both the **New Password** and **Confirm Password** fields empty. Click **OK** to cancel the old password.

Forgot Your Password?

There's no easy fix, but all is not lost. You need to send your entire Quicken file back to Quicken's Technical Support Centre. The easiest way to do this is to create a backup on floppy disk, as described earlier in this chapter. Just send them a copy of your data on disk or via email and they will return an unprotected file. If you are worried about someone seeing your data, investigate the Sanitize utility in the Tools folder on Quicken's CD-ROM. You can use this to scramble the categories in your file. When your data returns, use your copy of Sanitize to unscramble them once more.

For more information, get in touch with Quicken's Technical Support.

The Least You Need to Know

➤ You probably don't want to hear yet again about the importance of backups, why you should never avoid them, and why you should store those backups somewhere other than anywhere near your computer.

➤ In the words of one great marketing company, Just Do It!

Chapter 20

Program Options: Doing It Your Way

In This Chapter

➤ Customizing Quicken

➤ Setting program options

➤ Changing the way your register looks and behaves

➤ Setting options for writing checks

➤ Adjusting default settings for your reports and graphs

➤ Personalized reminders and billminding

➤ It's the Internet, your way

➤ Web connection options

➤ Rearranging the desktop

Customizing Quicken

Quicken is flexible. No doubt about it. In fact, compared to most other accounting packages, it's a gold-winning gymnast—a Nadia by nature, if not by name.

You can control substantial portions of the way Quicken looks and behaves through its Option dialog boxes. They're all tucked away under the Edit menu. Click **Edit** and select **Options**. You should see eight entries under that submenu. All of these open their own dialog boxes, and some open dialog boxes with multiple tabbed panes.

Quicken's options were included to help you change how Quicken behaves, manipulating it so that it works the way you do, rather than the other way around.

In this chapter I take you on a quick tour of all Quicken's options. Keeping in mind that they *are* rather numerous, you should probably also take the time to play with them on your own.

Each time you make one or more changes to a particular dialog box, click **OK** to exit and save those new settings, or click **Cancel** to leave things just as they were.

Where Are the Color Schemes?

Sadly, Quicken no longer supports color customization, at least not to the extent of the complete color schemes built into earlier versions. However, you can still change the colors used in your registers, as described later under "Setting Register Options."

Setting Program Options

To adjust Quicken's general options (those that are program-wide, or don't seem to fit anywhere else) open the **Edit** menu, click **Options**, and select **Quicken Program**. This opens the General Options dialog box shown in the following figure.

This dialog box is typical of most of those used to set Quicken's options. Click the tabs at the top of the screen to move from one panel of options to another.

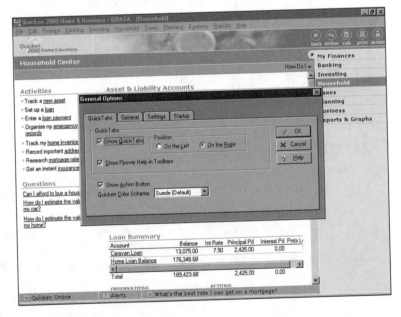

Changing the Quicken "Look"

You can customize many aspects of Quicken's operation including the layout of the screen. QuickTabs are the small tabs that appear to the right of each open Quicken window. By clicking a QuickTab, you select that window. Use the **QuickTabs** tab in the General Options dialog box to set the following options:

➤ **Show QuickTabs**   Turn the QuickTabs on or off.

➤ **Position**   Shift your QuickTabs from the right-hand side to the left.

➤ **Show Flyover Help in Toolbar**   Elsewhere in Windows, this style of help is known as tooltips, flyouts, or even screentips. No matter their name, they all do the same thing: pause your mouse over any icon or button in an active Quicken window (this doesn't apply to dialog boxes), to see a quick tip on what that function does. If you find the tips annoying, just click here to turn them off.

➤ **Show Action Button**   Select this to add an Action button to the group of buttons called back, online, calc, and print. This button provides access to a range of common tasks, but if you have used a previous version of Quicken, you'll notice these match the buttons that were included in the old icon bar. When you return to the main Quicken window, click the **Action** button and select **Edit Action List** to adjust existing actions or add new ones.

➤ **Quicken Color Scheme**   Take your pick from various color schemes. If you use Quicken on a laptop, you might find one that provides greater contrast, or you might just want to imbue Quicken with a little individuality.

Backups, Tax Categories, and Memorized Transactions

The **General** tab provides a broader array of options:

➤ **Use Tax Schedules with Categories**   Leave this option checked (that is, selected) if you want to assign specific Tax Form Line Items to your categories. This is especially important if you intend on using Quicken to help prepare your tax return. You can set up Tax Form Line Items using the Tax Link Assistant, described in Chapter 9, "Paychecks and Tax Categories."

➤ **Remove Memorized Transactions Not Used in Last *n* Months**   Every time you record a new transaction, Quicken adds it to its list of memorized transactions. You can recall that transaction in the future with just a few keystrokes.

The list is limited to 2,000 entries. When the software reaches that limit, Quicken turns off automatic memorizing. After that point, you must manually delete some memorized transactions to free up space and manually switch on memorizing by setting several register options (as detailed in the following paragraph).

An easier way to prevent a blowout in memorized transactions is to retire those that haven't been repeated within *n* months. To do so, simply type in the number of months in this field and select the check box. Now, Quicken clears the memory banks every time you start the program. (I usually set this to 13 months because that means certain annual transactions such as membership renewals are retained, even if they arrive a little late in the mail.)

➤ **Hide Advertisements in Online Financial Services Center**   Small advertisements are displayed throughout the Online Center. You can hide these when viewing your online banking transactions and performing other tasks within the center. Advertisements continue to be displayed when viewing online quotes and news for your securities regardless of this setting.

➤ **Turn On All Quicken Sounds**   Quicken's cash register "kachings" and other sounds are on by default. If you find them annoying, click here to turn them off.

➤ **Backup**   Use this section of the dialog box to specify how often you want to be reminded to backup, how many copies Quicken should store in the "backups" folder (that is, unless you send the backup elsewhere when creating it), and whether or not you want to see additional backup prompts besides those displayed when exiting the software.

Keyboard Mappings and the Fiscal Year

Use the **Settings** tab to change the following:

➤ **Keyboard Mappings for Ctrl-Z/X/C/V**   In almost every Windows program, **Ctrl+Z** stands for Undo Last Command, **Ctrl+X** stands for Cut, **Ctrl+C** stands for Copy, and **Ctrl+V** stands for Paste. This is not so in Quicken.

In Quicken, **Ctrl+Z** activates QuickZoom, **Ctrl+X** takes you to the other half of a selected transfer, **Ctrl+C** takes you to the Category & Transfer List, and **Ctrl+V** voids a transaction.

To use standard Windows keyboard commands rather than Quicken's equivalents, click **Undo/Cut/Copy/Paste**. After this, double-click with your mouse to QuickZoom any report or graph, use the transaction toolbar or **Edit** menu to void a transaction, and use the **Finance** menu to access the Category & Transfer List.

➤ **Working Calendar**   The options in this group have important financial ramifications. You are probably used to the U.S. financial year running from January 1 to December 31, but you can apply to the IRS to have your financial clock moved to a different date. If you work a nonstandard year (many companies choose to work from July 1 to June 30), click **Fiscal Year** and set the month your year begins using the drop-down list, **Starting Month**.

➤ **Multi-Currency Support**   Quicken usually assumes all dollar amounts are stored using a single currency. It doesn't matter whether this is the dollar, the drachma, or something stranger. As long as it's centesimal, it will work just fine. If you maintain overseas accounts, trade in foreign currencies, deal with foreign shares, or need to maintain an account in a different currency for whatever reason, select this option. The next time you create an account, you can specify the currency appropriate to that account. Transfers between accounts with different currencies are recorded with an additional dialog box that enables you to specify the conversion rate between one and the other.

Setting Foreign Currency Conversion Rates

If you use foreign currencies, you'll find it easier to generate net worth reports and record transfers between different currency accounts by setting default conversion rates. To do so, open the **Finance** menu and select **Currency**. (You see the Currency entry only after turning on multi-currency support). Select the appropriate currency from the Currency List and click the **Edit** button underneath the Currency List's title. Use the Edit Currency dialog box to specify the **Currency Name** and **Currency Symbol**, a **Currency Code** for online updates of that currency's value, a **Shortcut letter** you can use when recording transactions in that currency, and the conversion rate from (**x per $**) and to (**$ per x**) your usual dollar.

Startup Settings

Click the **Startup** tab to change the following:

➤ **Quicken Home Page when starting Quicken**   Select this option to always start with the Home Page in the Financial Activity Center when starting Quicken. This page warns you of upcoming scheduled transactions, notifies you of alerts, provides you with account balances, and more. It's a great way to start the day.

➤ **Reminders when starting Quicken**   Click this option if you prefer to see a concise list of reminders, alerts, and notes from your financial calendar rather than all of the information squeezed into the Home Page.

➤ **None**   You can choose to start without opening either of these windows.

When you finish adjusting your General options, click **OK** to save your changes or **Cancel** to discard them.

Setting Register Options

The register options are located on the Options submenu. Select the **Edit** menu, choose **Options**, and click **Register**.

These options help you customize Quicken's registers so they work exactly the way you need them to.

Changing the Register Display

Use the first tab, **Display** (see the following figure), to change the look of each transaction entry.

Using this dialog box you can change most aspects of Quicken's registers, including their colors.

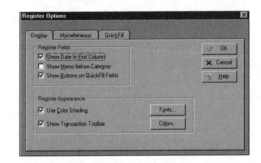

Use the first three options to adjust the Register Fields in the following ways:

➤ **Show Date in First Column**   Swap the Date field with the Num field in the transaction registers. Usually the date comes first, but you might prefer to record the check or transaction number and then the date.

➤ **Show Memo before Category**   Switch the position of the Memo and Category fields. This is a matter of personal preference, nothing more. Try them one way or the other.

➤ **Show Buttons on QuickFill Fields**   Turn off the small **Calendar** button that appears in the Date field, the down arrow that opens up the list of memorized transactions (even though you can still see the list), and the small **Calculator** icon that appears beside any amount field. This simplifies the data entry screen at the expense of some functionality.

You can also change each register's appearance overall using the remaining options as follows:

➤ **Use Color Shading**   Enables or disables the use of color in Quicken's registers. If you use a low-contrast laptop or notebook computer, you might like to select this to substitute Quicken's vibrant color schemes with an all-white transaction window. However, colors do make it easier to keep track of your place within each transaction.

➤ **Show Transaction Toolbar**   This is the group of three buttons that appear at the end of every transaction in progress in each register. If you clear them, you can use your keyboard and mouse instead. For instance, the Enter button duplicates pressing the **Enter** key on your keyboard; the Edit button achieves the same as clicking the **Edit** menu at the top of the screen and selecting **Transactions**; and the Split button is identical to pressing **Ctrl+S** or, while in the category field, clicking the down arrow to the field's right and clicking **Split**.

Finally, click **Fonts** to change the typeface used in the register window. Click **Colors** to select an alternative background shading for each type of register. If you are not satisfied with the light blue used for credit card accounts, you can change it here.

A Sight for Sore Eyes

The **Fonts** button under the **Display** tab in the Register Options dialog box is especially useful for boosting the size of Quicken's fonts for people with poor eyesight. You can set almost any size typeface using this dialog box, including your personal favorites. The default font is MS Sans Serif 8-point. Try changing this to a 10-point size if you have trouble reading the screen. There are, however, upper limits to the size you can use. For instance, a 12-point size is too large when used in conjunction with the MS Sans Serif typeface. If you choose one that's too large, Quicken lets you know and refuses to apply that change.

Miscellaneous Notifications

The next tab, **Miscellaneous**, is something of a catch-all.

Use the group under Notify to turn off Quicken's pesky requests for confirmation when working in registers:

➤ **When Recording Out of Date Transactions**   Warns you when you try to record a backdated transaction. That is, one dated before the current date.

➤ **Before Changing Existing Transactions**   Warns you when you try to edit previously recorded transactions.

➤ **When Recording Uncategorized Transactions**   Warns you when you try to record a transaction without specifying a category or transfer to another account.

The Data Entry section is handy for changing the way you record splits. Select **Automatically Enter Split Data** to record transactions from the Split window.

Changing the QuickFill Feature

The **QuickFill** tab provides two sets of options. The Data Entry group uses the same name as was used in the Miscellaneous tab in the previous section, but provides more specific options. It enables you to change the way you record your transaction data:

➤ **Use Enter Key to Move Between Fields**   Rather than using the Enter key just to record new transactions, check this option to use Enter to jump from one field to the next, like the Tab key.

➤ **Complete Fields Using Previous Entries**   Turns Quicken's auto-completion on or off. Auto-completion finishes a field based on the characters you have typed so far. It's truly one of Quicken's best time-saving features, so you should probably leave it on.

➤ **Recall Memorized Transactions (requires auto-completion)**   With this option checked, entering enough information to trigger an auto-completion also fills the amount, category, and memo fields with the details of the last transaction recorded to that payee or payer. This is another great time-saver if you regularly record the same transactions.

➤ **Drop-Down Lists on Field Entry**   Check this to drop a list each time you start typing in a Num, Payee, or Category field. If you turn this off, make sure **Show Buttons on QuickFill Fields** is turned on under the **Display** tab. Otherwise, you won't be able to access the memorized transactions and other pull-down menus available in each register window.

➤ **Auto-Capitalize Payee & Categories**   As its title suggests, this determines whether or not Quicken converts a lowercase starting letter in the payee and category fields to an uppercase letter.

Automatic List Updating changes the action Quicken takes after you record certain data:

➤ **Auto Memorize New Transactions** Clear the check mark from this option if you prefer not to memorize new transactions.

➤ **Auto Memorize to the Calendar List** Clear this option if you don't want newly memorized transactions to appear in the Financial Calendar's transaction list.

➤ **Add Address Book QuickFill Group Items to QuickFill List** If you use any version of Quicken other than Quicken Basic 2000, you can also add names and addresses recorded in the Financial Address Book to the list of memorized transactions. This makes it easier to use those names and addresses in Quicken.

When you finish adjusting your Register Options, click **OK** to save those changes or **Cancel** to discard them.

Setting Write Check Options

To adjust the options applicable to the Write Checks window, open the **Edit** menu, select **Options**, and click **Write Checks**. The dialog box shown in the following figure appears.

Check Options enables you to add extra messages, change the date checks are recorded, and adjust the automatic memorizing feature.

Although the Miscellaneous and QuickFill tabs are almost identical to those included in the Register Options dialog box, there are some important differences, as well as a few new settings.

Changing Dates and Check Options

The **Checks** tab includes the following groups of options:

➤ **Printed Date Style** Select between the **4-digit Year** and the **2-digit Year**. In other words, **2000** or just **00**. This is a matter of personal style and has no bearing on the dates actually recorded by Quicken. However, it does change the format printed on checks.

Will Quicken Crash at the Turn of the Year 2000?

The short answer is no. Quicken can store dates from 1950 through 2049 with no change in the way you work. Older computers might experience some difficulty with dates post-2000, but that is beyond Quicken's control. You can record dates for 2000 and beyond in the usual two-digit format. For example, December 31, 1999 would be entered as "12/31/99", and January 1, 2000 can be recorded as "1/1/00".

➤ **Allow Entry of Extra Message on Check**   Select this to be able to record a message in the Write Checks window that prints below the address, out of sight of the window in Quicken's window envelopes. This is useful if you want to include confidential information on the check, such as an account number.

➤ **Print Categories on Voucher Checks**   Specify whether your income and expense categories should appear on the detailed listing printed below the check. Hide these by clearing this option if those categories are for your own records only.

➤ **Change Date of Checks to Date When Printed**   Click this to adjust the date of the transactions recorded in your register to the date the check is printed. For example, let's say you record a transaction but don't want to print it until several days later. With this option checked, the transaction date in the checking account's register is changed to the date the check is printed.

➤ **Display Settings**   Check **Show Buttons on QuickFill Fields** to display Quicken's calculator, date, and pull-down menu buttons in the check writing window.

Miscellaneous and QuickFill Tabs

The remaining tabs are identical to those described for Register options with the exception that you can, using the **Miscellaneous** tab, set an automatic alert should you try to use an already used check number (check **Warn if a Check Number is Re-used**). Of course, this can't happen if you make a habit of selecting **Next Check Num** when filling out a checking account transaction, but it's a good way to find typos. This option is also useful if you hand-write your checks.

Incidentally, the options in the Miscellaneous and QuickFill tabs also link to those same tabs in Register Options, so selecting one here also selects it in the other.

All of the options under the QuickFill tab are identical to those under Register options previously listed.

When you finish adjusting your Write Checks options, click **OK** to save those changes or **Cancel** to discard them.

Setting Report and Graph Options

You can set your report and options as shown in the figure below by opening the **Edit** menu, selecting **Options**, and choosing **Reports and Graphs**.

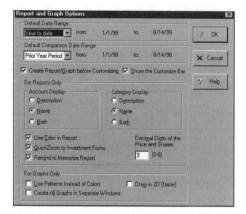

Use Report Options to change the defaults that form most of your reports.

This is a busy dialog box, but the options aren't too difficult to figure out:

➤ **Default Date Range**   Quicken's default report and graph dates can be set to almost anything you prefer, from the last year to the last quarter to any specific interval. If you like to concentrate on the big picture, you might set these to cover a year, but if you prefer the microcosmic approach, you might like to try a quarter or even a month. Note that the **Include all Dates** selection in the pull-down list forces the report or graph to extend from the time you first started using Quicken to the present day.

➤ **Default Comparison Date Range**   Comparison reports and graphs show the amount of change in a category or account over two time periods. For example, if you want to compare your accounts of this quarter this year with those of this quarter last year, set the default comparison to the earlier date and the **Default Date Range** to the more recent period. Figures from both will be compared onscreen.

➤ **Create Report/Graph Before Customizing**   Remove the check mark from this option to display a report or graph customization dialog box before the selected report or graph appears onscreen.

➤ **Show the Customize Bar**   Remove the customization bar from the top of the report and graph windows. Even with this removed you can still change the dates and other aspects of reports and graphs using the **Customize** button.

➤ **Account Display**   You can choose to have your accounts listed by their **Description** (Accounts Payable), their **Name** (for instance, Payables), or **Both**. This setting only applies to reports and doesn't affect anything else in Quicken.

➤ **Category Display**   The same options as above apply to categories, although you might find these more useful. For example, if you run your business through Quicken, use categories to track numerous income items much as you would an inventory, you can use category names to store the item's catalog code and the description to explain it more fully. By selecting **Both** here, your reports make far more sense, but it's also easy to work with those items through their coded shortcuts.

Use the remaining report options as follows:

➤ **Use Color in Report**   Check this to display negative amounts and report titles in color.

➤ **QuickZoom to Investment Forms**   This option takes you from a transaction you have double-clicked in an investment report to the form used to record that transaction. With this option cleared, you are taken to that transaction in your investment register instead.

➤ **Decimal Digits of the Price and Shares**   How many numbers do you want displayed after the decimal point? Two or three is usual.

You can also set the following options for graphs:

➤ **Use Patterns Instead of Colors**   Check this if you prefer to use patterns instead of colors to draw your graphs. This is an issue for anyone using a monochrome display, but Quicken sets this option automatically if it detects that to be the case. This option is also useful if you find that graphs print particularly slowly on your black and white printer. Selecting this to print patterns instead of colors might speed things up.

➤ **Create all Graphs in Separate Windows**   Check this if you want to create each new graph in a separate window rather than using one graph window for all of your graphs.

➤ **Draw in 2D (faster)**   Check this to view your graphs as 2D oblongs rather than 3D columns. This option's bracketed prompt suggests this is for speed reasons, but the difference on a Pentium computer or faster is not particularly noticeable. However, I find 2D graphs, although not quite as aesthetically pleasing as the 3D variety, easier to size up onscreen because the tops of the columns run parallel across the screen with only small gaps.

When you finish adjusting your report and graph options, click **OK** to save those changes or **Cancel** to discard them.

Setting Reminder and Billminder Options

Think of the Reminder options as a great place to fine-tune your memory. Unlike the other options in this chapter, you can only change one section—the number of days in advance that reminders and notes are shown—through this dialog box.

To adjust the advance notice you receive for reminders and notes, open the **Edit** menu, select **Options**, and choose **Reminders**.

Days Shown provides two settings:

➤ **Days in Advance**   Use this field to specify how many days notice you want on a reminder before it falls due. The reminder appears in your list of reminders that many days in advance.

➤ **Show notes for**   Choose the forward period over which you want to display calendar notes in the reminders window.

When you've finished, click **OK** to save your changes or **Cancel** to discard them.

Additional options for Reminders and Quicken's Billminder are available under the Reminder window's **Options** menu. To change them, select **Reminders** in the **Finance** menu. When you see the Reminders window on your screen, locate and click the **Options** drop-down menu.

Use the **Reminders** submenu as follows:

➤ **Show Reminders when starting Quicken**   Select this option to jump immediately to the Reminders screen each time you start Quicken. This is the same as the identically named option that appears in Quicken's General Options under the Startup tab, as discussed at the beginning of this chapter.

➤ **Show Reminders from Other Files**   Select this option if you would also like to see reminders from other Quicken files. Quicken searches for reminders, alerts, and notes in all files contained in the same folder (or directory) as the current file. It also keeps track of other files you have opened, even if they are in a different area of your computer or even on a completely different hard drive located elsewhere on your network. Searching through other files is particularly handy if you keep your home and business data separate and need to make sure you don't overlook an important payment in either file. Unlike the reminders in the current file, you can't actually open or work with those in other files without first opening the files to which they pertain. However, this is a small price to pay for an almost unparalleled memory.

➤ **Days Shown**   Open the same dialog box as described for the Reminder Options above.

The second entry in the Quicken Reminders window's **Options** menu is used to adjust Billminder's parameters. Use this menu to set the following options:

➤ **Show Billminder when starting Windows** Select this option to view the Billminder utility each time you start Windows.

➤ **Show Scheduled Transactions** Use this option to display scheduled transactions in the Billminder window.

➤ **Show Checks To Print** Select this option to show all checks waiting to be printed. This includes online payments you have made but not yet sent.

➤ **Show Online Payments** Select this to also show your online payments waiting to be written and added to the send list.

➤ **Show Investment Reminders** Investment reminders are just like other scheduled transactions and displays, for example, a share purchase or a sale forward-dated to the day you want it enacted. Investment reminders don't include stock price alerts, but these are included in the Alerts and Calendar Notes window in the lower half of the Billminder window.

➤ **Show Calendar Notes** Select this to include Calendar Notes in the Billminder window.

Setting Internet Options

Access your Internet connection options by opening the **Edit** menu, selecting **Options**, and clicking **Internet Connection**. You see the dialog box shown in the following figure.

Your Internet Connection controls when Quicken connects to the Internet, as well as what happens after it has completed updating.

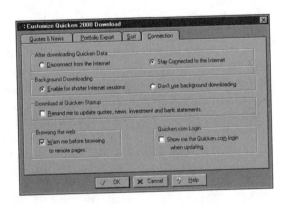

These options control Quicken's connection to the Internet for downloading pricing data, news updates, transaction statements, and so on. There are four groups under the **Connection** tab of this dialog box:

➤ **After downloading Quicken Data**   Select **Disconnect from the Internet** if you don't want Quicken to maintain an online connection after it has completed downloading or **Stay Connected to the Internet** if you would prefer it did. The retained connection means you can then use other Internet software after Quicken has completed updating, or even while it is still doing so. You can't adjust these items if you are using other than a dial-up connection to the Internet.

➤ **Background Downloading**   The options in this section control the Quicken Download Agent. You can only change them if you have already set up Quicken to access the Internet. When the agent is active, a small Quicken logo appears in the small panel to the left of the Windows taskbar. The agent activates whenever it detects an active Internet connection and, if **Enable for shorter Internet sessions** is selected, quietly downloads program updates and other data during lulls in your Internet session. Quicken doesn't have to be running while this occurs. If you would prefer more control over the updates, click **Don't use background downloading**. This means you need to manually initiate updates using Quicken's One Step Update.

➤ **Download at Quicken Startup**   The single option in this group controls the display of a small reminders dialog box that displays each time you start Quicken. If it annoys you, leave this option cleared.

➤ **Browsing the Web**   Quicken stores several of the opening pages to its related Internet content on your computer. You can load these through your browser and view them without actually connecting to the Internet. You can move from these to actual pages on the Internet with nary a pause, but if you use a Dial-Up connection, you might prefer to receive a warning before Quicken initiates the dial-in process. In that case, leave **Warn me before browsing to remote pages** selected.

➤ **Quicken.com Login**   You need to register with Quicken.com before you can use the Internet services such as updating an online portfolio that are associated with that site. (This is not the same as the registration you had to perform the first time you used Quicken. That registered the software, entitling you to upgrades and discounts. The Quicken.com procedure registers you with an online service, enabling you to store your portfolio on their pages and use the numerous other facilities provided online.) With **Show me the Quicken.com login when updating** deselected, Quicken automatically supplies your registered username and password each time you access the site. If you are concerned about other people viewing your personalized online data, make sure you leave this option checked.

Use the remaining tabs in this dialog box as follows:

➤ **Quotes & News** Customize your quotes and news downloads here. You can edit securities, add ticker symbols and, by clicking the left-hand column of the list of securities, select those that should be updated online.

➤ **Portfolio Export** Select the accounts you want to include when exporting your portfolio to Quicken's Web site.

➤ **Sort** Change the order in which items are downloaded from the Internet.

When you've finished, click **OK** to save the changes to these options or **Cancel** to discard them.

Setting Web Connect Options

The *Web Connect* options are used to determine how Quicken behaves after transferring online transactions from the Quicken.com Web site to your computer. Transactions are sent as a package of information that needs to be loaded into Quicken before they can be accepted into your registers.

To set these options, open the **Edit** menu, click **Options**, and choose **Web Connect**.

The Web Connect Options dialog box provides the following choices:

➤ **Give me the option of saving to a file whenever I download Web Connect data.** Quicken opens and processes downloaded transactions as soon as they arrive hot from the Web. Select this option if you would like the opportunity to save the downloaded transaction data first. You might do this if you are concerned about losing transactions in transit or you need to copy them to another computer.

➤ **Verify that Quicken is the default Web Connect application when it is launched.** If Quicken isn't the default Web Connect application, there's a possibility the downloaded transaction data could be sent to another application where it might be processed incorrectly and discarded or swallowed and made to disappear. With this option selected, Quicken makes sure it has been registered as the destination for the downloaded data each time it is launched. This option is an important data security consideration, so it is selected by default.

➤ **When Quicken is launched by my browser, don't close it after Web Connect completes.**   Your browser launches Quicken if it isn't already running to process the data that has just been downloaded. If Quicken has been launched in this way, it closes as soon as it completes. You might prefer to select this option so that Quicken keeps running, enabling you to check over the transactions and accept them into the registers.

When you have finished, click **OK** to save your changes to these settings or **Cancel** to discard them.

Setting Desktop Options

It's easy to rearrange your desktop so that it opens with the window you want to see already there on your screen.

Usually, Quicken keeps track of whichever windows were open when you last exited the program. The next time you start, it reopens all of those windows. There's a good chance you won't find this ideal. During a typical Quicken session you will probably open more windows than you close—especially if you're giving the software a good airing—cluttering the QuickTabs the next time you start.

The alternative is to create and save the perfect set of windows, telling Quicken to open these each time you start a new session. These windows might include your favorite Register, the Investment Portfolio, a Write Checks window, and your Reminders.

To save this set up, open you windows and arrange them as you require (drag the **QuickTabs** up and down the list); then click the **Edit** menu, select **Options**, and choose **Desktop**), select **Save Current Desktop**, and click **OK**. The next time you start, the windows are just as you arranged them. The first setting, **Save Desktop on Exit**, is the default behavior. Select this if you decide you would rather return to the previous mode of operation.

Click **OK** to exit when you've finished.

The Least You Need to Know

➤ Options are a great way to imbue Quicken with a little personal charm, so take the time to explore all of the option dialog boxes. They're a great way to customize Quicken so it works not only for you, but also with you.

➤ There are many ways to change the way Quicken looks and behaves, but you'll find some of the most useful in Program Options. From here you can adjust color schemes, help tools, sounds, backups, keyboard mappings, and more. You can also use the Program Options dialog box to turn on multi-currency report—perfect if you need to track overseas investments or earnings.

➤ Look to your register options to adjust the order of data you record in your registers. You can also clean up the display, change typefaces, and customize QuickFill so it works the way you need it to.

➤ Clear the Print Categories setting in the Write Checks options if you don't want your income and expense categories to appear on checks that you print. Hiding the categories is a good idea if you desire additional financial privacy.

➤ Use the Report and Graph Options to define the report and graph defaults. This is the best place to set default dates around which you want reports and graphs created.

➤ Many of the Internet Options are available in the One Step Update dialog box but, as with reports and graphs, this options dialog box provides a great place to set your defaults.

Inventing an Inventory

Quicken Home Inventory

Quicken Home Inventory tracks the smaller things you own; for example, televisions, stereos, furniture, personal valuables, rare books, and really, just about anything you own.

Home Inventory is included with Quicken Deluxe and Quicken Home & Business. However, it isn't actually part of Quicken. It's more a separate application that integrates with Quicken to a limited degree.

How limited is limited? Well, the value of any item recorded in the inventory is represented in Quicken through a specialized inventory asset account. That's about it.

Unfortunately, while the value is reflected, that reflection is more like a one-way mirror, so you can't adjust the contents of Quicken's inventory account and expect to see those changes reflected back in Home Inventory.

Despite its limitations, Home Inventory remains a very complementary addition. You can use it to not only track the goods in your home, but also those of your business.

The inventory database enables you to track information such as how much, where, and when you paid for the item, as well as warranty information, serial numbers, insurance details, and current resale and replacement cost. This makes Home Inventory ideal for keeping records on high-value items such as electronic equipment, artwork, and furniture. Of course, if you do use Home Inventory for insurance information, you should always store a backup of your data off the premises, along with printed reports that replicate that same data in a universal format. (That's paper-based, just in case you were wondering.)

Need Insurance? Can't Stand the Sales Pitch?

If you're connected to the Internet, you can grab quick quotes and other insurance information for your home, car, business, and other assets through Quicken's InsureMarket. To visit the market, open Quicken's **Finance** menu, select **Quicken on the Web**, and then click **Quicken.com**. From the Quicken.com site, click the **Insurance** heading under a section called Departments. To go there through any Internet browser, just type in the address www.quicken.com/insurance.

Starting Quicken Home Inventory

The best way to start Quicken Home Inventory is from within Quicken itself. Just click Quicken's **Household** menu and select **Quicken Home Inventory**.

The first time you start the inventory software (or create a new inventory file), you should click **Continue** to move past the introductory screen and to open the main Inventory window.

Short on Screen Space?

The List View window is a little crowded in its default mode. To make it larger, click the **Maximize** icon in its title bar. That's the small window control button second from the right on top of the screen. This opens the central window up to its full size. Most of the figures you see in this chapter were taken with the window maximized.

The buttons that make up the Icon bar provide quick access to Quicken Home Inventory's most useful features. Table 21.1 lists each icon and its function.

Table 21.1 Icon Bar Buttons for Quicken Home Inventory

Button	Name	Function
	Locations	Opens the list of locations. These are areas in which you keep your belongings such as Living Room, Shed, and Garden.
	Categories	Opens the list of categories. Each item is grouped by category. Typical categories include Appliances, Clothing, and Electronics.
	Policies	Opens the list of policies. Quicken Home Inventory can track multiple insurance policies.
	Claims	Creates or edits an insurance claim.
	Find	Finds an item by description or notes.
	Move Item	Moves an item to another location.
	Update	Updates the balance of Quicken's Home Inventory account.
	Goto Qkn	Launches Quicken.
	Help	Gets Online Help.

The inventory is made up of items, categories, and locations. For example, that CaffeinePlus espresso machine given to you by your spouse last Christmas—it's so good you haven't slept a wink since you received it—is part of the electronics category whose location probably is your kitchen, but might also be your office, depending on its centrality to your working day.

As you can see, items are assigned to categories that group your possessions by type. Items are also cataloged by the location in which they are stored. Just how you choose to use those categories and locations lends Quicken Home Inventory a great deal of flexibility, and also some complexity.

The inventory window provides two views: List and Detail.

The List View is the default view (see the following figure), showing all items by location or category. It displays them in a table and includes the item's name (referred to in the List View as its Description), the category to which it has been assigned, its replacement cost, and its resale value.

Click here to maximize this window.

Quicken Home Inventory opens with the List View window. You can use this to immediately begin recording your assets.

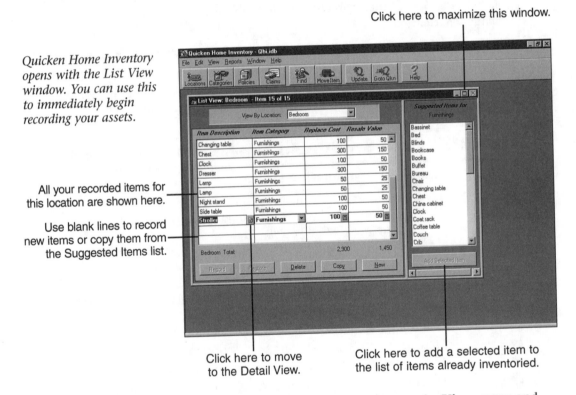

All your recorded items for this location are shown here.

Use blank lines to record new items or copy them from the Suggested Items list.

Click here to move to the Detail View.

Click here to add a selected item to the list of items already inventoried.

To change how the List View filters the items it displays, open the **View** menu and select **By Category** or **By Location**. Then use the pull-down list at the top of the List View window to select the category or location you want to view. In the remainder of this chapter, it is assumed you have retained the default setting of viewing by location.

Access the Detail View from the List View by clicking the small **Detail View** icon beside any item description. The Detail View (shown in the following figure) provides more specific information about an item such as the date and place of purchase, which insurance policy applies to that item, the location of receipts and other records, and also enables you to change that item's location within the lists. Click **Return to List View** when you're finished. This button is in the top-left corner of the Detail View screen.

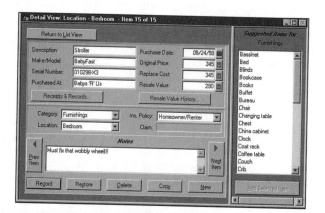

This is the Detail View for the Stroller item. Use the Notes field to record free-form information about the current item.

Exiting and Backing Up Your Inventory

Backing up your inventory is much like backing up your other Quicken data; get your formatted floppy disk ready!

To exit Inventory, open the **File** menu and select **Exit**. After you exit, you are asked if you want to back up. It is recommended that you back up your inventory data regularly. To do so, click **Backup**, select a **Backup Drive,** and make sure the drive contains a disk. Specify a filename—the default, QHI.IDB, should do just fine—and click **OK** to create the backup.

You can also initiate a backup from Inventory's **File** menu. Just select **Backup** and follow the above procedure.

After you've created your backup, store that data in a very safe place.

Restoring an Inventory You Previously Backed Up

To recover the data you've previously backed up, open the **File** menu and select **Restore**. Locate the file named QHI.IDB (or whatever you named your backup) in the file selection dialog box. If you backed up to a floppy disk, you need to insert that disk and select it using the **Look in** pull-down list (before you see the backup file) and click **Open**. Because Home Inventory keeps its file linked to your current Quicken data, you have to click **OK** to confirm that it should overwrite the existing file. However, after you've done so, you should see your original data restored.

Creating Your Inventory

You can create a new inventory item in two ways. The hard way (in so far as it involves more typing) is to do so starting from scratch. The easy way is to use one of the hundreds of inventory items already built into each inventory category.

Let's look at the easy way first. Incidentally, the fastest way to move from field to field within the inventory is to press your **Tab** key. As is the case throughout Windows, **Shift+Tab** moves you back one field.

Hundreds of existing items are already defined in the Suggested Items list.

To create an inventory item based on a Suggested Item, first make sure you have the List View window open on your screen. If not, open the **View** menu and select **List View**.

Select a location from the **View by Location** pull-down list at the top of the List View window. Then select an Item Category from the second column of the first blank line in the List View window. The easiest way to do this is to click anywhere on the **Item Category** entry. The category controls the contents of the *Suggested Items for* list to the right.

Removing the Suggested Items Pane

If you don't require any of the items in the Suggested Items pane, you can remove that entire section of the window by opening the **View** menu and clicking **Suggested Items**. This gives you more room for the entries in your List View or the data in the Detail View. To restore the pane in the future, simply select the same menu entry again.

From the *Suggested Items for* pane, locate the item you want to add and either double-click it to copy it across to the inventory table, or select it and click the **Add Selected Item** button at the bottom of the pane. The data copied across is simply default data and is probably not very representative of the values of your own items. You should change the values as described in the following numbered list. It should go without saying that this is particularly important if you need to make an insurance claim.

1. In the **Replace Cost** field, enter a replacement cost calculated on what it would cost to replace that item with a new, equivalent item.

2. The **Resale Value** field is set to 50% of the **Replace Cost**, but you may edit this as required.

3. Click **Record** to move on to the next item.

4. To create a new inventory item from scratch, make sure the List View window is open.

5. Before recording any details, select a location from the **View by Location** pull-down list at the top of the List View window. You can change this later if it's not quite right or if you need to create a more specific location to house the item, but for now just pick the most appropriate placement so you can get started.

Items That Don't Suit Any Location

If you have an item that doesn't seem to suit any location—for example, a portable CD-player—simply specify it as **Unassigned**. Although an Unassigned location is a location unto itself and so, in one sense, this entire suggestion falls apart through a self-induced paradoxical loop, this doesn't concern the inventory. It treats Unassigned items in your reports and claims just like any other.

6. For each item you decide to record in that location, provide the following details:

➤ **Item Description**   Give this item a name. You can be as terse or descriptive as you like, and you can even use real spaces between words (rather than something like "Table_dining_oval" you can simply put "Oval dining table"). If you have more than one item of this type, make sure you add enough information to clearly distinguish between each of them.

➤ **Item Category**   Select a category from the list. You learn how to edit your category list in the following section called "Editing the Location and Category Lists." When you view your item list by category, this field shows Item Location instead.

➤ **Replace Cost**   This is what it would cost right now to replace this item with a new one. Note that this field does not allow for sentimental value. Nothing's irreplaceable, unless the jury says so.

➤ **Resale Value**   Automatically calculated at 50% of the replacement cost, but you can change this if you believe the value of the goods to be greater or lesser.

7. After you've completed all the fields, click **Record** at the bottom of the List View window or press the **Enter** key to write this item into your inventory. If you move to another item without recording the existing edits, Home Inventory brings up a friendly reminder. Click **Yes** to confirm saving those changes.

Changing an Item's Location or Category

You can change an item's location or category from the List View window or the Detail View, but it's easier from the List View, especially if you need to change many items at once.

Before you start, check that the List View is open and that it is set to view by location. To ensure you are viewing by location, pull down the **View** menu and try to select **By Location**. If you are already viewing by location, this menu entry appears grayed out.

Find your item in the List View window and change the category by selecting it from the pull-down list in the Item Category column. Click **Record** to save those changes when you're finished.

To change an item's location from the List View window, make sure it has been set to view by category. You can do this by pulling down the **View** menu and selecting **By Category**.

Then find your item in the List View window and change the location by selecting it from the pull-down list in the Item Location column. Click **Record** to save your changes.

Using the Detail View

Simply creating a list of items is not enough to establish an insurance claim. Although the inventory doesn't replace the need for physical documentation such as purchase or credit card receipts, you should always check your insurance policy so you know exactly what might be required by way of additional supporting evidence.

This is where the Home Inventory excels. You can associate extensive background information with every item entered into the List View. Just select that item, open the **View** menu, and choose **Detail View**, or click the small **Detail View** icon beside that item's entry in the List View's **Description** column.

The Detail View provides the following fields:

➤ **Description**   This is the same field provided in the Description column of the List View window.

➤ **Make/Model**   Use the manufacturer's code as printed on the item, rather than that taken from the packaging or an arbitrary decal or screen-print.

➤ **Serial Number**   Again, copy this from the item itself. This is especially important in the case of a claim for theft.

➤ **Purchased At**   Be precise: it might be the only way to make a claim, should you lose your purchase receipt.

➤ **Purchase Date**   As important as the place purchased.

➤ **Original Price**   The original price you paid for this item.

➤ **Replace Cost**   The details for this field are taken from the List View window, although you can edit them if required.

➤ **Resale Value**   Again, these are taken from the List View window, but can be changed here.

Fill in as many of the fields as you can, especially for those items against which you might need to file a claim. For all the major items you should at least record the make/model, serial number, place purchased, purchase price, and, depending on your policy, either replacement cost or resale value.

Use the remaining functions in the Detail View window as follows:

➤ **Receipts & Records**   Click this button to open the Receipts and Records dialog box. Use this to indicate the type of records you have to support your claim of ownership for each item. You can also indicate the location of those records. When you're finished, click **OK** to return to the Detail View.

➤ **Resale Value History**   Click this button to open the Resale Value History dialog box. The value of most items changes over time (depressingly, most often in a downward direction), so use this feature to record those changes. You can use the Resale Value History dialog box to take note of appreciation or deprecia-tion, as discussed in the section titled, "Tracking Depreciation and Appreciation," later in this chapter. Simply click **New** to create a new entry, or **Edit** or **Delete** entries as required. When you're finished, click **Close** to return to the Detail View.

➤ **Category**   This drop-down menu enables you to change the item's category.

➤ **Location**   Use this drop-down menu to change the item's location.

➤ **Ins. Policy**   Select another insurance policy through this drop-down menu. When you need to make a claim, Quicken Home Inventory can automatically produce a summary or detail report, as described in "Tracking Depreciation and Appreciation," later in this chapter.

➤ **Claim**   This field displays the name of any claim you have assigned this item. Although you can edit items you've already assigned to a claim, you cannot delete them until you have removed them from the claim. (Claims are discussed in "Making a Claim," later in this chapter.)

➤ **Notes**   Use this text box to store additional data such as warranty information or anything else you believe could prove useful.

The buttons running along the lower edge of the Detail View window are used to manage the items in the list. They perform the following functions:

➤ **Record**   Saves any updates made to an existing item.

➤ **Restore**   Discards any changes made while editing this item.

➤ **Delete**   Deletes this item.

➤ **Copy**   Copies this item's details to a new item.

➤ **New**   Creates a new item.

Click **Return to List View** when you're finished editing the item. If you modified but did not record your changes, you are asked in another dialog box to click **Yes** to record or **No** to discard.

Alternatively, use the large scrolling arrows labeled **Prev Item** and **Next Item** (they're on either side of the **Notes** text box in the Detail View window) to move back and forth through the list of items already stored for that location or category. Click **Return to List View** after you've finished.

Updating Quicken's Inventory Asset Account

When you finish recording your inventory items, click **Update** in the Icon bar, or open the **File** menu and select **Update Quicken**. This takes the total resale value of your assets entered to date and places that value into a read-only Quicken asset account called Home Inventory. (You have to confirm the update each time you select it.)

Now, whenever you create a Net Worth report through Quicken, you also see the value of the goods stored in your inventory.

Tracking Depreciation and Appreciation

You can track depreciation and appreciation through Quicken Home Inventory, but there are some issues you should know before you begin.

Techno Talk

Depreciation and Appreciation?

Depreciation occurs when an object loses value. For example, it is widely recognized that a new car depreciates some 30% as soon as you drive it out of the lot. Appreciation occurs when an object gains value. Typically, art and antiques appreciate, but appreciation is by no means limited to those items. (Your appreciation of art and antiques might also appreciate, but that's just confusing the issue.) Both appreciation and its depressing opposite need to be tracked for tax and insurance purposes. Depreciation gains you a deduction, although schedules published by the IRS limit this to a certain percentage per year depending on the item. Appreciation is important for capital gains purposes, although, of course, capital gains tax isn't payable until that item is sold. However, if you don't track the appreciation in Home Inventory, you might miss out on the accrued value should you need to make a claim.

Home Inventory depreciates or appreciates an item's value as you see fit to tell it, but those changes are only reflected in the balance of the Home Inventory asset account in Quicken. In other words, the changing values are not reflected in, say, a depreciation expense account.

This might cause some tax problems. For instance, although major purchases by a business are classified as expenses, and can therefore be claimed as a deduction, some items must be depreciated over several years rather than claimed in the first. This is particularly true of larger items such as manufacturing equipment (sometimes known as "capital goods").

Any depreciation on business goods must be done through Quicken rather than the Home Inventory. That enables you to deplete the item's asset account through a depreciation expense category. As long as that category is marked as tax-related, it appears on the reports you prepare for your return and enables you to claim the deduction.

Straight-Line and Accelerated Depreciation

Yes, there are two types of depreciation. Straight-line depreciation uses a generally accepted rate over a specified period. For example, a computer depreciated over five years is depreciated by 20% of its purchase price each year. Accelerated depreciation assumes larger depreciation at the beginning of an item's life followed by a slower rate for the remainder. It enables corporations to write off more than the cost of their purchases in the early years, and in some cases, was combined with other tax laws to actually reverse the flow of tax dollars. This helped some companies earn hundred-million dollar tax rebates after making pre-tax profits of several billions of dollars. Nice for some!

For the home, depreciation generally makes no difference because most home purchases don't qualify as a tax deduction. However, it still reflects the market value of those goods.

In addition, you might have some items that enjoy appreciation, something I'm sure you also appreciate.

On this level, it's easy to record appreciation or depreciation. To do so, find the item in Quicken Home Inventory's List View window, select it, open the **View** menu, and choose **Detail View**.

From the Detail View window click **Resale Value History**.

The Date and Price columns in the Resale Value History dialog box obviously provide this item's price history. Use the **New**, **Edit**, and **Delete** command buttons to adjust these values and click **Close** when you're finished. You don't have to adjust the price on a regular basis, although Quicken makes use of this history when creating Net Worth reports or graphs that show, say, a year's worth of data.

Above all else, remember that depreciation is a very serious taxation issue. In fact, there's only one thing worse than applying depreciation to goods that shouldn't have been depreciated—and that's failing to do so when they could have.

So that you don't miss out, make sure you talk to your taxation professional about your major purchases. You could be in for a very pleasant tax break.

Editing the Category and Location Lists

The category location lists are useful not only because of the way they help you to organize the items you record. Open the list of categories, and Quicken Home Inventory can show you how many items have been used in each category, as well as their combined replacement or resale value. This is a great way to quickly ascertain how much value you have in electronic goods, personal jewelry, art, and so on. The location list provides the same information organized by location rather than category. You can use this to see the total replacement or resale value of items in the living room, shed, basement, or similar.

To view and change your categories, click the **View** menu and select **Category List**. To view and change your locations, select **Location List** instead. Alternatively, click the **Locations** or **Categories** icons.

Using each list is easy. Click **New** to add a new category or location. Simply enter the name and click **OK**. To change the name of a category or location, click **Edit**, type it, and **OK** the new name. All items marked as belonging to the previous location or category now belong to the edited version. To delete a category, click **Delete** and confirm the deletion. If you delete a category that already contains items, Home Inventory marks the items as "unassigned". The same thing goes when you delete a location that already contains items. To edit these items, open the category or location named "unassigned", select them, and change them as required.

Click **Close** to return to the window you were using before opening the category or location lists.

Editing the Policies List

Open the **View** menu and choose **Policy List**, or click the **Policies** icon.

The Policies window lists the inventory's default policies.

As with the category and location lists, it also shows the number of items covered by each policy, as well as their total replacement cost. The amount shown in the Difference column is important. This is the difference between the amount covered by the policy and the items you are trying to insure. Bear in mind that although insurance companies generally don't pay more than the value of the goods insured, they certainly won't replace them at all if you haven't insured using a sufficient dollar value. A negative value shows a shortfall in insured value. If you see this, you should consider upping the dollar value to cover the shortfall—at least after checking the replacement value of the items covered to make sure you haven't over-valued them.

You can add, change, or remove policies using the **New**, **Edit**, and **Delete** buttons at the top of the window.

You should at the very least check the automotive and household policies and adjust the **Coverage** amount so that it equals the maximum claim possible according to your policy.

You should also click the **Claims >>** button in the Edit Policy dialog box if you are currently making a claim under this policy, and record the adjuster's contact details.

After you complete adding or editing a policy, you see a dialog box similar to that shown in the following figure. Most of the fields are quite straightforward. They are chiefly of interest when you need to make a claim, ensuring you have all the information you need to contact the insurer.

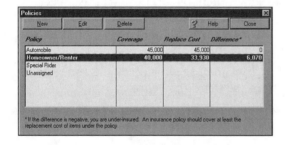

Use the Insurance Policy list to check if your assigned items have hit the limits of their policies.

When you're finished, click **Close**.

Incidentally, the only way to add items to a new policy is to go back to that item's Detail View and select the new policy using the **Ins. Policy** drop-down list. (You read about this earlier.)

Making a Claim

After you finish updating your inventory and adjusting the insurance policies, you have one final step remaining before you can consider your inventory truly complete.

If the worst happens and you need to make a claim, you need as much supporting evidence as you can lay your hands upon. Besides the receipts, warranties, credit-card statements, and other items that will help you to establish proof of ownership, you should print a detailed report that summarizes all of the information you have entered into the inventory package.

Quicken Home Inventory can print six different reports. These are shown in Table 21.2, and are also available under the **Reports** menu on the menu bar.

Table 21.2   Home Inventory Reports

Name	Purpose
Inventory Value Summary	Totals items by category, location, or insurance policy.
Inventory Detail	Shows detailed information on each item, sorted by category, location, or insurance policy.
Insurance Coverage Summary	Displays items sorted by policy including their replacement cost, resale value, purchase date, and purchase price. Includes totals and policy contact information.
Insurance Coverage Detail	Shows detailed information on each item sorted by insurance policy. Includes policy contact information but no totals.

In general, print the Inventory Value Summary report sorted by Location. Then generate another copy sorted by Category. Finally, create and print Insurance Coverage Detail. This provides you with information based on the types of goods that are in your inventory—which is handy when you need to break down the claim by electrical, clothing, and so on. It also shows them by location—this is especially useful if faced with a localized theft, fire, or flood—as well as all of the information entered into each item's detail window. This helps support your claim, and that, after all, is the chief purpose of the Quicken Home Inventory.

After you print the reports, make a backup of the inventory file and store them both in a safe place, preferably away from the items they cover.

To prepare a claim, open the **View** menu and select **Claims List**, or click the **Claims** icon.

From the Insurance Claims dialog box click **New**, read the New Claim Instructions, and click **OK**.

Now you need to define your claim:

➤ Click inside **Claim Description** and briefly summarize the reason for this claim. For example: Burglary, Fire, Act of God.

➤ Press **Tab** and select from the list or type the **Date of Claim**.

➤ Press **Tab** and select from the list or type the **Date of Event** that caused the loss.

➤ Press **Tab** and select the appropriate policy from the **Policy Name** drop-down menu.

➤ Press **Tab** and enter a **Claim Number**. If you don't have a claim number for this claim, contact your insurance company to obtain one.

Click **Items** to open the Select Items for Insurance Claim dialog box. Click each item to be added to the claim (hold your **Control** key to select more than one or click **Select All** for—and I really do hope this isn't the case—the lot), and click **OK** when you're done.

Each item you select is listed in the New Claim form, along with the replacements and repair costs. Select each item and click **Adjust Cost** to change the price basis used for that item in the claim. You can choose to use either the replacement or the repair cost, but this depends on your insurance policy and whether your insurance company has indicated it will write-off the items rather than attempt repair. Obviously, if an item is beyond help, you can base the claim on replacement cost, but you will need to talk to your insurer. Select **Use Replacement Cost** or **Use Repair Cost** and verify the claimed value. Click **OK** to return to the New Claim form.

Enter additional **Notes** and click **OK** to save the claim.

Quicken Home Inventory offers to create the report immediately. Click **Yes** to go ahead or **No** to go back to the main window. You can create this same report from the **Reports** menu by selecting **Insurance Claim Summary**.

After your insurance claim has been paid, return to the Claims List by selecting **View**, **Claims List** and click **Paid**. This opens the Claim Paid dialog box. Enter the date the claim was paid and the amount paid and click **OK**. Quicken again prompts you to create a claim report. Click **Yes** to create the report, or **No** to manually create the Insurance Claim Detail report at a later time. Quicken then returns you to the main inventory window. Meanwhile, the software returns any items to the inventory that have been marked on the original claim as using a repaired price basis. It also deletes any items paid on a replacement basis.

After you have purchased the replacements for the items that were written-off, you need to create new inventory items for each.

The Least You Need to Know

➤ Quicken's Home Inventory can help you make a more successful insurance claim by compiling all of the data associated with the items in your house.

➤ The best way to start the Home Inventory is to do so from within Quicken.

➤ Once you have it open on your screen, maximize the main window and take the time to explre the items already provided in the Suggested Items List.

➤ Use the Suggested Items List to speed up your entry of items and details.

➤ Use the Policies and Claims system to help satisfy your insurance obligations and speed up your claim. However, always keep your receipts and other supporting evidence of your purchases and warranties in a safe place, preferably away from your house. You can use Quicken's InsureMarket to find cheaper insurance rates on the Web.

Chapter 22

Searching and Replacing Data

In This Chapter

➤ Finding transactions fast!

➤ Searching and replacing transactions

➤ Using wildcards

Searching Questions

Need to find that transaction in the haystack? Need to find it fast? Then step this way.

Quicken provides an extensive range of search and replace facilities. Frankly, if you can't find what you're looking for with these, it's probably lost for good.

You can use the search and replace functions to fix mistakes, combine or split registers, change dates, and to correct things on a global basis—that's global as far as your file is concerned; the world's ills take a bit more work.

All Quicken's search and replace tools live under the Edit menu. However, you need an open register before you can see them all. Without worrying about opening a specific register, press **Ctrl+R** to open the last register you used. Then select the **Edit** menu and take a look at **Find and Replace**. You should see the following entries:

> ➤ **Find** This is Quicken's quickest search tool. It takes you to the nearest match in the current register with no fuss and no bother. You can learn about it later in this chapter, "Finding and Replacing Transactions."

➤ **Find Next** This is only available after you have made a match using the **Find** tool. Select this entry to take you to the next matched instance of the data you were searching, ad infinitum. By the way, you can achieve much the same result as Find Next by repeatedly clicking **Find** in the Quicken Find dialog box discussed in the following section, "Find It Fast!"

➤ **Find/Replace** This tool generates a list of transactions that match a certain criteria. You can also use it to replace data contained in those transactions with any other data you specify. You can learn about this tool later in this chapter in the section, "Finding and Replacing Transactions."

➤ **Recategorize** This tool helps you to replace one category with another, scanning through all your transactions. For more on recategorizing your transactions, see Chapter 4, "It's a Category and Class Thing."

Find It Fast!

The Find tool is a powerful method for searching through any register for data based on several conditions. If you are familiar with spreadsheets or databases, you will recognize this tool as a true querying system. Admittedly, it doesn't have as many options as your typical *SQL* engine, but it is powerful nonetheless.

To search for a transaction, open the register you need to search. Then open the **Edit** menu, select **Find and Replace** and click **Find** (**Ctrl+F**). The figure below shows the Find dialog box.

From here you can define your search criteria. Use one or more of the fields provided as follows:

➤ Use the **Find** field to indicate part or all of a name, account, amount, memo, or whatever you need to search for. To access the Calculator or Calendar icons, first select a date or amount field from the **Search** drop-down list.

➤ Use the **Search** drop-down list to search only for that information within a specific field (for example, Amount, Payee, Memo, or similar) or select **All Fields** to search every field at once.

➤ Specify the criteria that must be met to trigger a match using the **Match if** drop-down list. This list provides several useful options, including finding items that are greater or lesser than a specified amount or date, and also text that starts with, contains, or ends with the letters or words you provide.

To find one instance of that criteria in the current register, click **Find**. Click it again to find another. Quicken usually searches backward because you are placed, by default, at the end of the register. To search forward, click **Search Backwards** to remove the check mark.

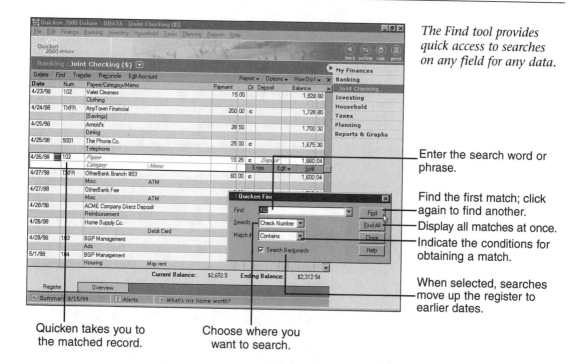

The Find tool provides quick access to searches on any field for any data.

Enter the search word or phrase.

Find the first match; click again to find another.

Display all matches at once.

Indicate the conditions for obtaining a match.

When selected, searches move up the register to earlier dates.

Quicken takes you to the matched record.

Choose where you want to search.

To find all instances of that criteria across all your registers, click **Find All**. Quicken treats this as something of a special occasion, opening the Quicken Find pane shown in the figure below if it finds transactions that match the search criteria. Double-click any transaction to jump to its entry in the register. Click the **Find** tab in the QuickTabs list to return to the Quicken Find pane where you can inspect another.

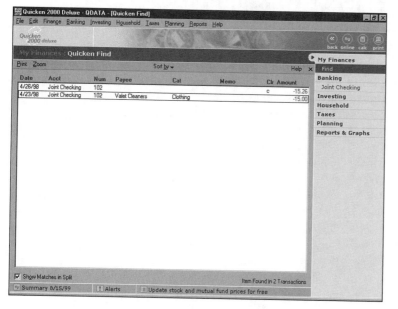

*Clicking **Find All** shows all transactions matching the search criteria, in this case two checks with identical check numbers. As you can see, the Find tool is a useful way to diagnose problems in your books; for example when accounts won't reconcile.*

The Call of the Wildcard

Quicken supports *wildcards* in all its searching facilities. Wildcards are special characters, such as ? and .. and ~, that stand for, in the first case, any single letter and, in the second, one or more letters. Quicken reads the two question marks as standing for anything—in this case, any date. The double period (..) can be used when you don't know what or how many letters need to be in the search criteria. They can be mixed and matched to provide extraordinary flexibility in your searching. For example, to find all transactions recorded during the month of October 1999, you could use the criteria "10/../99", searching for exact matches within the Date field. This finds both one- and two-digit days within that month. For the question mark, a search on "B??t" would find Boat, Beat, and Bait. However, because each question mark equals one letter, "B??t" would not find But, Bat, or Bot.

The third case, the tilde (~), tells Quicken to find everything except the text following that mark. Therefore, a search by date using ~97 as the criteria would find every transaction except those recorded in 1997.

Finding and Replacing Transactions

If you think the transaction search tools are great, you're going to love the ability to search and replace.

Considering a simple example, if you had recorded a series of transactions to a consistently incorrect payee, fixing the error takes but a moment. Simply perform a search for every transaction paid to that payee, mark those you need to change, provide the replacement payee's name, and tell Quicken to do its thing.

What Can't Find and Replace Do?

Chiefly, it can't move transactions between accounts. To do that, you must export the transactions to a separate file and then import them into the destination register. You can learn how to do this in Chapter 25, "Talk Fest: Importing and Exporting Data."

Also, it's not very good with dates. You can search for transactions made on a certain date, but you can't automatically assign those transactions another date.

You can also search for one criterion and replace something completely different. For example, you can search for all transactions that occurred on a certain date, but instead of correcting that date, you can tell Quicken to recategorize each of those transactions.

This can take some getting used to because it's so different than the search and replace function built into most other software. However, it's a great idea, and although it takes some time to learn to make the most of it, it isn't difficult to use. Sophisticated searches and effortless replacing are but a few steps away.

To begin, open the register that contains the data you want to search. Open the **Edit** menu, select **Find & Replace**, and then **Find/Replace**. The following figure shows a find and replace in action.

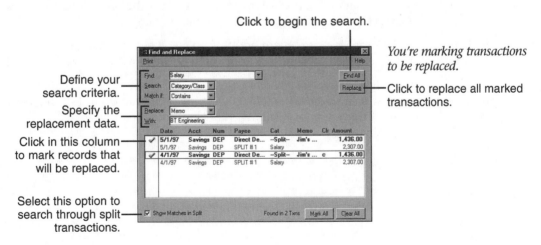

Click to begin the search.

Define your search criteria.

Specify the replacement data.

Click in this column to mark records that will be replaced.

Select this option to search through split transactions.

You're marking transactions to be replaced.

Click to replace all marked transactions.

Define your search in the following way:

➤ **Find**   Enter all or part of the search text. If you first select **Date** or **Amount** with the **Search** field, you are able to use Quicken's Calendar and Calculator tools for the **Find** field.

➤ **Search**   Select the field you need to search, or select **All Fields** to search every field at once.

➤ **Match if**   Choose the match criteria. If you're not sure how this works, see the "Searching Questions" section at the beginning of this chapter.

➤ **Replace**   Which field do you want to replace? As mentioned, this doesn't have to be the search field. For example, you might have searched by **Date** but can choose to replace using **Category**.

➤ **With**   What do you want to record in the replacement field?

Selecting **Show Matches in Split** causes the replace facility to search through the components that make up every split transaction. This is usually selected because it means you can search through transactions paid to a single source such as a supplier of goods for your business when that transaction contains numerous transactions assigned to many categories. You should click **Show Matches in Split** to remove the check mark if you want to ignore the components that make up a split transaction.

Click **Find All** to find all transactions matching the search criteria. Quicken lets you know if it can't find any matching transactions. However, if it does, they flow into the list box in the lower part of the Find and Replace dialog box.

Click in the left column of each transaction you want to alter with the replacement criteria. The check marks indicate that they will be replaced. Alternatively, click **Mark All** to mark every transaction or **Clear All** to remove those marks and start over.

When ready, click **Replace** to perform the replacement on every marked transaction. Quicken displays one final dialog box asking you to confirm the procedure. Click **OK** to go ahead or **Cancel** to return to the Find and Replace dialog box.

The Find and Replace tool is an excellent addition to Quicken's arsenal, but use it with caution. It is all too easy to wipe out hours of good work with one swipe of that **OK** button.

The good news is that it is almost as easy to correct mistakes that occur in numerous existing transactions. To my way of thinking, that's not too poor a trade.

The Least You Need to Know

➤ Although Quicken provides a specialized recategorization tool, you can achieve the same results and, indeed, many more by using the Find and the Find & Replace tools.

➤ To quickly find a transaction, press **Ctrl+F** and set up the criteria. Click a field within the transaction to use that as the default search field.

➤ Wildcards are great ways to find information when you are unsure of the spelling, or you need to find all instances of transactions that occurred within a certain month or year.

➤ If you can't seem to find and replace certain transactions, even though you know they are there, make sure the option to search within a split is selected within the Find/Replace dialog box.

Chapter 23

911: Emergency Records

In This Chapter

➤ Tips for managing emergency records

➤ Recording and updating records

➤ Printing emergency reports

Organizing Your Emergency Records

"Operator, operator! What's the number for 911?"

Only Homer Simpson could so memorably forget the number for 911. On the other hand, you are almost certain to find a use for Quicken's Emergency Records Organizer.

You can use the Emergency Records Organizer to store critical information about you and your family, including personal contacts, medical records, the location of important legal documents such as your will, desired funeral arrangements, passports, and more.

There are two situations when the Emergency Records Organizer proves vitally important. The first is if tragedy strikes; the last thing you want to be doing is searching drawers and filing cabinets for elusive documents.

The second is when you need information in a hurry. Maintaining a list of allergies, important medical contacts, and other known medical conditions for all the members of your family is clearly a task everyone should undertake.

The Emergency Records Organizer gathers this and other important information around a central point, making that information easy to find in an emergency.

However, before you begin recording your vital facts and statistics, keep the following points in mind:

➤ It's okay to store this information in Quicken, but don't forget you should also maintain paper copies, preferably with your attorney or in a safe-deposit box.

➤ Print the Detail Report as described in the next section so you or your relatives have the report readily accessible without turning to Quicken. In fact, if you password-protect your files, they won't stand a chance of seeing that information anyway.

➤ Keep a current backup of all your Quicken data, storing the disks well away from the computer.

➤ Don't assume that just because you specify your funeral arrangements here, they must be legally adhered to. You must still create a legally acceptable will, duly signed and witnessed. The requirements vary from state to state, so seek the advice of a legal eagle.

Of course, the organizer can be used for much more than "disaster-related" information. By exploring the different areas, you'll see that you can turn it into the perfect organizer for recording everything from your children's school contact details and daily schedules to the phone numbers and addresses of physicians, contact details, and account numbers for your bank and investment accounts, and more. It's like a handy database where most of the work in setting up and defining fields has already been done.

Creating and Updating Emergency Records

To open the Emergency Records Organizer, open the **Household** menu and select **Emergency Records Organizer**.

The first thing you see is the Introduction screen. Go to the top of the window and click the **Create/Update Records** tab. This takes you to the screen shown in the following figure.

How Can I Save My Emergency Records?

Your emergency records are stored with the rest of your Quicken data, so there's no need to specifically save them. If you have password-protected your Quicken file, all the copies of your emergency files on your hard drive and in your backup system are password-protected as well.

Click this tab to
open your records.

Select a general area to
begin recording data.

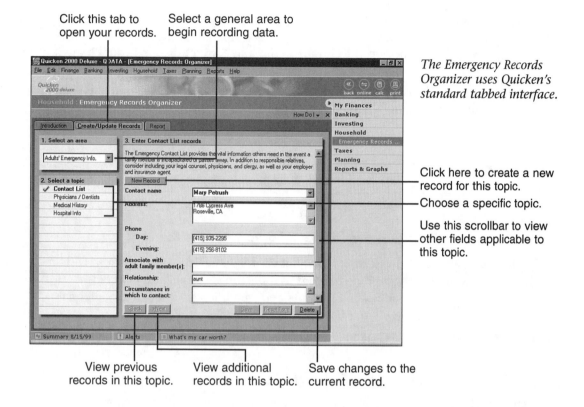

*The Emergency Records
Organizer uses Quicken's
standard tabbed interface.*

Click here to create a new
record for this topic.

Choose a specific topic.

Use this scrollbar to view
other fields applicable to
this topic.

View previous
records in this topic.

View additional
records in this topic.

Save changes to the
current record.

The **Create/Update Records** screen consists of three main areas, much like the Tax
Deduction Finder. You use these to indicate the broad area of information you want
to target, then to select a specific topic within that area, and to provide the information for that topic in the form of one or more records.

Starting with the portion of the window labeled **1. Select an area**, click the drop-
down arrow to display and select from the list of categories. You cannot add to this
list, but it's made up of a wide variety of categories that are well worth exploring. You
might even find it quite inspirational in helping you store other forms of information.

In the area labeled **2. Select a topic**, choose the specific type of information you
want to store. The list changes according to the category selected in step 1. When
you select a topic, the pane on the right changes to reflect the type of information
you need to record for that topic. If you have already recorded information for a
topic, a check mark appears to its left.

Use the pane on the right labeled **3. Enter Contact List records** to enter information for the topic. Each field prompts you on what is required. If there are more fields
than fit on the screen, use the scrollbars to move up and down. If you already have
recorded something for this topic, click **New Record** to start a new blank record.

After you have completed the record, click **Save** to write those details to your Quicken file. As soon as you have done so, a check mark is added to the topic list in the left pane. **Delete** deletes the current record and **Cancel** discards your changes.

Edit your records by using the **<Back** and **>Next** buttons to move through all the records you have entered for any topic. After you've found the correct one, simply change each field as required and click **Save**.

Does Quicken Create Some Records for Me?

It certainly does. You will notice that details from your accounts appear in certain reports even though you didn't record that data in the Emergency Records Organizer. These include account names and credit limits, although the information does not include current balances.

Printing Emergency Reports

After you finish entering your records it's time to consider printing a report. As mentioned at the beginning of this chapter, you should try to keep this report in a safe place. If your house has a fireproof safe or room, that's a good option. Otherwise, consider filing them with your attorney or placing them in a safe-deposit box. Obviously, the necessity of this depends on the type of records you have entered, but if it's anything your family or other loved ones might require one day, consider its storage very carefully. Most importantly, don't forget to tell them where these records are stored.

Printing an Emergency Records report is easy. Simply click the final tab, **Report**.

Select the type of report you want to create by using the pull-down list under **Report Type**. Table 23.1 provides a guide to each report and its contents. You can also **Sort by family members** and **Print topics with no data entered**.

Table 23.1 Emergency Records Organizer Reports

Report Title	Contents/Purpose
Emergency	Combines all the information contained in the topic **Adults' Emergency Info**. Obviously, this is for use in an emergency.
Caretaker	Uses the **Home/Auto/Property** topic. As its name suggests, this is ideal for printing out a copy and giving it to whoever looks after your home while you're away.

Report Title	Contents/Purpose
Survivor's	If you lose a family member, the Survivor's Report includes their personal information taken from the **Adults' Important Info.** and **Personal & Legal Docs** topics.
Summary of Records Entered	Combines all records entered so far, but includes only the most important information from each.
Detail Report	Combines all topics and records, printing everything you have recorded to date.

Reports are usually sorted by topic. I prefer to sort by individual family members, bringing together all the records for each person. This provides a grouping that is more convenient for fast access. Printing topics with no data seems like a good idea if you're not near a computer and need to write information by hand into the report. Unfortunately, each field in each topic for which you have failed to supply information prints with a bold **(No data entered)**. This option isn't particularly useful.

The report appears in the lower window. Preview it onscreen, as shown in the following figure, using the scrollbars to move up and down the report. Produce a hard copy of the report by opening the **File** menu and selecting **Print List** (**Ctrl+P**).

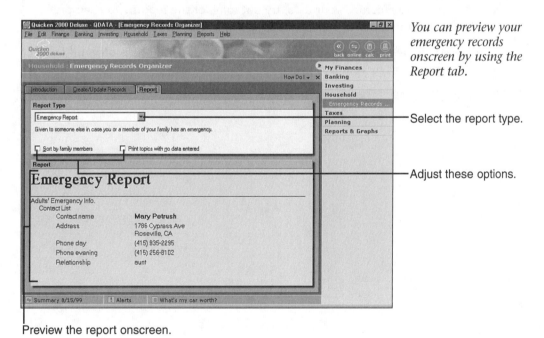

You can preview your emergency records onscreen by using the Report tab.

Select the report type.

Adjust these options.

Preview the report onscreen.

That's it! By using the Emergency Records Organizer diligently, you make everyone's life easier in a crisis, but keep in mind that it can also help you day-to-day with your most important phone numbers and contact addresses.

As always, you should obtain professional advice when planning your estate, constructing a will, or determining the future of your loved ones. Most of all, remember to never ask an operator for the number to 911.

The Least You Need to Know

➤ The Emergency Records Organizer is a wonderful crisis management tool in that it puts all the emergency information you need at your own, or someone else's, fingertips.

➤ There's no need to fill in every possible information category, but make sure you cover those most relevant to your situation.

➤ Most of the categories are for multiple records. You can view these using the **Next** and **Back** buttons, if shown.

➤ After you have recorded your data, try out some of the reports. You can preview them onscreen and print them using the File menu's **Print List** command.

➤ Always keep a paper copy of Emergency Records. This will help others if they can't gain access to your computer.

Chapter 24

Making Contact with the Address Book

In This Chapter

➤ Opening and closing the Address Book

➤ Creating new records

➤ Grouping and searching records

➤ Printing mailing labels, return addresses, address book entries, and more

---

Introducing the Address Book

The Address Book built into Quicken Deluxe and Quicken Home and Business helps you manage your personal and business contacts. It's a great tool that acts as a handy electronic organizer, and can also print mailing labels suitable for marketing or personal purposes.

The Address Book is also useful because it offers a place in which to store information that goes beyond the basic mailing address you might use when writing checks in Quicken. You can store data such as the name and position of your contacts within various organizations, as well as their cellular telephone numbers, the names of their spouses and children—even their birthdays!

Of course, it takes some time to record all that information into the Address Book, but you do have a slight head start. If you attach addresses to the checks you post, the addresses are already recorded in the Address Book. The Address Book also reflects changes made to your memorized and scheduled transaction lists, but it doesn't include your online payees.

If you use Quicken Home and Business, you can also see the contact information you have recorded on your invoices appear in the Address Book, but you might want to check that Quicken is set up to do this. Just open the **Edit** menu, select **Options**, and choose **Register**. Click the **QuickFill** tab in the Register options dialog box and click to place a check mark beside **Add Address Book QuickFill Group Items to QuickFill List**.

Where's the Search Facility?

The old Financial Address Book provided a far more comprehensive search facility than the new Address Book. In fact, in just one glance you'll notice a host of differences.

However, the good news is that this has been more than made up for by much tighter integration with Quicken. In fact, you'll find it easier than ever before to create truly effective marketing campaigns.

Starting and Exiting the Address Book

To get started, open the **Finance** menu and select **Address Book**.

A window similar to that shown in the following figure appears.

After you start the Address Book, there are several tasks you will probably want to perform. These include:

➤ Recording new and editing existing contacts

➤ Searching for contacts that meet certain criteria

➤ Grouping your contacts to make them easier to manage

➤ Printing lists of addresses and mailing labels

Let's look at each.

Enter a search term for the
current selected column.

Select or view existing
records using this list.

Filter the list by
one or all groups.

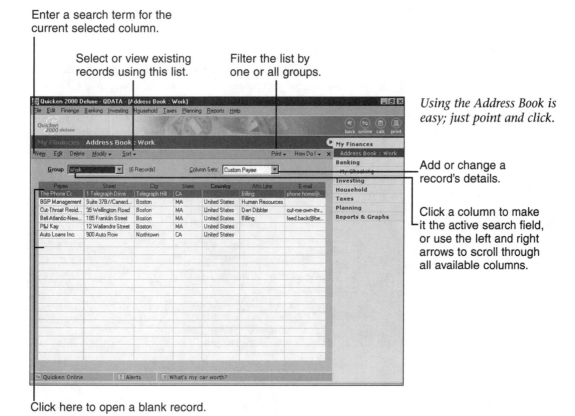

*Using the Address Book is
easy; just point and click.*

Add or change a
record's details.

Click a column to make
it the active search field,
or use the left and right
arrows to scroll through
all available columns.

Click here to open a blank record.

Recording and Editing Contacts

To start recording a new record, click the **New** button at the top of the Address Book
pane.

The dialog box shown in the following figure appears.

Now, there are many fields scattered around the various tabs in this dialog box, and
nearly all are perfectly self-explanatory.

Instead of explaining each one, the following bulleted list just shows you a few tricks:

➤ You don't have to fill in all the fields, but make sure you explore those that are
available. For example, the Notes field under the Miscellaneous tab is a great
place for addresses that don't fit the standard fields. If you do put an address
there, click the **Format** button and select **Use First 5 Lines of Notes
instead of Address**.

➤ To make your contact part of one or more groups, click the **Group** button and select the ones you require from the list. You can learn more about groups in the later section, "Grouping Your Contacts."

➤ Back on the Payee tab, select **Include this Payee in QuickFill List** to add this payee to the list Quicken uses to complete payee names while you type. Make sure you have also selected **Add Address Book QuickFill Group Items to QuickFill List** in your register options. (Open the **Edit** menu, select **Options**, choose **Register**, click the **QuickFill** tab, and then click on that option.)

Use the Tab key to move between related groups of fields. Most entries are optional.

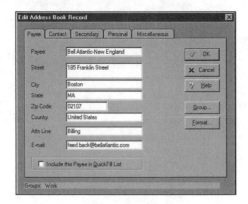

QuickFill List?

There is no place in Quicken that you can view this list. It is maintained internally to help you quickly complete payee names when recording transactions and checks. For example, if you type Sm Quicken could automatically complete the ith, assuming, of course, you have recorded Smith in an earlier transaction. Quicken completes the name by looking up those letters as you type them in its QuickFill list.

➤ To edit an entry, double-click its name in the list, make any changes, and click **OK** to save them.

➤ Quicken treats a payee's first and last names as an organization. You can convert existing entries imported from your existing Payee List by selecting them in the Address Book window, opening the **Modify** menu, and selecting **Switch**

Names and Organization. This cuts the data stored under the Organization field and pastes it into the Address Book's First and Last Name. These fields are located under the **Contact** tab in the Edit Address Book Record dialog box.

Adding Yourself to the Address Book

When you print labels from the Address Book, you can choose one of the records to become the return address. That means you should add yourself to the Address Book list, recording the return address in the address fields provided. One point, though: make sure you don't also assign yourself to a group, otherwise you might end up posting yourself a Christmas card!

Grouping Your Contacts

By grouping your Address Book records, you can more easily manage related sets of contacts. Grouping helps you to filter the list by one type of contact or another. This is handy if you need to print mailing labels for one set of contacts or another, but not all at once. For example, throughout the year you might regularly print mailing labels for your business contacts, but come Christmas you might instead only print mailing labels for everyone on your Christmas card list. (There's an old threat: "Huh! Now you're off my Christmas Card list". Do it for real!)

The Address Book has five predefined groups. The following groups are located under the **Group** pull-down menu in the Address Book window:

➤ **Family, Friends, Work, and Christmas List**   These are the default groups already built into the Address Book.

➤ **All Groups**   With this selected, every contact for every group is displayed simultaneously.

➤ **Unassigned**   These are all your contacts who haven't yet been assigned a group.

➤ **QuickFill**   This is used for contacts copied from Quicken's QuickFill List.

➤ **Selected Groups**   Selecting this group opens a Show Selected Groups dialog box. Use this dialog box to select all the groups you want to display at once. For example, you might want to view all records grouped as Family, Friends, or Christmas List. Selecting those groups here displays all the cards that are marked as any of those three groups.

➤ **New**   Select this to create a new group. Just provide a name and click **OK**.

➤ **Edit**   Select this to edit the name of an existing group or to delete groups from the list.

You'll also see groups for Customers and Vendors if you use Quicken Home and Business.

To change the assigned group of any one contact, select that contact in the list, open the **Modify** menu, and select **Assign to Groups**. Select each group this contact should be a part of and click **OK**.

To revert back to no group, click each selected group to deselect it and then click **OK**.

Finally, use the Column Set menu to change the columns that are displayed in the Address Book list. Try a few to see what they do, or return to the default Payee column set.

Printing Addresses and Mailing Labels

The Address Book makes it easy to create a list of clients, complete a marketing campaign, or speed up the annual Christmas card mailing frenzy.

You can print addresses or mailing labels for entries you manually select from the list (hold down the **Ctrl** key and click on each), or every entry within a group.

It is this functionality that turns the Address Book into a potentially powerful marketing tool.

To print labels, open the **File** menu from the Address Book window and select **Labels**.

The dialog box shown in the following figure appears.

Quicken can print a wide variety of label formats.

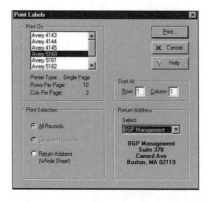

Select the appropriate Avery label formats and, for partially printed sheets, type in the **Row** and **Column** from which you want to start printing.

Under **Print Selection** choose one of the following:

➤ **All Records**   Print all the records displayed in the current list. If that list has been filtered using the Group pull-down menu, you only print labels for that group. Therefore, to target only your Christmas List, select that first from the Group menu and then select the **Print Labels** command.

➤ **Selected Records**   Print labels for only those records selected in the current list. You can select more than one record by clicking it while holding down the **Ctrl** key. To make a continuous selection, click the first record and, while holding down the **Shift** key, click the last record. This selects all the records in-between.

➤ **Return Address (Whole Sheet)**   Print an entire sheet of return addresses. This is handy if you have hand addressed your envelopes and just want to print your own address so that you can fix it to the back of each envelope. Note that if you select this option, you must also select your return address using the Return Address **Select** menu to the right.

When you are ready, click **Print**, set your final printer options, and either click **Preview** to show the results on your screen for a final once-over before you print or cancel the job, or click **OK** to send them to the printer straight away.

Changing Printers and Fonts

It's easy to change the printer and font used to print your envelopes. You can do so by clicking **Main Font** in the Print Labels dialog box (this changes the font for this single print run), or you can change the default font and printer by opening the **File** menu, selecting **Printer/Setup**, and choosing **For Reports/Graphs**. Select the envelope printer using the Printer pull-down list. Select an alternate font, style, or size by clicking **Body Font**. You can change fonts to go for something a little more festive, more in keeping with your business, or just right for a special occasion. Here's another quick hint: always remember that the plainer and more readable the font, the better chance it has of zipping through the postal service's automated sorting machines.

The Least You Need to Know

➤ The Address Book replaces the old Financial Address Book. Although it doesn't offer the same feature set as the previous Financial Address Book, it does a much better job of synchronizing the address book data throughout Quicken.

➤ The Address Book stores payees from checks on which you have included an address, and, if you use Quicken Home and Business, the debtors shown on invoices.

➤ Don't feel you need to provide all of the information prompted for by the Address Book's fields.

➤ If you have a particularly troublesome address that doesn't fit the usual fields, type it into the Notes field and use the Format settings to specify that the first five lines of the Notes field should act as the address.

➤ If your business has a strong corporate image, use the font settings to match the font used on the address labels to that used in the body text of the rest of your correspondence.

Chapter 25

Talk Fest: Importing and Exporting Data

In This Chapter

➤ Understanding QIF and other export methods

➤ Exporting reports via clipboard and disk

➤ Exporting transactions

➤ Importing transactions

The Well-Connected Computer

No computer is an island, and Quicken is no exception.

In fact, by using Quicken's export and import functions, you can work with other Quicken files, merging data or splitting off sections of your own accounts. You can also export your reports to other software for further manipulation.

You can import and export data in any of the following formats:

➤ **Importing or Exporting QIF Files**   The QIF (Quicken Interchange Format) system is most useful for copying data from one Quicken file to another or for moving transactions between accounts in the same file. QIF files are stored in an ASCII format, so you can look at them with your word processor or even the Windows Notepad. However, they won't make a lot of sense if you do. The coding used for these files was definitely designed to be read by machine, not human (well, except for particular programmers, and I'm going to give their humanity the benefit of the doubt), and they can only be understood by programs that specifically support the QIF format.

➤ **DDE**   Dynamic Data Exchange is a communications standard built into Windows that is used to transfer data between one application and another. DDE is fast and seamless. When add-on software such as TurboTax and TaxPlanner magically extracts data from your Quicken file, the transfer almost certainly occurs through the magic of DDE.

➤ **Windows Clipboard**   Although this is the most basic exchange mechanism, it's also the one you use the most. Most Quicken data can't be copied to the Clipboard, or if it can, it isn't understood by any other software. However, some data can be copied, including the text that makes up any report.

➤ **Printing To Disk**   Quicken can not only send print reports to your printer but also to a disk file. Anytime you click the **Print** button at the top of Quicken's report windows, you see a host of possible disk-based formats from which you can take your pick (see the following figure). An ASCII disk file is the simplest format, but a tab-delimited report is useful for importing that report into other applications.

Even the Report window's print facility can export your data to a disk file.

Exporting Reports

Quicken can export data through the Clipboard by printing reports to a disk file or via a QIF file. The system you use depends on your purpose. For example, QIF files are great for working directly with your Quicken data because they represent that data in its raw form—that is, on a transaction-by-transaction basis. However, unless you are exporting that data to another program that can read and work with the specialized QIF format (for example, TurboTax), it doesn't prove very helpful. The data in a QIF file simply doesn't make much sense when exported to other programs, such as your favorite word processor or spreadsheet package.

If you do need to work with your data in another program, do so using data that has already been processed in some way. Rather than playing with a list of transactions, you might prefer to manipulate the figures that show your spending by category. In other words, it is more useful for you to create a Profit and Loss report and export that than it is for you to export the individual transactions that comprise it. The report is data that Quicken itself has already interpreted, compiled, and turned into an interesting set of results. (If you do need information on a transaction level, you can still get to it by creating and exporting a Register Report.)

After you have created the report, copy the results into your word processor or spreadsheet and further manipulate them as required.

You have two ways to extract report data from Quicken: through the Windows Clipboard and by printing the report to disk. Knowing how to do this enables you to use the reports you export for any or all of the following:

➤ Exporting data to a word processing or DTP (desktop publishing) package ready to be turned into a slick, professionally presented report or table.

➤ Exporting data to a spreadsheet program such as Microsoft Excel or Lotus 1-2-3 where it can be further analyzed or used with that software's more extensive graphing tools.

➤ Exporting to a database, ready for long-term storage.

➤ Electronically transmitted across the Internet.

Exporting to the Clipboard

There is just one way to copy report data to the Windows Clipboard: Create the report in Quicken and click the **Copy** button near the top of the report window. This copies the complete report; in fact, you can't copy only part of a report. After you have copied the report to the Clipboard, you can simply paste it into the target document using that application's usual pasting facility.

The bad news is that at first sight you're likely to be disappointed by the results. Even when pasted into a word processor or a desktop publishing (*DTP*) package, the pasted material looks less like neat columns of figures and more like a mish-mash of scrambled digits. However, if you copy and paste the data into a spreadsheet, it should turn out okay.

I can't provide you with steps on how to make reports look great in your preferred DTP or word processing software, but I can give you some tips that should help you more quickly achieve great results with your copied reports.

Just keep the following in mind:

➤ Everything relies on tabs. Tabs must be used to align the columns in reports, and you can't achieve the same results by filling the gaps between the columns with loads of spaces. The spaces in proportional typefaces such as Arial or Times have a different width to the characters and it is next to impossible to arrange them so that they fall into neat, vertical columns. Although this isn't true if you use a nonproportional typeface, such as Courier, the results don't compare—at least, not too favorably.

How Can I Find a Nonproportional Typeface on My Computer?

All Windows computers include the nonproportional Courier typeface. However, you might also have others. You can pick them out if you look for a typeface whose letter and space characters take the same amount of horizontal room. (This is the definition behind nonproportional.) In other words, an "I" requires the same space as an "O", even though the "I" is actually much narrower than the "O". In a proportional typeface, such as the one used throughout this book, "II" takes far less room than "OO". The space between characters—the kerning—also changes in a proportional typeface from one pair of characters to the next.

Quicken assigns a tab to every column in the report—with one exception. All you have to do is either insert those tabs or shift their position until everything aligns. The exception is the area leading up to the first column. Any lines indented within that column are indented using spaces rather than tabs.

➤ Use decimal tabs for any column that deals with a monetary amount. Decimal tabs align columns of numbers according to the position of the decimal point, rather than an arbitrary setting such as the left or right edge of the text. This creates a precisely aligned column of decimal points.

If You Use Microsoft Word...

The easiest way to work with report data you have exported from Quicken is to paste the data into Word, select it, open Word's **Table** menu, and select **Convert Text to Table**. You might also find it helpful to turn on hidden characters so you can more easily see how Quicken uses tabs and spaces in the exported data. To do so, open Word's **Tools** menu, select **Options**, click the **View** tab in the Options dialog box, and select **Tab characters** and **Spaces**.

➤ Quicken doesn't export the report title or column headings, so you need to create your own. To export a report with these features, read "Exporting to a Disk File," in the next section.

➤ Use a thin font. Quicken truncates any text that spills into the next column, replacing the truncated letters with an ellipsis (...). A report copied to the Clipboard contains the full text from every column. To make the columns fit, you can either take the virtual scissors to them as per the Quicken method, or set the text in a tighter typeface, such as Helvetica Narrow or Futura Condensed. Experiment with your font list until you find one that works. In general, serif typefaces such as Times (or Times New Roman) squeeze more text onto the page (or within a column) than sans serif typefaces such as Arial. However, condensed versions of sans serif typefaces work better than serif typefaces, hence the availability of Helvetica and Futura in their compressed forms. If you can't find a thin font, try using a smaller type size. Although most computers use 12-point type as a matter of course, certain sans serif typefaces down to about 7 points in size should remain quite readable when printed on a 600-dpi or better laser printer.

To Serif or Sans Serif?

Serifs are the small curlicues (or spiky bits, to be less precise) and other artifices that adorn the letters of many fonts, including the text used for the body of this book. Sans serif (literally, "without serif") is a typeface with clean sides: for example, the font used for the headings within this book. Because of their clarity, these are more readable on a computer screen and, for the same reason, are more readable than serif typefaces when reproduced at a smaller size on the printed page.

➤ Set your page to landscape. Turning a page on its side is, of course, ideal for printing reports with numerous columns extending across the page. You should be able to do this from nearly any word processing or DTP package by opening the **File** menu and selecting **Page Setup** or **Printer Setup** (or occasionally both). If you continue to experience trouble squeezing the columns onto a single page, try decreasing your margins and the size of the font.

Exporting to a Disk File

If you don't want to work with the report data immediately, you need to send the report to someone else, or you simply need to store it somewhere for archival purposes, you should print the report to a disk file.

Quicken supports several disk file formats. These are:

➤ **ASCII Disk File** Unlike a copied report, the ASCII format writes the report to disk exactly as it would appear on your printer, complete with a report title and column headings. The ASCII format also replaces tabs with spaces. This means you don't need to worry about setting tabs to make sense of the columns. In fact, you should be able to drop this report into any word processing or DTP package, set it in a nonproportional typeface such as Courier, and expect it to come out just right.

These reports also have the distinct advantage of being perfectly DOS-compatible. The horizontal width is limited to 80 characters, and choosing **Portrait** or **Landscape** within the Print window makes no difference to the end result. You can look at these reports by using any DOS text-editing package and also through the Windows Notepad. To open the latter, click the Windows **Start** button, select **Accessories**, and then choose **Notepad**. These reports don't make much sense when viewed in a word processor unless you select the text and set it in a nonproportional typeface such as Courier. Quicken also truncates text spilling over the preset column limit.

What About the Windows WordPad?

Although ASCII reports look good when viewed through the Windows Notepad, you can achieve some simple formatting using proportional typefaces and tabs if you copy the report to the Clipboard and then paste it into Windows WordPad. The WordPad is located within the Accessories section of the Window Start menu, just beneath the Notepad. WordPad can import graphics and do a whole lot more to your reports. It's definitely worth exploring.

➤ **Tab-Delimited Disk File** The tab-delimited format is similar to the Copy to Clipboard function except that it saves the column headings with the report body. This format won't make much sense when viewed through a DOS editor or the Windows Notepad, but it does work if you reset it using tabs in a word processing or DTP package. Whether you use a proportional or nonproportional typeface is up to you, but usually the former looks better.

The tab-delimited format is ideal for importing the report into some spreadsheets, but not all. This is because Quicken saves the report using the full text contained in every column. In other words, it is saved without truncation. Because Quicken also saves the text with tabs and column headers, most spreadsheets have everything they require to import and recognize the report. Some, however, fail to pick up the difference between the report's text and its numerical elements.

➤ **123 (.PRN) Disk File**   This format was designed for Lotus 1-2-3 spreadsheets but works with any program that can read comma-delimited text. As this is as common a format as tab-delimited, chances are compatible products include your own spreadsheet software.

The comma-delimited format swaps tabs for commas. In addition, it surrounds the text with quotation marks but leaves the numbers as is. This is a universally recognized system, so don't let the "123" demarcation put you off. All three of the major spreadsheets understand this format, as well as many others.

Understanding the different formats was the hard part. To export a report to a disk file, simply follow these steps.

1. First create the report and adjust the dates or otherwise customize it until the data is just right.

2. Open Quicken's **File** menu and select **Print Report** (**Ctrl+P**), or click the **Print** button at the top of the report window.

3. In the Print dialog box, use the **Print to group** option to select a destination for your report. You have the following options:

   ➤ Your Printer

   ➤ ASCII Disk File

   ➤ Tab-Delimited Disk File

   ➤ 123 (.PRN) Disk File

4. Click **OK**. If you selected one of the disk file options, choose a **File name** and select the folder into which you want to write the file. Set the **Lines Per Page** and the **Width** as required. Leave **Lines Per Page** at 0 to print your report with no page breaks. This is useful when exporting the report to another program because it suppresses the header and footer information usually associated with page breaks.

5. Finally, click **Save** to generate the report.

Understanding QIF

Quicken's QIF format is ideal for shifting data between two or more Quicken files. However, for the reasons mentioned at the beginning of this chapter, it isn't much good at shifting data between Quicken and other software. Still, QIF is very flexible. You can use it to export not only existing transactions, but also account names, category names, and memorized transactions.

This proves very useful in all sorts of situations. Here are just a few examples:

➤ **Combining business and personal records**   Let's say you have always kept your business and personal records separate, storing your business books on the computer at work, and your personal transactions on the computer at home. Assuming you are self-employed, you have to combine both books to provide an overall picture at tax time. Fortunately, that's easy. Just export your business' accounts with full transactions and category names. Save the file on a disk, take it home, and import it into your personal accounts. That's all it takes.

➤ **Combining records after marriage**   What do two Quicken users do after they get married? Forget the honeymoon, forget the house, and forget the kids. For a commitment that counts, it's hard to beat merging both Quicken files. ("Repeat after me: I promise to maintain my Quicken file and make regular backups until death of hard disk us do part.") The QIF system makes this a cinch, although you have to decide which categories to keep and which to discard.

➤ **Creating an ideal set of accounts and categories**. This is a great tip for service-oriented accounting practices. Quicken's default categories are rather limited, more for simplicity's sake than any other. To give your Quicken users even better service, create a standard set of accounts and categories and supply them to new clients on a 3.5-inch disk. Have your users import these rather than create their own accounts and categories in ad hoc manners.

You can even customize the list for each client. At tax time, knowing your clients have been working to a certain Quicken standard makes everyone's job easier.

➤ **Correct a bookkeeping error**   The ability to shift transactions between one account and the next makes it possible to correct a range of bookkeeping errors. For instance, say you created an account of the wrong type and have been using it steadily for a week, month, or even the entire year. The fix is easy. Export the transactions from that account and import them into the correct account. Then go back and delete the original transactions or even the entire original account.

Knowing how to use the QIF export system is an important part of mastering Quicken. It can help you manage your finances in numerous ways.

Exporting with QIF

To open the QIF exporter, click the **File** menu and select **Export**. The QIF Export dialog box shown in the following figure appears.

Use this dialog box to define the data you want to export. For instance:

➤ **QIF File to Export to**   Either type in a filename or click **Browse** and select an existing file. If you are exporting to a new file, open the destination folder using **Browse**, enter the filename, and click **OK**. Note that Quicken understands the long filename format of Windows 95 and Windows 98, so you can get away with a filename such as My Exported Quicken Data.

Enter the export   ...or click here   Select dates to bracket
filename...   to browse.   your exported transactions.

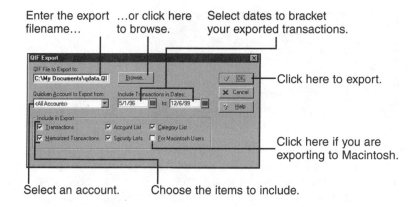

QIF exports from one
account at a time, but it
can include the full list of
accounts and categories.

Click here to export.

Click here if you are
exporting to Macintosh.

Select an account.   Choose the items to include.

➤ **Quicken Account to Export**   Select your account from the pull-down list.
To export all accounts at once—that is, every single transaction included in your
file—select **<All Accounts>** from the top of this list.

➤ **Include Transactions in Dates**   You can choose to export only those transactions between the dates you specify here. The default dates cover the earliest
to the most recent transaction dates.

➤ **Include in Export**   You can check one or all of these options. Obviously, if
you just want to export a list of category names, you should check only
Category List. However, if you also want to include transactions, make sure
you check **Transactions**. The option **For Macintosh Users** is an interesting
one. Quicken doesn't include historical stock prices in any of the standard
exports. In fact, there is no way to shift historical stock prices from one
Windows Quicken file to another. However, they can be exported to the
Macintosh version. Unfortunately, it doesn't work to export to the Macintosh
and then import that file into the Windows version. The stock history will not
follow through. If you plan to combine two files, select everything here except
the option **For Macintosh Users**.

When you've finished, click **OK** to export the file to disk.

Importing with QIF

The Quicken QIF importing screen is very similar to the exporting screen, but with
some important operational differences.

To import a file, open the **File** menu, select **Import**, and choose **QIF File**. This
opens the QIF Import dialog box shown in the following figure.

Select the file you want to import either by typing in its name or browsing for it
through **Browse**.

Use the **Quicken Account to Import Into** pull-down list to send the imported
transactions to a specific account or, by selecting **<All Accounts>**, to all your
existing accounts.

The QIF Import system is very similar to the export system.

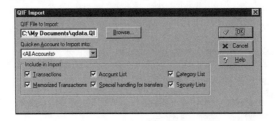

Even if the file you import includes account and category names, you must still have at least one account in your existing file. This makes it impossible to import a QIF file if you don't already have at least one register in place. However, if you do need to import data into an essentially blank file, create a dummy account while completing the New User Setup and select that account now from the pull-down list. The imported file can then create all the stored categories, accounts, and transactions. Delete the dummy account to revert to the real data.

Use the **Include in Import** options to specify the parts of the file you want to import. If you will be importing from several QIF files in an effort to re-create part or all of a set of books, you should also select **Special handling for transfers**. This matches up and links paired transactions that shift money between two accounts. If you want to combine two sets of accounts, just select every available option.

Finally, click **OK** to complete the import.

The Least You Need to Know

➤ Quicken can import and export data with almost no fuss or bother. Compared to most other accounting packages, it is remarkable how easily it accommodates accounts, categories, and transfers.

➤ When you export data, make sure you select **For Macintosh Users** if the file you are exporting will be imported into the Macintosh version of Quicken.

➤ Most tax professionals are only interested in data for the past financial year. Set the appropriate dates in the Date fields to only export that which is pertinent.

➤ The easiest way to combine two sets of Quicken data is to export **<All Accounts>** from one and then import **<All Accounts>** into the other.

➤ Finally, if you don't require them in the destination file, deselect **Memorized Transactions** when exporting. This can cleave a large file in two.

Glossary

401(k)   A retirement account set up on your behalf by your employer. The account is funded through deductions from your paycheck and is *tax-deferred* until you start to draw on those funds after retirement. Quicken provides a special form of account to manage your 401(k).

accelerated depreciation   Used by many corporations to achieve a higher tax deduction at the beginning of a product's purchase (usually a large capital item) followed by a steadily decreasing rate of depreciation. If the product was purchased on borrowed funds, it is possible to gain a larger tax deduction than the actual payments, making the tax dollars flow in reverse. The accountant who thought that one up has probably been inducted into the Tax Professionals' Hall of Fame. (See also *straight-line depreciation*.)

account   Quicken's accounts provide a register in which you can store transactions. You can use Quicken's accounts to build a copy of your real-world accounts (savings, checking, credit cards, and so on), or to create special purpose accounts to help you to track a loan liability, amounts you are owed, investments, and so on. It all depends on your taste for accounting.

accrual-based   An accounting method that recognizes expenses as they are incurred, rather than when they are paid. Accrual-based income is recognized as it is billed rather than when payment is received. (See also *cash-based*.)

Alternative Minimum Tax   This type of tax is applied by the IRS when a taxpayer appears likely to receive an unusually high and perhaps inequitable level of benefits due to itemized deductions and other exemptions. In other words, that's one loophole forever closed. AMT is figured using Form 6251, but Quicken's Tax Planner can also do it for you.

amortized loans   Loans that are repaid in two parts: interest and principal. Even though each loan repayment remains the same over the course of the loan, the interest component of each repayment is greater at the beginning but decreases over the course of the loan. Conversely, the principal amount starts small and gradually increases. You can view the varying amounts using Quicken's Loan Planner. Almost all mortgages and personal loans are examples of amortized loans.

annual yield   Also referred to as the yield, this investment term divides the annual dividend of a stock by its share price. So if a stock pays dividends of $6 per share over the course of the year and the share price is $80, the annual yield is 7.5%.

annualized   Financial data for part of a year projected forward to obtain an estimated total for the entire year. Therefore, income of $60,000 over three months becomes $240,000 annualized.

annuities   Tax-deferred investment vehicles often held with an insurance company or with insurance-like properties. Most annuities are called variable annuities. They pay either a fixed or variable rate of income for life after you retire. Income from annuities is subject to tax, which almost always is at a higher rate than the equivalent capital gains payable on other types of investments. This makes them a rather poor choice for retirees, no matter what the insurance companies claim.

appreciation   Something the author hopes the readers of this book feel. Sorry, it's really a rise in the saleable value of an item. The appreciation becomes part of a capital gains calculation when you sell that item and as such is subject to tax. The opposite of appreciation is *depreciation*.

asset   Something in which you have a financial interest. For example, a house or car, cash in the bank, securities investments, or money you are owed. Although an asset was traditionally the part you owned outright, or that part of the principal of a loan you had repaid, as long as you also track the liability, the actual amount you own shows up as *equity* in a *balance sheet* report. This means that the easiest way to track mortgages in Quicken is to create a liability account and attach to it an amortized loan.

asset class   A group of assets, such as securities of a specific type. Both Quicken Deluxe and Quicken Home and Business can download asset classes for those securities you create with a *ticker*.

balance forward   Applying payments to a group of invoices or bills by starting at the oldest and working towards the most recent until the amount has been allocated in full. This method is used most often for regular clients or those with an account. The alternative to balance forward is known as *open item*.

balance sheet   A report that shows the total of your assets at the top, and combined liabilities and equity below. If both amounts total, the books are said to be "balanced."

blue-chip   Large stocks whose market capitalization is approximately equal to their assets. These are considered stable stocks. The most exclusive group of blue-chip stocks are those that have been included in the Dow Jones 30—the stocks that make up the Dow Jones Industrial Average.

bonds   A form of security that you purchase for a fixed period of time such as 5, 10, 20, or even 30 years. Bonds promise pay interest at a fixed rate. When the time expires, you can redeem the bond and receive your money back. The value of bonds fluctuates in line with standard interest rates. For example, if interest rates offered on new bonds should go up, the value of previously issued bonds decreases. Conversely, if current interest rates go down, bonds issued with a higher rate increase in value. There are many tax-effective investments in bonds, including those offered by government-owned utility companies.

brokerage   The fee a broker charges to carry out your buy or sell transaction.

capital gains   The difference in the value in an item between when you purchased and sold it. (This is usually referred to as the item's appreciation or depreciation.) In the U.S. there are three forms of capital gains: short, medium, and long-term. The longer you hold onto an item, the lower the rate of tax you need to pay when you sell it. Some versions of Quicken include a Capital Gains Estimator that can calculate the different rates for you.

cash management account (CMA)   A type of savings account that usually includes checkbook facilities. Many brokerage accounts include the flexibility of a linked cash management account set up through a *linked checking account*. These enable you to draw checks on the available cash balance.

cash-based   An accounting system that counts expenses as they are incurred and income when it is received—rather than when you generate the invoice. This method of accounting is the opposite of *accrual-based* accounting and is used only in very small or micro-businesses.

category   These help you to group related transactions so you can later draw inferences from your registers through Quicken's reports and graphs. For example, by assigning all your gas purchases an "automotive:gas" category, you can quickly see how much money you spent on fueling your car over the year, no matter to which gas station you paid those funds. Categories are central to most of Quicken's functionality.

category groups   Previously called supercategories, category groups help you to draw together related categories for budgeting purposes. For example, all your non-discretionary expense items (mortgage, estimated tax, food, that sort of thing) can be defined as a single category group, making it easier for you to create a budget that considers both discretionary and non-discretionary items.

centesimal   Anything that can be divided into 100 units. Quicken is compatible with any centesimal currency. The dollar is one example, but so is the lire, the drachma, and many other currencies.

class   An alternate method of grouping transactions when they don't share the same category or where additional information is required. For example, the easiest way to track the running expenses of two different cars is to create a class for each (rather than two subcategories). Expenses for each can be summarized no matter to what categories those transactions were applied.

cleared transactions   Transactions that have been marked as appearing on a statement and therefore cleared through the bank. Cleared transactions are generally awaiting the completion of a *reconciliation*. Meanwhile, you can recognize them by the "c" that appears in the Clr column of their register entries. The "c" is replaced by an "R" after they have been fully reconciled.

compound growth   Growth that accelerates due to interest being repeatedly recalculated and added to the principal on a regular basis. This form of interest is known as *compound interest*. Over time, compounded growth can turn a very small seed capital into a spectacular pile of money. This has been related in the question, "Would you prefer to start with one cent and double your capital every day for one month, or receive $1,000,000 right now?" The answer, if you care to work it out, is that choosing the former will deliver over five times as much as the latter.

compound interest   A type of interest that adds to the principal, which results in even greater interest being added on the next calculation which results in an ever-increasing rate of growth. See also *compound growth*.

copy number   Used with classes to differentiate between income or expenses that belong on one tax-related form or another. If you are self-employed with two businesses earning you income, you need to create two classes with one assigned copy number 1 and the other copy number 2. Record all your income and expense transactions for these businesses as you normally would, but also make sure you specify the appropriate *class* in each category field. At the end of the financial year, Quicken Home and Business can generate two tax-related Schedule C forms—one for each business. Copy numbers are also useful if your receive more than one Form W-2 or prefer to combine you and your spouse's finances while using Quicken but actually file separately.

cost of goods sold (COGS)   The amount it costs you to prepare the items that generate your income for sale. Cost of goods sold can include packaging and preparation costs, but doesn't include items that are not integral to the product. For example, warehousing costs don't contribute to a product and are not a business expense. Packaging also isn't a business expense unless it is sold with the product. The cost of goods sold is of particular interest to the IRS because it helps define your gross profit.

debit card   Similar to a credit card, but one that must always contain a balance in your favor. The balance reduces each time you make a purchase or payment using the card and requires periodic topping up. It is easier to manage your debit card account if you set it up as a checking account rather than a credit card account.

deductible   Goods or services you buy that are tax deductible—that is, they reduce your total taxable income.

deductions   These are the amounts removed from your gross pay by your employer before that pay ends up in your own pocket. The deductions form the difference between your gross and your net pay and should be listed on every paycheck and summarized on the Form W-2.

depreciation   The opposite of *appreciation*. In other words, it's a decrease in the realizable sale value of an item, resulting in a negative capital gains. Many items can be depreciated for taxation purposes at a fixed rate.

dividend   A distribution made by a company to its stock holders, usually from excess profits. Dividends are paid at a certain amount per share, so the larger shareholders receive a larger portion of the profits.

downtick   A southerly movement in the price of a security. This might be momentary or part of a trend. In an effort to curb market manipulation, stocks cannot be shorted on a downtick.

DTP (DeskTop Publishing)   Although Quicken doesn't have any desktop publishing beyond that which you can achieve through customized reports, you can export data to a DTP package such as Microsoft Publisher, Adobe PageMaker, or even your word processor and turn it into something of publishable quality, adjusting colors, fonts, shading, and more.

Employee Stock Purchase Plan (ESPP)   Often part of a salary structure than enables employees to convert part of their wages into stocks in the company for which they work. This enhances employee loyalty because they become part owners. Employee Stock Purchase Plans have made many employees wealthy, especially those who started working early in the rise of high-tech companies such as Apple, Microsoft, and Dell.

employee withholdings   Amounts withheld from paychecks as an advance tax. You can request an extra amount be withheld from your paycheck in lieu of making extra estimated payments.

employer contributions   An amount paid by your employer on your behalf, usually through a mechanism known as the SEP, or Simplified Employee Pension. Employer contributions are above and beyond your base wage and are not counted as part of your income. Your employer is limited to paying up to the lesser of 15% of your salary or $24,000 into your *IRA*. You can add an additional $2,000, to top up the IRA.

equity   The amount you own. This is usually calculated on your assets minus your liabilities.

estimated tax   A quarterly payment used to fill the gap between the total withholding tax you pay and tax credits you use through the year, and the total tax for which you are liable. Quicken's Tax Planner can help you calculate your estimated tax payments or adjust your withholding so that the estimated payments are no longer necessary.

exemptions   An automatic decrease in the amount of tax you pay calculated based on yourself and the number of dependents you can claim. (You can claim each exemption only if the dependent passes five separate tests for eligibility.) Exemptions reduce as your income increases.

FIFO   An acronym for "First In, First Out". This is a method of valuing your inventory that assumes the first item purchased was the first item sold. It is important if the price of the goods you are purchasing have changed over time. If they were higher when you first started purchasing, using the FIFO method gives you a lower value inventory than the alternate *LIFO* method and a lower *gross income*, which means less tax to pay.

fiscal year   Also known as the financial year or tax year, this is the year you report on in your tax return. Nearly every tax payer's fiscal year runs from January 1 to December 31, but some overseas companies choose to run from July 1 in one year to June 30 in the next. The fiscal year can equal any bracketed selection of 365 days, but permission must be obtained from the IRS before you decide to change your own.

flyout   Pop-up display used in Quicken's graphs. It shows the actual figures that contributed to the bar, pie, or line segment of the chart currently under the mouse.

font   A typeface of a specific style and size. Taken from the Latin *font*, or basin, they at one time referred to the hollowed containers into which hot lead was poured to create a plate for the first commercial printing presses. (That is, those that didn't use carved wooden blocks.) In Quicken, a font refers to a typeface of any style and size.

foreign currencies   From Quicken's point of view, anything that isn't the USD. Quicken is compatible with any *centesimal* foreign currency, and you can even keep accounts in more than one currency at a time as long as you have selected multicurrency support in Quicken's General Options dialog box.

Form W-2   The standard wage income reporting form.

fringe benefits   Any unusual amount received by you in the course of your employment. For instance, travel and food vouchers, tips, commissions, and more. Fringe benefits represent taxable income. Also, I suspect, the world's most popular business name for a hair salon.

futures   An investment derivative molded into the form of a contract to buy or sell a commodity at a fixed date at the price specified on the contract. If you entered into a buy or "call" contract, and the base price of the commodity rose, you'd be able to purchase at a discount and immediately sell for a profit. The commodity can take the form of actual goods such as cotton, wheat, or soy, or it might be a cash-settled contract for something more nebulous such as a stock index or interest rate. Many futures contracts are sold by trade organizations because they help to guarantee a future fixed price. This helps farmer's plan for the future value of their crops, no matter what happens to the underlying price.

Ginnie Maes   Bonds offered by the Government National Mortgage Association (GNMA)—pronounce the acronym quickly and you'll recognize the genesis of the name. These bonds are repaid on a monthly basis and guaranteed by the association.

gross   Popular slang for *disgusting*. As in: "Dude! How can you eat a marmite and jelly ice? That's *so* gross!" See *gross income*.

gross income   Your total income, no matter its source. Gross income minus eligible deductions results in your taxable income.

gross pay   See *gross income*.

gross profit   Total business income less the *cost of goods sold*. The higher the cost of the goods sold, the lower your gross profit. If you maintain an inventory, see also *FIFO* and *LIFO*.

grouped transactions   A method of arranging scheduled transactions so that they occur as a group. This means you only need to confirm the single grouped transaction each time it falls due rather than a host of smaller but related transactions.

inflow   Amounts flowing into an account. This is the reverse of *outflow*. A bank account shows deposits as inflow. By subtracting your *outflow* from your inflow, you obtain the actual cash flow.

Intellicharge   This is the name of Quicken's now superseded online credit card system. It has been replaced by the *Open Financial Exchange*.

Internal Rate of Return (IRR)   Also known as the average annual total return, the IRR is the effective compounding interest rate by which your investment has grown. That is, if your starting capital had been placed in a bank, then the IRR would equal the fixed compound interest rate the investment earned each year to arrive at the ending capital. The IRR is of more than academic interest, as it provides you with a convenient way to compare the growth of your investments with simpler interest-bearing deposits.

Internet Explorer   Microsoft's World Wide Web browser. Internet Explorer 5.0 is included with most versions of Quicken. Internet Explorer 4.01 is also built into Microsoft Windows 98.

Internet Service Provider (ISP)   The person or business that provides you with your Internet connection.

Intuit   Developers and publishers of Quicken, QuickBooks, TurboTax, and other financial and legal software and online products, and all-around good guys. Intuit is a publicly listed company that trades under the ticker symbol INTU.

Intuit Market   An online service through which you can order checks, invoices, statements, and other Intuit and Quicken-compatible products.

Intuit Services Corporation   The company previously responsible for clearing online payments. Because online payments now use Open Financial Exchange, they can be cleared by any processing house specified by your financial institution, or through the Intuit Online Payment Service.

investment goal   An investment classification system similar to the asset class. You can use goals to group investments chosen for their similar purpose and view and compare the performance of different goals in your investment reports and graphs.

invoice items   Items created specifically to be used in the Invoicing subsection of Quicken Home and Business. You can define several aspects of any invoice item including its selling price, code, description, and related information. Having that information on hand within Quicken speeds up the time it takes you to generate invoices.

IRA (Investment Retirement Account)   A form of retirement plan whose contributions reduce your gross income and so are highly tax-effective. Contributions to an IRA are so effective they are limited to the lesser of $2,000 or 100% of your income—this last part simply means you can't claim a deduction greater than your income by also transferring non-income funds to an IRA in addition to all your income. However, your employer can also contribute to your IRA on your behalf through an *SEP*.

landscape printing   Printing across a sheet of paper rather than down the sheet—that is, with the longest side of the page forming the horizontal edge. Most modern laser and inkjet printers can print in a landscape orientation as easily as they can in a portrait orientation.

liability   Something you owe. Credit card debt, personal loans, bills that need to be paid, a mortgage, or any other funds due are all examples of liabilities.

LIFO   An acronym for "Last In, First Out". This method of valuing your inventory assumes that the most recent item added to your inventory is the first one you sell. If the purchase prices of the goods in your inventory have increased, using the LIFO method results in a lower value inventory than the *FIFO* method and a lower *gross income* with less tax payable.

linked checking account   A facility linked to a brokerage account that enables you to write checks against the available cash balance. Your broker might refer to this system as a *cash management account*.

long   The usual method of buying shares. This is an investment you have made in a security whereby you actually own those stocks, bonds, or whatever. The opposite of a long is a *short*.

loop (endless)   See *repeat*.

lots   A bundle of shares purchased or sold at one time. The only time you need to worry about lots is when you sell shares. Then you should worry lots and lots, because the specific lots you choose to sell have some bearing on your capital gains. The Capital Gains Estimator helps you determine which lots are most advantageous at the present time. It's almost as good as winning the lottery.

market indices   Indicators generated by brokerages, exchanges, and securities analysts that seek to reduce to a single value the movements of many different securities across the entire market or a particular market sector down. The best known of these is the Dow Jones Index (see *blue-chip*), but indicators exist for all the major market sectors.

memorized transaction   Quicken automatically memorizes all the transactions you record, recalling those transactions when you start to enter them once more through the QuickFill feature. You can tell Quicken not to memorize new transactions through the QuickFill tab under Register Options.

money market   A place you can buy and sell money using, well, money. It's also a short-term cash investment that might provide a better interest rate than a short-term deposit in a savings account. Some money market funds allow you to use a check-writing facility, making them as convenient as most savings accounts.

Motley Fool   An investment site and part-time religion championing the Dogs of the Dow approach to investing. You'll find Fool Headquarters at `www.fool.com`. Why do they call themselves fools? Because they aren't professional investors, yet their methods are historically proven and require as little as a few minutes' management each year.

mutual funds   Pooled funds set up for the mutual benefit of their subscribers. Only about 20% of mutual funds actually manage to outperform the market indices, but most of the managers haven't noticed because people just keep throwing money at them.

net pay   Your take-home pay—that is, what you get to put in your pocket after tax.

net worth   Your net worth or equity is calculated by subtracting your liabilities from your assets. If all of your assets were sold right now at their current market value and all of your liabilities paid out in full, you are worth whatever is left over. Let's hope it's a positive exercise.

non-deductible   An expense that cannot be claimed as tax deductible and so does not reduce your taxable income. See also *deductible*.

open item   Apply payments to specific invoices or bills rather than the receivables or payables balance as a whole. This method is the opposite of the *balance forward* system and is used for casual clients or those without an account.

opening balance   The balance used when you create a new Quicken account. Although many accounts start with a zero opening balance, there are some that might have amounts in them already. An opening balance is recorded as a transfer back to the same register, so it has no effect on any other registers or income and expense categories. You can edit the opening balance at any stage, even after you have recorded other transactions in that account.

operating system   The software that controls your computer's hardware, providing the framework through which other applications respond to your commands. This book should help you, the operator, control the software that controls the hardware. But who's controlling you?

options   Identical to *futures*, options enable you to purchase a number of shares at a future date at a future price. They come in two flavors: "calls", or rights to buy; and "puts", or rights to sell.

outflow   Amounts flowing from an account. If you record a payment in a deposit account, that amount is known as an outflow. By subtracting your outflow from your *inflow*, you obtain the actual cash flow.

pane   The main Quicken screen is referred to as a window, a standard screen element included in Microsoft Windows. When that screen is divided in two or more sections, such as when viewing an Investment Performance graph or the Emergency Records Organizer, each section is referred to as a pane.

payables   Amounts you owe. If you use Quicken Basic or Quicken Deluxe, you can set up a payables register by creating a new liability account. Quicken Home and Business includes a special Bills/Payables account type and register. Payables are the opposite of *receivables*.

payee   The person or entity to whom a payment has been made. The payer is the person making the payment. The hairy guy with the club is the debt collector.

portfolio   This generally refers to the complete set of securities you own. However, you might have one or more portfolios devoted to certain tasks such as growth or income. Quicken assumes you have just one portfolio, but you can manage groups of securities by setting investment goals.

portrait printing   The default mode for nearly all printers with the image—be it the text of a report, the graphics of a graph, or whatever—running straight up and down the page. In other words, the tallest side of the paper forms the vertical edge. Printing across the page is known as *landscape printing*.

postdated   A transaction recorded using a future date. Quicken doesn't count that transaction's contribution to a register until the clock in your computer says that day has been reached.

principal   In loans, the amount remaining to be paid of the original sum you borrowed. In *amortized loans* the amount of principal repaid early on is relatively little compared to the interest expense. However, it grows increasingly larger until the final repayments are almost all principal and no interest. At least, that's the principal behind them.

proxy server   A network gateway that translates the addresses used on Internet communications so that they are routed to the appropriate computers. You probably don't need to worry about your proxy settings unless you need to access the Internet through a network, or you use a cable modem or ADSL. You can enter a proxy if applicable when following the Internet Connection Setup.

QIF (Quicken Interchange Format)   An *export* and *import* protocol that makes it easy to copy transactions and entire registers between different data files and computers.

Quick Key   Quicken's term for keyboard shortcuts. A typical Quick Key is the **Ctrl+O** combination that launches the Open File dialog box. The most useful Quick Keys are displayed on the tear-out card at the front of this book.

QuickBooks *Intuit's* small business accounting package. Although it's a totally different product than Quicken (although there are many similarities between the invoicing module in Quicken Home and Business and that in QuickBooks), it sports an equally friendly interface and is very fast, efficient, and flexible. If you find Quicken not up to your small business tasks, do yourself a favor and investigate QuickBooks.

Quicken.com A comprehensive online service accessible from within Quicken and also from any Web browser anywhere. You can obtain personal financial and personal investment advice on Quicken.com, as well as access the latest news, feature articles written especially for Quicken users, and a whole lot more.

QuickEntry This utility ships with all versions of Quicken besides Basic. It enables you (or someone else) to record transactions and, depending on how you've set your options, store them for later acceptance into Quicken's registers.

QuickFill A generic term for the function that works with numerous fields throughout Quicken's registers and dialog boxes to automatically complete the current entry if it recognizes a unique candidate from the characters you have typed up to that point.

QuickPay A payroll package developed by *Intuit* for small business that links to Quicken and simplifies the management of a business payroll. Any paychecks you receive should be recorded with the Paycheck Wizard instead.

QuickTab The tabs that run down the right-hand side of Quicken's screen. Each tab corresponds to an open window. Click the tabs to navigate from one window to the next.

receivables Amounts you are owed. In the business sense, each receivable corresponds to an invoice. These may be referred to as accounts receivable or even just A/R. You can create a receivables account using any standard asset account, or, if you use Quicken Home and Business, create a Receivables/Invoices account that provides specialized invoicing and debtor-management functions. Receivables are, of course, the opposite of *payables*.

reconciliation Performing a reconciliation involves marking those transactions that have cleared through your bank statement. After you have taken all deposits and withdrawals into account, your bank account and your Quicken account should be in balance. Confirm the reconciliation and those transactions are marked as reconciled. If you see an "R" in the Clr column of any transaction, you know it has been reconciled. See also *cleared*.

register Each account you create also creates a unique register. Registers are used to record all transactions that change the balance of that account. Each time you receive a statement from your financial institution for any register, make sure you also perform a *reconciliation*. That ensures the transactions you have recorded match those made in the real world.

repeat   See *loop (endless)*.

return on investment (ROI)   The percentage growth in your investment over the entire time you've held it. ROI isn't a performance measure because it doesn't take the time you've held your investment into account. However, ROI is an important part of capital gains calculations. To compare your investments by their performance, examine the *Internal Rate of Return* instead.

scheduled transaction   A transaction set to occur at a future date. You can create scheduled transactions through the Scheduled Transaction List or the financial calendar. You can also create *grouped transactions* out of two or more scheduled transactions.

shares   Every company is made up of one or more shares. The number of shares and the current price of each define that company's capital. Not all shares in the same company are equal. For instance, a company might choose to issue more than one class of shares and attach different rights to each. When you purchase shares in a company, you become a part owner of that company. (The amount you own is equal to the percentage of the total pool of shares you own. Therefore, if you own 10% of all shares currently on issue, you own 10% of the company.) Depending on the class of shares you purchased, you might have rights to receive dividends generated by the company from its profits and to cast your vote at annual and other meetings. If you choose not to vote, you can assign your right to a proxy, who may do so in your stead.

short   The opposite to buying a share *long*. When you sell short, you sell the *shares* before you actually own them on the promise that you will replace those shares at a later date. You hope the share price will fall rather than rise so that you can purchase the same number of shares later for a lower price, replacing the ones you borrowed and pocketing a profit. This concept is behind the phrase "to sell oneself short", because you do so in the sad expectation your worth will fall.

split   In Quicken's world, a split is a split transaction. These are transactions that have been assigned to more than one category or transfer. For example, if you buy milk for your home and home office, you could split that transaction, assigning the appropriate percentages to a work category and a personal category. Just don't let this penny-pinching drive you to tears. After all, there's no point crying over split milk.

SQL   An acronym for Structured Query Language, a highly standardized data definition and manipulation language used for relational databases. Many enterprise-level accounting packages are compatible with SQL, but it's going to be quite some time before that happens to Quicken.

stock split   When stocks split, the total number of issued shares is adjusted by a set ratio. Often stocks undergo a 2 for 1 split, where the number of issued shares is doubled and the price of each halved. However, stocks can also split the other way, canceling half the issued shares and doubling the price. Splits can operate at other ratios as well, such as 3 for 2 or 1 for 1.5.

straight-line depreciation   This is the type of depreciation with which most people are familiar. The product is depreciated at a fixed rate each year, be it 15%, 33.3%, or whatever. The rates are fixed for taxation purposes according to the category into which the product falls.

supercategories   A defunct term replaced by *category groups*.

Taskbar   The bar that holds the Windows Start button. You can use it to launch and move between your open applications. The Quicken Download Agent icon appears at the far right edge of the Taskbar area.

tax shelters   Investments designed to minimize your tax liability. Finding the right shelter has become something of a recreational pastime, both for Congress who is trying to encourage people to save for retirement, and high-income earners who are willing to go to great lengths to reduce their tax. The best known tax shelters include *IRA*, *SEP*, and Keogh Plans. These are *tax-deferred* plans.

tax-deferred   Describes the situation where the income tax payable on the funds you have invested is deferred until you start to draw on those funds after retirement. This encourages saving for retirement. By not paying tax up front, you are given a marvelous opportunity to invest and keep investing more capital than you otherwise could.

tax-related   An income or expense *category* whose transactions have some bearing on your tax. The category you use to record your salary or wages is obviously tax-related, but even if you use a category to track the money you spend going to ball games, this has no bearing on your tax situation, so that category shouldn't be indicated as tax-related.

ticker   The symbol assigned to a stock or other security. When you know a security's ticker symbol, you can access price updates and news releases through Quicken's Internet connectivity. This said, please don't have a heart attack over a stock with a faulty ticker.

transaction   Records the movement of money into, out of, or between accounts. Transactions also record the purchase of shares, assets, and anything else that may adjust the balance of an account. They are, in fact, the only reason Quicken's accounts have registers.

Transaction toolbar   The small set of tools that appears at the end of any transaction you create or edit. You can use the Enter button to record your changes or additions, the Edit menu to pull down a range of transaction-specific commands, and the Split button to open the *split* transaction dialog box.

transfer   To shift funds between one account and another. This is achieved by specifying the destination account in the *category* field of that transaction. When recording a transfer, specify the destination account by placing a square bracket on either side of its name, as in: "[mortgage]".

TurboTax   Tax preparation software developed by *Intuit*. TurboTax ships in many different versions including those for personal and business use, and in federal and state variants. It is highly compatible with Quicken and, if you have used the appropriate *tax-related* categories, able to generate your tax return almost automatically.

typeface   A set of characters of a particular style. For example: Times New Roman and Arial. See also *font*.

void   A canceled transaction whose contribution to your accounts has been negated. You can void any transaction by clicking on it and selecting Void Transaction from the *Transaction toolbar* Edit menu. **VOID** is placed in front of the *payee* and the transaction total blanked.

Watch List   A set of securities on which you are keeping a close eye, possibly with a view to trading in the near future. Quicken's *portfolio* management makes it easy to create and update a Watch List.

withholding tax   Tax withheld from a paycheck according to the appropriate *marginal rate*. The appropriate amounts are indicated in the Tax Tables published by the IRS and included in the Tax Planner utility built into Quicken.

WordPad   A Windows 95 and Windows 98 accessory that offers basic character and paragraph formatting. WordPad can open much longer files than the Window NotePad. It can also open files stored in some Microsoft Word formats.

Zero-coupon Bonds   Bonds you purchase at a discount to their redeemable value. The longer you hold them, the more interest they earn. However, even though this interest counts as income (and must be reported), you don't receive it until you actually sell or redeem the bonds.

Index

375